AMERICAN
OVERDOSE

Chris cGreal is a reporter for the *Guardian*. A former corres-
ponde in Johannesburg, Jerusalem and Washington DC, he
now v es from across the United States.

F has won several awards, namely for his reporting of
the R ndan genocide, Israel/Palestine, and on the impact of
econo ic recession in America. He received the James
Came n prize for 'work as a journalist that has combined moral
vision nd professional integrity'. He was awarded the Martha
Gellh n Prize for Journalism for reporting that 'penetrated the
establ ed version of events and told an unpalatable truth'. He
is a fo ner merchant seaman.

AMERICAN OVERDOSE

THE OPIOID
TRAGEDY
IN THREE ACTS

CHRIS MCGREAL

FABER & FABER

First published in 2018
by Faber & Faber Limited
Bloomsbury House
74–77 Great Russell Street
London WC1B 3DA

First published in the USA in 2018
by PublicAffairs
Hachette Book Group
1290 Avenue of the Americas, New York, NY 10104

Printed and bound by CPI Group (UK) Ltd, Croydon, CR0 4YY

A CIP record for this book
is available from the British Library

ISBN 978–1–78335–168–8

FSC
www.fsc.org
MIX
Paper from
responsible sources
FSC® C020471

2 4 6 8 10 9 7 5 3 1

For my sons, Braam and Zenzo

Contents

ACT II   HOOKED

ACT III   WITHDRAWAL

Acknowledgments

This book would not have been possible without those across the United States who gave generously of their time to speak to me so fully and frankly about living with addiction, the trauma of losing someone to opioids, and the impact of the drugs on their communities. I regret I was not able to include all of their names and accounts, but their insights framed and infused this book.

Among those who took the trouble to speak to me repeatedly over the years were April Rovero, Sandra Kresser, Avi Israel, Sherrie Rubin, and Emily Walden. Besides those quoted in the text, I'm also grateful to Travis Bornstein, Robert Eaton, James Fata, Aimee Dunkle, Gary Mendell, Margie Borth, Erin Finkbiner, Jan Lovett, Maureen Kielian, and Gayle Saks.

Jim Cagle in Charleston, West Virginia, shared his knowledge and research in helping me understand events in Mingo County. Besides those quoted in the text, a number of people who choose to remain anonymous offered valuable insights into events in Williamson and Kermit.

Eric Eyre, a talented reporter at the *Charleston Gazette-Mail*, was generous with his time and information. Eric won a Pulitzer Prize for his groundbreaking exposure of the scale of opioid pills flooding West Virginia.

I'm indebted to the many people who offered their perspectives on the workings of, and complex relationships between, the pharmaceutical industry, federal regulators, and the medical profession. I will not name them all here as they are quoted in the text or identified in the sources, unless they wished to remain anonymous. But Dr. Margaret Hamburg was alone among former FDA commissioners in agreeing to an interview.

Several people still employed by the government were obliged to speak to me off the record. Members of the congressional staff helped me understand the workings of the relationship between Congress and federal health regulators and between Congress and pharmaceutical lobbyists.

Professor Marcia Meldrum at UCLA shared her extensive knowledge of the history of prescription opioids and insights into the shift in her own thinking on their use as well as her impressions of Dr. Russell Portenoy.

I am also grateful to Dr. Jennifer Plumb, Dr. Grant Baldwin, Carol Moss, Robert Childs, Dan Bigg, and Adam Winstock who each offered important insights. Penney Cowan and Cindy Steinberg spoke to me about the perspective of patients in pain.

Others who made contributions to this book in different ways include Mary Sue Connolly, Craig Mayton, Alan Wald, James Myburgh, Molly Bingham, Ruaridh Nicoll, Rita Sabler, Sarah Boseley, and John Mulholland.

This book was set in motion by a phone call from Clive Priddle, the publisher at PublicAffairs. He asked about heroin and ended up discussing opioid prescriptions. Since then he has provided valuable guidance, insights, and pithy comments that have helped shape this book into what it is today. Annette Wenda did a fine job of editing the copy. Thanks also to my agent, Zoë Pagnamenta, who was an enthusiast for this project, an excellent guide through the forest of contracts, and a top-notch negotiator.

Introduction: An Epidemic Foretold

The first time I looked into the face of opioid addiction, it was of a heavily made-up woman in her late fifties at a food bank in eastern Kentucky.

Karen Jennings had once been a manager at McDonald's. Walking home one day a little the worse for drink, she fell into a creek and broke her back. The doctor prescribed painkillers to ease her through the pain of recovery.

Even as her injury healed, the narcotics drew Karen in. The drugs worked on her brain to demand ever larger doses of opioids with the promise of a few hours' bliss. But if she failed to deliver, the narcotics exacted a perverse price. They caused her body to replicate the very pain they were supposed to fight. They tortured a fix out of her.

With that, Karen's life spiraled into a perpetual hunt for pills, costing her her job, destroying marriages, and taking a harsh toll on her family. She is haunted by a suspicion that her drug use contributed to the depression endured by her son, a bank vice president, who took his own life. By the time Karen emerged from her addiction fifteen years later, she was living on the breadline and amazed to find herself still alive.

Karen Jennings's story is a personal tragedy, but that is not how she told it. She cast herself as a survivor plucked from a sea of dead, lost to a modern-day plague engulfing the communities around her. She was sucked in at the beginning, in the late 1990s, just as what was to become the biggest drug epidemic in American history was taking hold. In time, the contagion infiltrated almost every corner of the United States.

The ascendancy of prescription painkillers was driven, at first at least, by one drug, OxyContin—the most poweful narcotic pain-killer ever released for routine prescribing. It wasn't the only opioid, but it was the game changer because of its strength and because the manufacturer, Purdue Pharma, unleashed a marketing campaign like no other to make it the go-to drug for pain treatment. In the parts of rural Appalachia first blighted by OxyContin, the pills were known as "hillbilly heroin" for a reason.

The clues to the scale of the catastrophe were in the details long before the death statistics were taken seriously: the firefighters called out more often for overdoses than fires; the teachers buying food for the growing numbers of students neglected by parents spending their time and money on drugs; the pharmacies popping up in small towns where other shops were in retreat for lack of business; the surge in babies born with withdrawal symptoms and cared for by grandpar-ents; the firms unable to find enough workers to pass a drug test.

Karen Jennings was a witness to all of this. What mystified her was that so many others seemed blind to the unfolding devastation for so long. How was it that this tragedy began when Bill Clinton was president, surged through the years George W. Bush occupied the White House, but only began to be given the attention it deserved when Barack Obama was wrapping up his second term? Even then, no one seemed to do very much about it.

In time, I heard people across the United States ask versions of Karen's question. Men and women blindsided by a plague many did not know existed until the moment it tore into their lives, struggled to understand how it happened. As grief gave way to anger, the families of the dead and the survivors wanted to know why those Americans expected to protect them—the medical profession, the government, the federal regulators—seemed to stand idly by, or worse, as the bodies piled up year after year.

This book is an investigation of those questions and one in particular: How was the greatest drug epidemic in American history allowed to grow virtually unchecked for nearly two decades with no end in sight?

The crude calculation is that prescription painkillers have claimed more than a quarter of a million American lives, although there are good reasons to believe the toll is higher because of under-reporting and stigma. Opioids now kill more people in the United States each year than AIDS at its most destructive, and more in a single year than all the American soldiers who died in the Vietnam War. By the time the opioid epidemic has run its course, the number of deaths may well have doubled or more, compounded by a second wave of heroin and synthetic opioids such as fentanyl.

Other countries look on in alarm and wonder if the American experience is the start of a global wave of addiction about to engulf them.

There are good reasons for caution. Opioid-related deaths are up sharply in the United Kingdom. Scotland has the highest reported drug-related death rate in the European Union with more than half of overdoses involving morphine or heroin. In England and Wales, opioid prescriptions have doubled over a decade, driven by the dispensing of tramadol. Two million Britons have taken a painkiller that was not prescribed for them. Deaths involving opioids have more than doubled since 2012 in England and Wales, driven by a surge in heroin use.

Tramadol is ever more popular in West and North Africa where it is used by farmers to counter the toll of fieldwork on their bodies, and is mixed with energy drinks to boost sexual performance. In

Nigeria, the drug is favored by fighters for and against the jihadist group Boko Haram. Much of the illicit tramadol used in Africa is manufactured in India and smuggled by criminal gangs, leading the Indian government in 2018 to impose tighter production and export controls.

In Australia, deaths from fentanyl are up sharply as the Chinese manufacturers look for markets beyond the US. In South Africa, heroin is responsible for more than one-third of drug-related deaths.

Then there are the pharmaceutical companies themselves which, just like big tobacco, look to the developing world for new markets as prescribing of opioids comes under increasing scrutiny in the richer nations.

But, for now at least, the US epidemic remains an overwhelmingly American crisis for reasons that serve as a warning to other countries.

The US consumes more than 80 percent of the world's opioid painkillers yet accounts for less than 5 percent of its population. A former head of the Food and Drug Administration has described this mass prescribing of narcotic painkillers as "one of the greatest mistakes of modern medicine." But it is neither a mistake nor the kind of catastrophe born of some ghastly accident. It is a tragedy forged by the capture of medical policy by corporations and the failure of American institutions to protect the public. That in turn is the result of a medical system run not as a service for the public good but as a business for corporate profit—a forewarning to the UK's National Health Service about the hazards of privatization.

The dangers of superstrength opioid painkillers were not a secret to the medical establishment, government or drug manufacturers. The surge in addiction and overdose was identified not long after OxyContin went on sale and the alarm was sounded clearly. But the warnings were shunted aside by corporations steering medical policy. They wrote the pain treatment manuals used to train doctors and continued to drive up the prescribing of opioids.

The profits of addiction are stamped on museums, galleries and research institutes around the world. OxyContin earned billions of dollars for Purdue Pharma and, in turn, for the family that owns the company. Opioids have made the Sacklers, who put down roots in the US and the UK, among the richest in America. The family built a reputation for philanthropy. The Victoria and Albert Museum in London, the University of Glasgow and Kew Gardens are among scores of institutions that have accepted a slice of the money made from America's opioid epidemic in return for stamping the Sackler brand onto their institutions. But while the family was happy to see its name in lights, the connection to Purdue Pharma and OxyContin was kept in the shadows.

Told for the first time, this is the story of how greed trumped the practice of medicine: of bad people driven by avarice, of good people led astray by a misguided self-belief, of the negligent and the heroic. Together they fed the greatest drug epidemic in US history. It began small, as a series of fires, before the inferno. They were lit across the country, but none burned more brightly than in a rural corner of West Virginia.

ACT I
DEALING

CHAPTER 1

The Undertaker

EVEN AS A teenager Henry Vinson wanted to be an undertaker. He liked the dead and the rituals for dispatching them. "My life's overriding ambition was to become a funeral director," he wrote years later with a turn of pride in knowing he was unorthodox.

At the age of nineteen, Vinson landed an internship at a funeral parlor in his hometown of Williamson, West Virginia, and then a place at the College of Mortuary Science in Cincinnati. Within three years, he was running his own undertakers back in Williamson, one of those places that calls itself a city even though it's not much more than a main street with a part-time mayor's office. Ghost shops and an abundance of storefront injury lawyers—"Been in a wreck and need a check?"—long ago supplanted the department stores and haberdasheries. An iron bridge over the Tug Fork river marks the border between West Virginia and Kentucky, a block from the old city courthouse. Where Sears once stood sentry at the turn off from the bridge onto Williamson's main street, the New Beginnings Ministry now runs a Christian school.

Just about everyone in Williamson knew of Vinson. He was pushy in a way that didn't go down well among West Virginia's courtly business class. Ambition made him the state's youngest county coroner even though he had no medical training, and it won him no friends among rival funeral directors, who frowned on his ways of snatching up business.

The undertaking dream started to unravel when Vinson was forced to quit as coroner amid a flurry of accusations of professional and criminal misconduct. He was convicted of making harassing phone calls to a rival funeral director. An elderly widow accused him of refusing to release her husband's unrefrigerated body for six weeks because she was too poor to pay Vinson's bill. The state investigated him for fraud over the provision of coffins for pauper funerals.

"None of that is true," he told me years later.

Vinson said a local prosecutor gave him a choice—resign as coroner or face charges of misappropriating state funds. He quit and left Williamson, blaming his travails on homophobia, a conspiracy by rival morticians, and the hostility of a local newspaper that he said "made me out to be the Beelzebub of funeral directors."

But Williamson was, he later concluded, "just a dress rehearsal for my sojourn to Washington, DC."

Vinson landed a job at the biggest undertakers in the Washington area, the W. W. Chambers Funeral Home. Getting out of West Virginia meant he could be more open about his sexuality, and that offered its own business opportunity.

How Vinson got into the escort business depends on whom you believe. His own version is that he became friends with a man who told him about the money to be made in sex work. Vinson claims he saw the potential not as a prostitute but as a pimp and bought an escort service called Ebony and Ivory for $10,000 from a man dying of AIDS. He calculated that by applying the business skills he had learned in mortuary school, he would make the money back within weeks.

The owner of another escort business, Donald Schey, told a different story. He said Vinson signed up for sex work at his agency when he was told he could make $600 a day, way above his pay at the funeral parlor. Schey said Vinson became one of his busiest escorts.

Whatever the path, before long Vinson was running his own agency. He advertised in the city's weekly newspapers as Dream Boys, Jack's Jocks, and Man to Man and bought up the phone numbers of defunct escort services still listed in the Yellow Pages.

Once the calls started, they didn't stop. Vinson installed a rack of phone lines in his apartment and kept a phone hidden under the lid of a casket at the funeral home. By the end of 1987, he was taking more than a hundred calls a day from clients, with twenty escorts working for him on any given night.

"At the sprite age of twenty-six years old, I was a funeral director by day and a DC madam by night," Vinson recounted in a memoir.

Later, when his life was in free fall, Vinson blamed his woes on the prominence of some of his clients. They included politicians, and a scattering of Reagan administration and congressional officials. Vinson claimed former Central Intelligence Agency (CIA) director William Casey "was a frequent flier of my escort service."

But by far Vinson's most lucrative client was a former ABC reporter in Vietnam turned Washington lobbyist, Craig Spence, who spent up to $20,000 a month on escorts. On a visit to Spence's home, Vinson noted the prominently displayed photographs of his host posing with President Ronald Reagan and Senator Bob Dole. Spence claimed off-duty Secret Service agents worked as his security guards and told Vinson he was spending vast sums on escorts to buy influence.

Spence hosted dinner parties attended by a clutch of Reagan administration officials. His influence extended to arranging a midnight tour of the White House for six friends in July 1988, including two of Vinson's escorts.

All of this was bound to attract the attention of the guardians of the state. But when the Secret Service finally came banging on the front door of Vinson's colonial-style house in an upscale northwestern Washington cul-de-sac, it was ostensibly over something much more mundane: credit card receipts.

Vinson had become rich fast. He bought a plane and then a helicopter. But he kept the source of his sudden prosperity at arm's length by persuading his mother, a bus driver who also owned the ambulance service around Williamson, to run credit card payments for his escorts through her company. He told her he was in the entertainment business. Later he got Robert Chambers, a son of the family running the funeral home, to launder payments. Charges for sex were billed under "Professional Services" and listed as urns and funeral accessories. Robert took a 20 percent cut until his family found out and fired him.

As innocuous as funeral home ornamentals might seem, they still looked out of place when they started turning up on official credit cards. Unfortunately for Vinson, not only was the Secret Service responsible for the security of the White House and its orbit, but, as a branch of the Treasury Department in those days, the service also had a hand in investigating financial fraud.

The Secret Service accused Vinson of forging signatures and double billing some clients, knowing they would not be in a hurry to complain to their credit card companies. Compounding Vinson's difficulties, the federal agents demanding entry to his house had the local police in tow after DC's vice squad received a tip about escorts working from an upmarket hotel near Dupont Circle. The room was registered to Vinson.

A search of the house revealed lists of clients, their sexual tastes and a pile of credit card receipts.

As the scandal unraveled in public, the city's two daily newspapers, the *Washington Post* and the *Washington Times*, went at each other over the truth about Spence and his payments to Vinson's prostitution ring. The *Times* laid out a story of orgies, drugs, and blackmail. The *Post* claimed the investigation was no more than a fraud case and that Spence's parties were dull gatherings of important people talking about trade policy.

In the midst of the investigation, newspapers across West Virginia published death notices for Vinson. Investigators wondered if it was an attempt to disappear with the $1 million profit they estimated he made.

Vinson needed a lawyer. Greta Van Susteren, the future Fox News presenter, came recommended, but Vinson said he began to lose confidence in her after, expecting to face relatively minor charges of running a prostitution ring and receive probation, a grand jury handed down a forty-three-count indictment typically used against organized crime with the potential for several life sentences.

Vinson saw that as determination on the government's part to prevent him from telling what and whom he knew. His suspicions were reinforced by the judge's refusal to allow Van Susteren to name Vinson's clients in open court.

His fears of a judicial lynching, and fading confidence in Van Susteren to get him off the hook, led to a plea deal. Vinson admitted lesser charges and agreed to cooperate with the government, including a long debriefing session with the Secret Service, which, by then, was interested in talking about a lot more than credit card fraud.

Vinson said Van Susteren made reassuring noises about probation and encouraged him to placate the judge by going into rehab. The judge was not inclined to show leniency. He sentenced Vinson to five years and three months in federal prison.

The case had devastating consequences for some of his former clients; careers were ruined, and one White House liaison caught up in the scandal committed suicide. Spence moved to New York, living in an Upper East Side hotel with a twenty-two-year-old male escort. A few weeks after he was arrested in possession of cocaine, a gun, and a crack pipe, Spence killed himself in a Boston hotel room.

HENRY VINSON'S FOUR-YEAR tour of the federal prison system came to an end at a medium-security facility in Kentucky in July 1995. His parole officer signed off on the newly released felon moving in with his mother, Joyce Vinson, but balked at letting him work as manager of her commercial properties in Williamson.

An old friend of Joyce's stepped up. Dr. Diane Shafer had known Henry as a teenager and offered him a job as the file clerk at her downtown practice. It put Vinson back exactly where he did not want to be, in a small town where his recent past had done nothing to change minds about his character. But he was trapped. The parole officer gave his approval to the plan with, apparently, little scrutiny of Shafer's own record.

Shafer had been an orthopedic surgeon in neighboring Kentucky until its state medical board suspected she was running a scam, by overprescribing drugs and overcharging the government under a workers' compensation scheme.

The board appointed Gregory Holmes, a Kentucky assistant attorney general, to investigate. Shafer set about getting to know Holmes. Before long they were taking trips to Las Vegas, the Caribbean, and Mexico and living together on weekends. The couple married even though Holmes already had a wife—his secretary at the attorney general's office. Shafer's wedding gift to her new husband was $42,000. Ten days after the marriage, Holmes submitted his official report dismissing the accusations against his bride as unfounded.

The medical board was not persuaded and so began an investigation of the investigator. "Holmes later denied the relationship and the travels, but witnesses were able to easily identify the pair because he was blind and stocky, and she was over 6 feet tall," a court observed.

The police raided Shafer's home and found the marriage certificate. Holmes claimed to know nothing about it and accused his unlawful wife of forgery. Prosecutors concluded Shafer wrongly thought a wife could not be charged with bribing her husband.

They were both convicted of bribery, and Holmes of bigamy and theft, and sent to prison. The medical board revoked Shafer's license to practice as a doctor.

In 1995 an appeals court overturned the convictions on technical grounds. Rather than face a new trial, Holmes pleaded guilty to lesser charges and was barred from practicing law. Shafer rejected a plea deal and was not tried again. But Kentucky refused to reinstate her medical license, so she moved to West Virginia, where she was still permitted to practice, and opened a clinic in a two-story house on Second Avenue in Williamson, just down from the city's courthouse.

Shafer probably did need a file clerk because business was brisk from the beginning. She worked long hours, beginning each day at the local hospital, where she typically saw a couple dozen patients before facing the lines at her practice downtown.

Many of the faces were familiar. A large and loyal clientele followed Shafer from her clinic in Kentucky, where she was regarded as a generous prescriber of the painkillers a lot of men working in the mines or in logging relied on to get them through the day. Over-the-counter drugs such as ibuprofen didn't cut it. Tylenol 3, with a dose of an opioid, codeine, was a good first stop on the prescription route, but Shafer's patients were usually looking for something stronger after a few months, so they were moved onto hydrocodone.

Shafer's patients assumed prescription drugs were safe. People passed around the over-the-counter aspirin, ibuprofen, and Tylenol all the time. The prescription drugs, they calculated, were the same—only better.

The Drug Enforcement Administration (DEA) classifies each drug according to how dangerous it is. Vicodin and similar hydrocodone pills were placed in a lower category than painkillers made from another opioid, oxycodone, even though there was little practical difference. That created a perception among some doctors that hydrocodone was more effective than over-the-counter medicines but safer than oxycodone and so a natural first stop for prescribing. The classification also allowed doctors to write scripts for a supply of up to six months and renew prescriptions by phone. Vicodin rapidly became the go-to painkiller for doctors alongside another hydrocodone pill, Lortab.

VINSON OBSERVED THE lines outside Shafer's clinic and quickly grasped that there was a tidy profit in painkillers. The business skills honed in the mortuary trade and applied so effectively to running escorts were now turned to what looked like the perfect money spinner—turning doctors into drug dealers. Best of all, as far as Vinson could see, it was all legal because it involved a physician, a patient, and a prescription.

Vinson just needed doctors and somewhere to put them. Happily his mother, Joyce, owned a cavernous old warehouse a couple of blocks from Shafer's office. Henry Vinson continued to run Shafer's clinic while converting the warehouse into medical offices. Before long the Williamson Wellness Center was born. Then he began scouting for doctors. Vinson had a nose for the right kind.

Among his first recruits was Dr. Katherine Hoover. She had been practicing in Florida but was in a legal battle with the state medical board after it suspended her license for prescribing exceptionally large numbers of opioids, some of them to indigent patients whose bills were paid by welfare programs. Several pharmacists in Key West gave evidence against her. Two doctors who reviewed her prescribing record said she gave patients potentially lethal doses of narcotics. But an appeal court sided with Hoover and overturned the medical board's decision in part because it said she had acted within accepted medical practice. By then she'd settled back at the family home in Lost Creek, West Virginia, and was practicing at a nearby clinic. But she got into trouble there too after the state medical board took up a complaint that she solicited a seventeen-year-old female patient to have sex with her son and even went so far as to demonstrate sexual positions the young woman might use. That's when Vinson came knocking.

He also called up a physician he got to know while serving part of his sentence at the federal institution in Morgantown, on the other side of West Virginia. Bill Ryckman was the prison doctor. "I was friends with Bill Ryckman," Vinson told me years later. "Bill had an office in Pennsylvania, and he was looking for a different opportunity."

The two men disagree on how the doctor came to be in Williamson. According to Vinson, Ryckman decided of his own accord to set up a medical practice in a former warehouse in rural West Virginia.

The former prison doctor characterizes it differently. He said Vinson hired him on contract as a "consultant" after flying him down to Williamson on a private plane. All Ryckman needed to do was show his face in the clinic once or twice a week. What Vinson needed more than the doctor's presence was use of the number issued by the Drug Enforcement Administration that each physician required to write prescriptions for narcotics.

Years later, Ryckman was asked under oath if the setup at the Williamson Wellness Center was that of "an undertaker that hires doctors to run clinics." He agreed that it was.

Vinson completed the collection of doctors with another physician with an impeachable reputation. Armando Acosta had been convicted of fraud for hiding property from creditors after he declared bankruptcy. The West Virginia state pharmacy board had warned as early as 1996 that Acosta was "prescribing controlled substances excessively," and his license was suspended a year later for failing to keep records on his patients. He was a perfect fit for Vinson.

The finances of the Williamson Wellness clinic were straightforward, at least on paper. The doctors rented consulting rooms fitted out with medical equipment. Vinson provided the staff—he hired Myra Miller, the wife of a policeman, as office manager—and ran the administration. He also handled the money, and there was a lot of it.

The clinics charged $250 cash for a first appointment, which included the taking of vital signs and a consultation to diagnose a condition requiring an opioid prescription. After that, it cost $150 a month to renew the script. Patients were discouraged from asking to see a doctor after the first appointment by being made to wait for hours for any follow-up visits.

Before long, the doctors were getting through hundreds of patients a day. There were simply not enough hours for them to see all the people for whom they were writing prescriptions, so to speed things up, the doctors presigned hundreds of scripts, leaving the date blank. The receptionist filled it in when the patient came in and handed over the money.

At Williamson Wellness, there was so much money changing hands that Vinson installed a chute for the cash to a counting desk. Shafer took to stuffing the money into drawers and cupboards and carrying it home in great bundles.

Vinson was a savvy businessman. He saw opportunities, but the experience in Washington, DC, taught him to also look for risks. He realized he had no control over what happened to the prescriptions after they left the clinics, and that carried dangers. What if pharmacists were bothered by the scale of the prescribing? They might refuse to fill the scripts or, worse, notify the DEA or state medical board. Vinson didn't need that kind of scrutiny.

The key was to keep the big-name operations, like the Walmart pharmacy across the river in Kentucky, out of the picture. But some small pharmacies had a taste of the money to be made. Vinson and the doctors reeled them in with the lure of profits beyond the dreams of any local drugstore.

Williamson Wellness and Shafer both insisted patients could collect prescriptions only from a list of "preferred pharmacies." Hurley Drug, a short walk up the street from the clinic, was one of them. So was Family Pharmacy, a few hundred yards across the Kentucky border in South Williamson. Later, the most notorious of them all—Tug Valley Pharmacy—opened just a couple of minutes' walk from both clinics. It had a drive-through window, and cars were often lined up and down the street. The drugstores were later described as "both very lucky and among the most grossly negligent pharmacies in America."

With the delivery end sorted out, Vinson focused on growing his clientele.

Neighboring Kentucky has a generous state-run personal injury protection scheme that funds treatment for people hurt in car or work accidents. The scheme paid up to $1,000 for treatment by a doctor and a further $10,000 in physical therapy and recovery care. The personal injury lawyers soliciting business on Williamson's main street, one as the "Car Wreck King," were well versed in procedure. First, clients had to establish an injury, so they were packed off to one of Vinson's clinics. After that, they were frequently referred for long-term treatment. That provided another opportunity for Vinson.

Ryckman introduced him to a man called John Kazalas in 2000. The pair founded the Aquatic Rehab Center, offering physical therapy in another of Joyce Vinson's buildings across the street from the Williamson Wellness Center. Most of the fees were paid by insurance companies or state compensation.

The circle was complete. The money rolled in. Tens of thousands of dollars a day was carried to a local bank for deposit. There was so much money, Vinson bought an electronic banknote counter.

By the early 2000s, Shafer and Hoover were writing prescriptions for opioid painkillers that outpaced some West Virginia hospitals. West Virginia had one of the most productive pill mills in the country.

CHAPTER 2

Junk Science

A FEW MONTHS AFTER Henry Vinson's release from prison in 1995, the queen of England knighted two American doctors for their generosity.

Mortimer and Raymond Sackler were born to Jewish immigrants from Poland who established themselves as grocers in New York. The sons came of age in the 1930s intent on being physicians, but America's leading medical schools maintained quotas for Jewish students and they were turned away.

In 1937 Mortimer boarded a ship to Britain, sailing steerage—the lowest rung on the maritime class ladder—and enrolled to study medicine in Glasgow. Raymond followed a year later. The brothers stayed in Scotland for a while after Britain declared war on Hitler, cementing an enduring and fateful attachment to the country. Mortimer spent a good deal more of his life living in London than the United States; his third wife was English. But by the 1950s the brothers were working in New York, where they specialized in psychiatric disorders at the Creedmoor Psychiatric Center, exploring an interest in the use of drugs to address schizophrenia and other mental conditions.

Their older brother, Arthur, was a psychiatrist too, although by the time he qualified, he had discovered another talent: sleight of hand.

Arthur helped pay his way through medical school working as a copywriter for a small New York advertising agency. He later joined his brothers at Creedmoor, where the three of them wrote pioneering papers on the use of medicine in psychiatric treatment. He was ahead of his time as a vigorous opponent of smoking and in establishing the first racially integrated blood bank in New York.

But Arthur had also proved an adept adman and alongside his medical responsibilities acquired an advertising company, the Williams Douglas McAdams agency. The agency ran a newspaper, the *Medical Tribune*, which pioneered the clouding of lines between journalism and promotion. Pharmaceutical companies advertising in the paper were assured the *Medical Tribune*'s stories would promote their drugs to the hundreds of thousands of doctors said to read the publication, even if it meant fabricating claims. Arthur designed an ad for an antibiotic made by Pfizer with an array of doctors' business cards next to a claim that physicians endorsed the drug. The doctors were invented.

Arthur was not all he seemed in a myriad of ways. The communist journalist A. B. Magil remembered him from the 1930s as something of a left-wing firebrand who had been manager of a strike paper when students walked out at Sackler's medical school. "I was told by a reliable source that all three Sacklers had been [Communist] party members early on, but not for long," Magil wrote to an American academic, Alan Wald in 1991.

The Sacklers were forced out of Creedmoor at the height of Senator Eugene McCarthy's anticommunist witch hunt in the 1950s for reasons that remain murky. One version has it that they refused to inform on suspected leftists, although there was speculation that suspicions about their own past caused the breach.

Arthur appears to have retained some sympathy for his old comrades as they were cornered by McCarthy. He took on several at the

Medical Tribune when they found it difficult to find jobs elsewhere. They included Mel Barnet, a journalist and former Communist Party member fired by the *New York Times* in 1955 for his refusal to name names to McCarthy's committee. Barnet worked at the *Medical Tribune* until he retired as associate editor two decades later.

Arthur's moral code was complex, though. He was also not above what amounted to influence peddling. The head of the Food and Drug Administration (FDA)'s antibiotics division, Henry Welch, was forced to resign in 1959 after one of Sackler's companies paid him $300,000 to quietly promote particular drugs.

But there was no denying Arthur's commercial genius. He quickly grasped two key concepts in selling prescription drugs. One was to get doctors to sell them for him. In those days, patients had a respect for physicians often bordering on awe, so if a doctor recommended a medicine, it was as good as sold. The other realization was that the way to make real money wasn't to sell a drug to those who needed it when they would probably buy it anyway. The key was push it on those who didn't.

Arthur perfected the technique with a new tranquilizer in 1963. The manufacturer wanted to sell Valium without cutting into the market for another of its antianxiety pills. Arthur solved the problem by inventing a new market. He set about persuading Americans they had far too much stress in their lives and what they needed was a tranquilizer. Trouble sleeping? Take Valium. Stomach upset? Worried about exams? Heartburn? Whatever it was, Valium was the answer. One ad for the drug purported to show a woman being treated for "psychic tension."

There was nothing in the studies that the manufacturer, Roche, submitted for the FDA's approval of Valium to suggest any of this was an appropriate use of the drug. But it didn't matter what the label said, so long as patients asked for it and doctors prescribed it. Within a decade Valium was the most prescribed drug in the country, as millions of people could apparently not get through the day without it. By 1978 it was selling more than 2 billion pills a year and was immortalized in the Rolling Stones song "Mother's Little Helper."

Arthur, who effectively took a cut of every sale, became very rich. Much later, after his death, the Valium campaign earned him a spot in the Medical Advertising Hall of Fame. By then, the idea of a pill dissolving away the strains of life was well entrenched in American society and medical culture.

While Arthur was busy promoting drugs, his brothers had other businesses to run. In 1952 the Sacklers acquired a small firm, Purdue Frederick, once known for selling tonics and cures with more than a whiff of quackery. Soon laxatives and ear-wax remover were added to the range and at the height of the Vietnam war an antiseptic the US Army bought in bulk to treat wounded soldiers. The company pulled in a tidy profit. The three brothers had an equal stake, but Arthur left Mortimer and Raymond to run the pharmaceutical business.

Raymond stayed in Connecticut, overseeing Purdue Frederick. Mortimer returned to the United Kingdom to run the family's British operation, Napp Pharmaceuticals. In 1974 he renounced his American citizenship and took the nationality of his then wife to become an Austrian.

Napp owned a subsidiary in Scotland, Bard Pharmaceuticals. In the early 1970s it developed a formula to slowly bleed a pill's medication into a patient's system. This "prolonged release technology" was applied to several drugs, including a treatment for asthma. It caught the eye of a pair of doctors in London who thought it would be useful in their groundbreaking work if it could be made to work with a morphine pill.

The scientists at Napp went to work, little knowing they were taking the first step toward unleashing the greatest drug epidemic in the history of a country thousands of miles away, the United States.

AT THE TIME, American doctors regarded morphine with suspicion to the point of hostility. Whatever its qualities as a painkiller, it was viewed as so addictive and life destroying that the medical profession refused to countenance its use even for the dying. This fear was rooted in an addiction epidemic that shaped modern US drug policy.

By the time of the Civil War, morphine was a standard treatment for traumatic pain, and millions of pills were dispensed to soldiers for wounds, disease, and battle stress. But the drug was taken orally and was notorious for causing stomach pains.

The rise of the hypodermic needle changed that. Historian David Courtwright has likened a syringe of morphine to a magic wand that for the first time in the history of medicine could deliver almost immediate relief from pain.

Civil War veterans were among the first to benefit, but before long morphine injections were dispensed by doctors as a routine response to pain and the medical use of opiates tripled in a decade. Courtwright estimated that by the 1880s, more than half of those hooked on the drug were middle- and upper-class white women. Some looked to doctors for morphine injections to relieve menstrual pains. Tinctures of opium and alcohol were popular as a daily pick-me-up. Opiates and other addictive drugs were stuffed into a vast array of Victorian treatments, lining drugstore shelves or touted in traveling medicine shows. One Night cough syrup mixed morphine, cannabis, and alcohol. Mrs. Winslow's Soothing Syrup used morphine to treat teething babies. With no restrictions on their sale and little guidance on dosages, Americans were left to take as much as they saw fit or craved.

The government realized it had a wave of addiction on its hands driven by doctors. Hundreds of thousands of people were hooked on opiates. At first, the public mood was sympathetic because most of those addicted were war veterans or from more privileged classes. Addiction was largely regarded as a medical condition. It was, as ever, also a financial opportunity. Sanatoriums sprang up, although many were of dubious value and their treatments were crude.

As the twentieth century dawned, new users came on the scene, including young immigrants moving into the bigger cities who were regarded with suspicion. "Gone was the stereotype of the addicted matron; in its place stood that of the street criminal," wrote Courtwright.

A prohibitionist movement took hold alongside opposition to alcohol. In 1908 President Teddy Roosevelt appointed the country's first opium commissioner, Dr. Hamilton Wright, who described Americans as "the greatest drug fiends in the world" and opium and morphine as a "national curse." "The habit has this nation in its grip to an astonishing extent. Our prisons and our hospitals are full of victims of it, it has robbed ten thousand business men of moral sense and made them beasts who prey upon their fellows, unidentified it has become one of the most fertile causes of unhappiness and sin in the United States," he told the *New York Times* in 1911.

After sporadic legislation to tax and limit opium imports, the US Congress passed the Harrison Act in 1914 to restrict distribution to prescribing physicians. Because the law involved taxation, the Treasury Department was left to enforce it. Drawing on its absolute lack of medical expertise, the Treasury made a moral judgment that addiction was not a disease but a human failing. It ruled that doctors would not be permitted to prescribe narcotics to people who were hooked even if it was to help them shake their addiction. The Supreme Court upheld that position, and it prevailed for a half century.

The decline in sympathy for those addicted to opioids was matched by a similar diminishing of concern for people struggling with chronic pain. By the 1920s, the US medical establishment increasingly regarded them as malingerers and not in any particular need of relief. Medical education steered new physicians away from opiate prescribing.

People addicted to morphine and its variants came to be seen as deviants in an age quick to judge those who strayed outside society's norms. That some of the most famous heroin users—Billie Holiday, who was jailed for her drug use, and Charlie Parker, whose addiction contributed to his death at thirty-four—were African Americans and jazz musicians only reinforced the view of drug users as degenerates.

Racially tinged attitudes dragged into the 1970s as heroin took hold
in black inner cities, feeding a prejudice lingering to this day that
regards African Americans as more prone to drug addiction. That
heroin was widely thought of as a black drug only fed the popular
stigma against opiates.

But by then pain specialists in the United States and overseas
were questioning the virtual prohibition on morphine. Opioids had
been regarded as a godsend a century earlier for a reason. Surely, they
still had a role to play if the medical profession could keep a tighter
rein on them?

In the 1970s the greatest challenge to the prohibitionists emerged
from two key centers on different sides of the Atlantic. In Britain,
Cicely Saunders, a nurse and social worker who later qualified as a
doctor, had worked with the dying since the 1940s. She watched a
husband die in pain and founded the world's first purpose-built hospice, St. Christopher's, in London in 1967.

Saunders concentrated on pain relief as part of palliative care,
regarding it as a matter of medical ethics. In the words of the *British
Medical Journal*, Saunders "more than anybody else, was responsible
for establishing the discipline and the culture of palliative care." She
placed an emphasis on pain management and a focus on the dignity
of the dying. "She put paid to the notion that dying people should
wait until their painkillers had worn off before they received another
dose, and scotched the notion that the risk of opiate addiction was an
issue in their pain management," the *BMJ* said.

Saunders sought to fill the gap in knowledge by appointing Dr.
Robert Twycross in 1971 to research the most effective use of narcotics alongside the other strands of palliative care, finding the balance
between alleviating pain and keeping the patient functional enough
to still have a life. As a body of research and experience built up,
Saunders and Twycross promoted the scaling up of opioid doses and
advocated for a powerful mix of morphine and gin known as the
Brompton cocktail to give patients relief and dignity in their last
days.

The two doctors set aside the issue of addiction because it hardly mattered to patients who were about to die. It was Saunders and Twycross who approached Napp about the time-release pill.

The modern hospice movement was on the move, but it was a meeting in Italy in 1982 that propelled it to worldwide significance, resulting in the adoption of a scale for rising doses of opioid in palliative care by the World Health Organization (WHO).

Twycross was at the meeting. So was an American doctor, Kathleen Foley, who was doing her own groundbreaking work at the Memorial Sloan Kettering Cancer Center in New York. Foley emerged as a strong advocate of opiates to treat cancer pain after watching the suffering endured by dying patients. The WHO position bolstered her argument against the prohibition on opioids.

A couple of years after the gathering in Milan, a young doctor, Russell Portenoy, took up a position at Sloan Kettering. Foley was his boss. The pair worked together to bring the vision of pain-free and dignified death developed by Saunders and Twycross to the United States and with it a challenge to the old ideas about opioids. But they took it further.

Foley and Portenoy watched how effective the drugs were for people consumed by cancer and in easing the last weeks of life in the dying. They questioned why, if escalating doses of opioids were so helpful to the terminally ill, they could not be made to work for the millions of people living with chronic pain and its toll on physical and mental health. As Portenoy saw it, opiates had been an effective pain killer through most of recorded history, and it was only misplaced fears about addiction rooted in ignorance and stigma that was preventing them from still playing that role.

In Salt Lake City, Dr. Lynn Webster, one of a handful of doctors across the country to pioneer a now standard technique of delivering opioids using epidurals, took notice. "We thought we could restore the life of these people who are suffering so much by essentially eliminating their pain. We thought opioids were the answer. They had been the gold standard for centuries in the treatment of pain," he said.

Others took up the issue with religious zeal, including a doctor at Emory School of Medicine, David Haddox. But they needed evidence to overcome the hesitation of the US medical community. It came in 1986. Foley and Portenoy looked back over the medical histories of thirty-eight cancer patients who used opioid painkillers for several years. The results were mixed. While the drugs gave relief to more than half, fourteen still complained about pain levels.

The opioids also failed to greatly improve daily life. They didn't seem to make getting around any easier or help get their users back to work. To that extent, the paper was not a great testament to the effectiveness of narcotic painkillers.

But Portenoy and Foley focused their conclusions on a different set of numbers. They homed in on the statistic showing that only two of the patients became addicted and probably because they had previously abused drugs.

The two doctors took their findings to the medical journal *Pain*, claiming them to be evidence that opioids were not the dangerously addictive drugs so long feared by the medical profession. If there was a risk, it lay not with the drug but with patients with a history of addiction. All that was required was to make sure the two did not meet. "We conclude that opioid maintenance therapy can be a safe, salutary and more humane alternative to the options of surgery or no treatment in those patients with intractable non-malignant pain and no history of drug abuse," they wrote.

Pain rejected the article. The study was small and lacked the usual scientific rigor of control groups using alternative therapies or placebos. Portenoy pleaded the case, saying the paper was merely a counter to the prevailing view that opioids "always produce problems." The medical journal relented.

The two doctors saw the article as pushback against more comprehensive studies by institutions such as a Mayo Clinic report reinforcing the established view that opioid painkillers were not particularly effective for long-term treatment of pain, had debilitating side effects, and caused addiction. Even for those who got some comfort from the drugs, the clinic concluded that patients required escalating doses as tolerance grew and ultimately did better without opioids.

Years later, Portenoy said the *Pain* article was not trying to say more conventional findings were invalid. He just wanted to disrupt established thinking. "It should have been a little paper like a snapshot of a clinical experience and published and promptly forgotten," Portenoy told a University of California researcher, Marcia Meldrum. Portenoy might now wish it had been forgotten, but back then he was happy to see his "little paper turned into an important paper."

A prominent pain specialist, Richard Sternbach, wrote a scathing letter to the editor of *Pain*, accusing Portenoy and Foley of failing to grasp the complex nature of pain—that there are often psychological and behavioral causes—and of a fixation on opioids for relief. The exchange unleashed an intense and unusually sharp debate within the medical profession about the future of pain care. "The anger that that paper generated, and people buttonholing me at conferences and telling me that I was a bad guy and stuff that makes that even sound good. It was really an interesting time to live through," said Portenoy.

The lines were drawn for a battle over opioids that divided the medical profession and was still running two decades later.

Portenoy and Foley had tapped into a frustration among a group of younger pain doctors at their inability to offer anything more than superficial relief to the march of patients whose lives were dominated and destroyed by debilitating pain. To many of those doctors, opioid treatments were a magic bullet kept beyond reach.

The *Pain* paper marked the start of a revolution that turned attitudes to opioids on their head and brought about a fundamental shift in medical culture. Portenoy and Foley thought the long stigma against opioid treatment needed to be broken down. They had fired the opening shot with a paper that seemed to pull the rug from under the old arguments.

Years later, Portenoy admitted that the paper was not all it was cracked up to be. His sweeping conclusions were based on "weak, weak, weak data.... It was the weakest data there is."

He also acknowledged that his claims for the effectiveness and safety of opioids—assertions that would go on to become an important pillar on which an entire medical policy was constructed—were overblown at best. But that did not stop him running with them. He toured the country, calling opioids a gift from nature, and pushed access to the drugs as an ethical argument. People had a human right to be pain free. With it, the doctor helped create a new image of the good pain patient. They were no longer malingerers or whiners but silent sufferers, their tribulations little understood by wider society.

Portenoy needed more than his own paper to press the case. He put together a clutch of other shaky studies. Key among them was a brief letter in 1980 to the *New England Journal of Medicine* cited by Portenoy in his article with Foley.

Two doctors at Boston University Medical Center, Jane Porter and Hershel Jick, thought the *Journal*'s readers might be interested in numbers they'd crunched about addiction. The letter said that of 11,882 hospital patients treated with opioids, just 4 became addicted, and they all had a prior history of dependence. It appeared under the headline "Addiction Rare in Patients Treated with Narcotics," a bigger claim than the letter made.

There was no additional data to draw on nor information as to why the patients were treated with opioids. As they were in the hospital, it was likely they were treated for acute pain after surgery or an accident. Not only were they given the narcotics for a limited period, but it was under the supervision of medical staff who ensured they did not exceed their doses, quite different from the long-term prescribing and escalating doses advocated by Portenoy for chronic pain patients who might need the drugs for years or even life.

The 101-word letter was entirely accurate in its interpretation of the statistics, but all it offered was a snapshot of a particular set of patients in a hospital setting. That did not stop advocates of looser use of opioids from doing a quick calculation and pronouncing the Porter and Jick letter as evidence that less than 1 percent of prescription narcotics users became addicted.

In time, this spurious interpretation became a favorite with pharmaceutical companies, pain specialists, and pressure groups. It infected a slew of professional studies. It was misrepresented in the *Scientific American* as "an extensive study," called a "landmark report" in a medical textbook, and touted in *Time* magazine as evidence that fears of addiction to opioid painkillers were unwarranted. The letter was cited hundreds of times in scholarly papers. In time the "less than 1 percent" mantra even made its way into official guides for doctors.

Portenoy touted other claims rooted more in wishful thinking than scientific evidence. One theory had it that patients genuinely experiencing pain could not become addicted to opioids because the pain neutralized the euphoria caused by the narcotic. That in turn was used to back up a claim that there was no upper limit to the amount of opioids that could be prescribed, permitting ever-larger doses without risk.

There were no scientific studies to speak of to back up any of this. One supposition was built on another to construct a new orthodoxy in favor of unshackling the prescribing of opioids.

Although Portenoy was careful in his academic writing to qualify his claims by saying that the data on the long-term use of opioids was thin, and that close monitoring of patients by doctors was essential, he was less cautious in speeches and interviews to wider audiences. In 1993 he spoke to the *New York Times* of a "growing literature showing that these drugs can be used for a long time, with few side effects, and that addiction and abuse are not a problem."

Long after the epidemic took hold, Portenoy admitted that there was little basis for this claim and that he was more interested in changing attitudes to opioids among doctors than in scientific rigor. "I would cite six, seven, maybe ten different avenues of thought or avenues of evidence, none of which represented real evidence. And yet what I was trying to do was to create a narrative so that the primary care audience would look at this information in toto and feel more comfortable about opioids in a way they hadn't before. In essence, this was education to destigmatize and because the primary goal was to destigmatize we often left evidence behind," he admitted years later.

"Clearly, if I had an inkling of what I know now then, I wouldn't have spoken in the way that I spoke. It was clearly the wrong thing to do. And to the extent that some of the adverse outcomes now are as bad as they have become in terms of endemic occurrences, of addiction, and unintentional overdose deaths, it's quite scary to think about how the growth in that prescribing, driven by people like me, led in part to that occurring."

Portenoy was not alone in allowing his enthusiasm for his cause to justify a cavalier attitude toward scientific evidence and disdain for those who disagreed with him. In 1989, Dr. David Haddox, a physician with Emory University School of Medicine working as a consultant for drug manufacturers, coauthored a paper purporting to show that what looked like addiction is not addiction at all.

It said that cancer patients who appear to be craving more opioids because they are hooked are actually desperate for more drugs to kill the pain. As Haddox explained it, the pain, not the drug, created the hunger. If the behavior that looked like addiction went away when patients were given more drugs, it was not because their craving had been relieved but because the pain was diminished. Haddox called his theory "pseudoaddiction."

In time other prominent pain doctors came to regard pseudoaddiction as pseudoscience. Skeptics noted that Haddox based his entire study on observing a single cancer patient. But it slotted nicely into the new thinking. Doctors could not only set aside evidence of addiction but also prescribe ever-larger doses of opioids. If patients appeared to become hooked, the symptoms were to be dismissed as pseudoaddiction. Pseudoaddiction was a get-out-of-jail-free card for opioids.

By the early 1990s, Portenoy, Haddox, and a clutch of other determined doctors, convinced of the righteousness of their cause, were ready to unlock opioids from their confines and unleash them on an unsuspecting America.

PHARMACEUTICAL COMPANIES ARE not slow to spot an opportunity, and the opioid debate had not gone unnoticed at

Purdue. After Saunders and Twycross approached Napp Pharmaceuticals in the United Kingdom, the company had its Scottish subsidiary develop a time-release morphine tablet for cancer patients it called MST. A few years later, the drug was licensed in the United States as MS Contin—"contin" for "continuous," because it promised between eight and twelve hours of pain relief through its slow-release mechanism. It was Purdue's first step into the narcotics market.

By now Raymond Sackler's eldest son, Richard, also a doctor, was playing a leading role in the management of the company. In 1991, Purdue Frederick subdivided and created Purdue Pharma to focus on treatments for pain. Richard, who worked in research and development, channeled Arthur Sackler as he pushed for a wider sales base, encouraged by the changing mores on opioids promoted by Portenoy and his colleagues.

But MS Contin was on borrowed time. In 1990 Purdue's vice president for clinical research, Robert Kaiko, warned in an internal memo that with the drug's patent about to expire, it was only a matter of time before generic versions of the drug stole its market. The company needed to develop an alternative. For Purdue, the money lay in its ownership of the unique time-release formula, so Kaiko proposed switching it to another drug, oxycodone, and filing a new patent.

Oxycodone was a strange beast. While the public had heard of morphine and tended to have views about it, oxycodone was far less well known. Because of its name, physicians sometimes confused oxycodone with codeine, a weaker and commonly prescribed opioid.

Keiko's memo laid out some of the possibilities for a time-release oxycodone pill that could be prescribed for wider use than cancer pain. It also contained a revealing admission that "relatively little is known regarding the clinical pharmacology of oxycodone." No one really knew much about the effect of taking it for months or years, although there were warnings if the company had chosen to look for them. "It is interesting to note, however, that in the State of Connecticut and perhaps other states, the substance abuse officials consider oxycodone combinations among the most abused of Schedule II narcotic analgesic drugs," the memo added.

Kaiko, Richard Sackler, and two other Purdue executives whose names would feature prominently in the coming years—Paul Goldenheim and Michael Friedman—mapped out a plan for a new oxycodone pill. It was built around the time-release mechanism that meant it could be supercharged with exceptionally high doses of narcotic because, in theory at least, it would slowly bleed the drug into a patient's system over many hours.

Two months after the queen knighted Mortimer and Raymond Sackler, without the "Sir" as they weren't British or Commonwealth citizens, for donating a slice of their already considerable wealth to benefit medicine, science, and the arts in the United Kingdom, they learned they were about to be able to afford a lot more branding of institutions with the Sackler name.

The FDA had approved Purdue's new pill, Purdue's OxyContin.

CHAPTER 3

Pilliamson

E VEN BEFORE OXYCONTIN reared its head, Willis Duncan
had discovered opioids.

Painkillers got him through the day, deep underground, his body
relentlessly tested by life down the mines. "Sixteen hour days on your
knees in mud to your eyeballs. Your hands would be raw. You hurt.
Hurt bad all over at the end of the day." Duncan trickled the words
out slowly in a thick West Virginia accent. "Those pills, people were
depending on them."

There's not much on display at Duncan's cabin in a clearing
about twenty minutes' drive north of Williamson to suggest a particularly prosperous life, but it's a spacious home and he owns it outright. Over the years he earned good money as a contract electrician
on the coal mines. The work wasn't always consistent and sometimes
it was hours away, even as far south as Texas, but mining paid well
because it was demanding and dangerous.

The miners, like the loggers in the forests or up at the sawmill,
had long found one sedative or other to ease their physical strains.

At one time it was morphine or moonshine. Then marijuana. Until each ran up against official sanction. The mines began drug testing around the time Duncan started working in the pits in the 1980s. When First Lady Nancy Reagan made opposition to drugs her personal crusade, a positive test was a job killer.

For a while, miners who didn't want to take the risk relied on over-the-counter painkillers and relatively weaker prescription drugs such as Tylenol 3. But the use of prescription painkillers—Vicodin and Lorcets or the oxycodone tablet Percocet—climbed as word spread among those doing physically demanding labor that they were a lot better than anything else they could lay their hands on.

Duncan, like other miners, thought that if the drugs were on prescription they must be safe, and relative to what was to come, they were. By the time OxyContin made its appearance, Duncan and plenty of the men he worked with were already steeped in a culture of opioid painkillers. It was to prove fertile ground for the new drug.

DUNCAN SPREADS THE family photos across the kitchen counter. He smiles at the sight of his boys. His eldest, Brian, gap toothed under a pudding-bowl haircut at seven years old. Brian's younger brother, Jonathan, snapped some years later as a new father holding his baby daughter. He pauses over a picture of himself, more youthful in sunglasses and a lumberjack shirt, leaning on the trunk of his Chevy with Brian.

But the picture Duncan lingers on is a close-up of his wife, Debbie, looking as if she's caught on the hop by the camera as she gives half a smile, her red hair pulled back behind ears decorated with round gold rings. "Pretty as a doll," he murmurs.

Willis Duncan can't remember who first sent him off to see Dr. Diane Shafer in the early 2000s. Another of the miners probably. She'd write prescriptions for 60 or 120 Lorcets. If Duncan was short because he hadn't made it to the clinic to renew his prescription, there was always someone in the pit with a spare pill or two to tide him over. Lortabs were passed around like aspirin and ibuprofen. When the drug testing came around, it didn't matter if it turned up opioids, provided the miners could wave a prescription.

The pills worked well. Perhaps a little too well. Duncan felt physically better than ever when he was on them. The pain melted away, and he took the demands of the mine in his stride even after periodic batterings. He survived three roof collapses and was once seriously electrocuted. But he started to notice it was harder to get going before his shift without his pills, and when he didn't get them he sometimes skipped days at work. Duncan saw that he wasn't alone. "You get to seeing your fellow workers, they wouldn't come to work either. It wasn't just me. They wouldn't show up if they didn't have pain pills. Lorcets, Norcos, Roxycodone. Whatever people could get to get them through the day," he said.

Opioid prescribing climbed across rural Appalachia through the 1990s and nowhere more so than southern West Virginia. For a few years, Duncan needed the pills more than he admitted to himself at the time, but they weren't dominating his life until in 1998 Debbie Duncan fell ill and had an emergency operation. "She was bleeding femaley-wise, and they took her up to the hospital and they did a partial hysterectomy on her. That sucker changed her life at thirty-eight." Duncan struggles to explain the change in his wife, but before long she was prescribed Xanax for depression.

A year after Debbie's operation, Duncan was caught in a rock fall underground. It crushed his sternum and broke ribs. After emergency surgery, a doctor offered to sign him off work so he could claim disability benefit. But Duncan's children had plans to go to college, and he knew he would never be able to afford it if he wasn't working. He left the hospital with a month's worth of opioids and an instruction to get more when he needed them from the Williamson Wellness Center, run by Henry Vinson.

A few weeks after the operation, Duncan was sitting in front of Dr. Katherine Hoover. The drugs he was using weren't working terribly well. He was still in pain. His years of popping Lorcets on the mines had built up his tolerance to opiates and made the painkillers less effective. He needed higher doses to overcome the pain of the operation and recovery of his broken bones. Hoover wrote a prescription for stronger pills and added muscle relaxants to the mix.

They worked, and Duncan was soon back for more. When the insurance stopped paying, he stumped up $250 in cash to see Hoover. She told him there was no need to see her again unless he wanted to increase the dosage. He could just pay $150 at the front counter and collect a new prescription when his pills ran out.

> I didn't see a doctor but four times at Henry Vinson's place, and I went there eight years. You didn't see a doctor. To see a doctor, you had to be raising your medicine, and it would take hours to get in. You had about four receptionists in there. They'd check your blood pressure. My grandmother's Cherokee Indian, and I inherited all the junk they had. High blood pressure is one of them. It never mattered. After a while they quit taking blood pressure. "Everything all working fine? Yep. Where you want your medicine called in?" You tell 'em. Pay $150. Out you go.
>
> You could tell them your dick hurts, and they would write you a script. The doctor's signature was already on it when you went in. You just went in there and didn't even see the doctor and got your script. From five o'clock in the morning to nine o'clock at night, they were full speed ahead. It was swinging doors, jukebox. You get there at five o'clock in the morning. They didn't open till eight o'clock, but at five o'clock there would be a hundred people there waiting.

A couple of blocks away, Debbie Duncan was seeing Diane Shafer for her Xanax prescription. Duncan isn't sure when his wife started taking opioids and whether she was raiding his supply before she also started getting them from Shafer. But soon Debbie was filling the medicine cabinet with hundreds of her own pills.

AT THE TIME Debbie Duncan was recovering from her operation at the end of the 1990s, Wilbert Hatcher was quitting his job as a guard at an Ohio jail specializing in the drug addicted. He'd watched the torment of a human body torturing itself to extract a hit, and it scared him because now he was seeing it inside his own home.

Before Ohio, Hatcher worked six years at a West Virginia treatment center, seeing people recycled through the system, rotating through highs and detox, their lives consumed by the struggle to find drugs or to get off of them. Everything else—relationships, work, dignity—cast aside in the perpetual pursuit of sating the beast.

Now here was his wife in the grip of amphetamines and alcohol. Hatcher knew the markers. The changing personality. The deceptions. The absences, even when she was present. They were already tearing at his family and taking a toll on their two young sons. Hatcher gave his wife an ultimatum. "I had doctors I worked with that were willing to treat her. I said to her, 'You have to go get help. You have a year to get yourself together. These two boys are coming with me,'" he said. "She was a very beautiful lady. Blonde hair, blue eyes. The last time I seen her she looked like she was sixty."

In the late 1990s, Hatcher moved to Williamson. He'd grown up there and thought the rural life would be better for his sons, away from the traps of the city. He landed a job as a guard at the regional jail.

Williamson was not the city he remembered. The circus around what was commonly known as "Henry Vinson's place" and Diane Shafer's clinic a block and a half around the corner seemed to dominate the place. Hatcher even had occasion to go to Shafer's when he broke a finger. He was seen by Dr. William Ryckman, who prescribed a few painkillers. Hatcher was clued into the dangers and stopped taking them after a few days. He described himself as "totally against the pill thing, fanatically."

Hatcher got himself a job at a motel the other side of the iron bridge to Kentucky. One day in 2003, while helping a guest locked out of a room, he slipped down the stairs. As it was an employment accident, Kentucky's workers' compensation scheme covered his treatment, so he applied through one of the storefront injury lawyers in Williamson. The lawyer told Hatcher that to claim, he needed to establish a record of treatment showing he had an injury and pointed him to the Aquatic Therapy Center gotten off the ground by Vinson. The front desk told Hatcher he could not be seen without a referral by Vinson's clinic across the street.

Hatcher found himself standing in front of Dr. Katherine Hoover. She checked him over, gave him a referral to the physiotherapy facility, and prescribed Lortab painkillers.

Hatcher was welcomed at the aquatic center and the clinic for the next few weeks, but then the workers' compensation payments for physiotherapy dried up and he couldn't afford to pay on his wages. The state of Kentucky would keep paying for prescriptions, though.

Hatcher had not forgotten the lessons learned working at the rehab center years earlier, but his back wasn't getting any better and he really needed something for the pain. He talked to Hoover. She doubled the dosage. "I'm a well-rounded, educated individual who thinks that I don't have an addictive personality. That is a concept that you think. I worked in a psychiatric hospital for six years, and I worked around substance abuse. So an addictive personality, I don't have that. But when they're pushing it, and they feed it and feed it...," he said.

Within months he could not do without the daily hit of narcotic, and the doses escalated rapidly from thirty every two weeks to sixty and then ninety. The pills began to consume Hatcher's life.

Six months into it, it became a problem because I was looking for it. I had to have it. My body hurt. It wanted it. When you take a pill and there's no relief, when you're taking them just to function in life and get up, that's the problem. It's no longer for the pain; it's for every second of your day to function.

Your body craves. Craves it. It's just like being hungry, but it comes with physical pain. To go without it, the physical pain, oh, gosh, you're jerking, your hands and stuff is jerking, you feel the cramps in your arms and your legs. It's real bad. The anxiety, the muscle cramps. You're trying to

figure out, "What am I going to do here? What am I going
to do?"

Hatcher's days revolved around his pill supply. He collected a prescription from the Wellness Center twice a month. By then Hoover
had added Valium and a muscle relaxant along with the opioids, but
mostly he didn't see her. On the occasions he did, she barely asked
about his condition. She was more interested in hearing about how
things operated up at the jail where Hatcher once worked. Hoover's
son had been arrested and died inside the jail, and the doctor was
suing for wrongful death. "She wasn't about my condition. She wasn't
worried about my back or my neck. She was getting her money. I
paid cash, $300 a month. They had the scripts ready for you when
you went in. There were times I didn't even see her. I went two years
without seeing her. I went in. They do your blood pressure. They ask
a couple of questions on the form. And then, here you go," he said.
"There's times I didn't even fill out anything. It was ready. Who am I
to say stop doing this? You've already got me."

Every time Wilbert Hatcher went to the clinic, the lines seemed
longer and the circus seemed louder. "The line to get in there would
run for a block and a half. They were from Virginia, from Tennessee,
from Ohio. You had people out there in the parking lot trading their
meds, selling."

Everyone seemed to come to Williamson. The accidentally
addicted. The hard-core addicted looking for ever-greater highs.
The teenager looking for fun who got hooked by way of the parents'
medicine cabinet. Some were already addicted and saw an easy way
to feed their habit with what they regarded as legal heroin. Others
arrived looking for medical help never having taken a drug illegally
in their lives.

The patients in the Wellness clinic's records included coal truck drivers, shop assistants, forklift operators, waiters, sawmill workers. They
came looking for relief from bad backs and arthritis, migraines and
school sports injuries. Or to feed their addiction. It didn't matter what
the condition was, there was pretty much only one treatment. Pills.

People took to calling the town Pilliamson. Opinion on its streets was divided. The complaints about out-of-state cars clogging the streets rarely let up. People tried to detour past the clinics to avoid the drugged up and the dealers. But the out-of-towners were good for some local businesses, and a slice of the profits pulled in by the pharmacies boosted the city tax coffers.

Hatcher's prescriptions were faxed to Family Pharmacy, a five-minute drive the other side of the river, just inside Kentucky. Hatcher noticed that it was often Ryckman's name as the prescribing doctor on the bottle of pills, even though he never saw him. But he didn't care. Just so long as he got his Lortabs. "In your mind you think there's something wrong here, but the addiction part of you tells you, 'I don't care. They're giving it to me, and I have it now,'" he said.

As Hatcher's tolerance grew, he popped the pills at an ever-faster rate. The dosages kept rising until even what he could get on prescription was not enough. So he turned to the street.

Williamson was awash in pills. Dealers brought people by car and minibus from out of town to line up at the Wellness Center. Some turned over their entire prescription for cash just to make money. Others, who needed a fix too, kept some of the pills for their own use and made money on the rest.

Hatcher knew which doors to knock on. "There are people in my life that I would never have associated with. There are people that couldn't get five minutes of my time because I knew what they were doing. But now these people are in my interest circle because I'm knocking on their door to get it," he lamented. "You knew who it was. You knew who had them."

The hunt for pills took over his life. It took his money, and it took his time. "You do the job. You make dinner for the kids. But there's the constant nagging. Where are the pills coming from? You bang on doors. No answer. You wait. Even when there is an answer, you wait. The dealer doesn't have what you need. But he will in three or four or five hours. Waiting," he said.

Hatcher found himself standing in line with the kind of people he used to help. The kind of people he used to guard. They were from all over. Young, old. More men than women but still plenty of women. Mostly white, although Hatcher himself was African American. He saw that he was looking at himself, yet he could see no way out.

In 2005 Hatcher landed a job as an assistant manager at the Walmart on the other side of the Tug Fork river. It paid well for the area at $40,000 a year, but the hours were long and after a couple of years, he realized that the demands of the job and the constant search for pills meant he wasn't spending time with his children. Something had to give if he was to be a better parent, and it wasn't going to be the drugs. Hatcher quit Walmart in 2007 for a job paying $10 an hour in an auto-parts store. His income halved. Now he had time to see his kids, but what money he had was going to buy painkillers. Hatcher spent a couple of hundred dollars a week, half his income. "My family lost a lot. I could have given them a lot more than what they had. I've lost a truck. I've lost a Jeep. I've lost a lot. But time is the biggest thing I lost. The money, that stuff"—he shrugs—"time, and being able to tell you exactly what was going on in my life at the time."

IN THE MID-2000S, Willis Duncan was still earning decent money. Up to $10,000 a month on some jobs, but much of it went on ever-increasing numbers of painkillers for himself and Debbie. The more they used, the more their tolerance to opioids built and the more pills they needed. Willis was addicted, but so long as he got his drugs he could still function. But Debbie was by then taking such large doses that she was frequently out of it. "I'd be so mad, I'm talking about boiling mad, 'cause she'd be on 'em when I'd get home and I'd have a day off to spend time with her, and she would be all *fubar* [fucked up beyond all recognition]. You couldn't understand nothing she said. A foreign language," he said.

Some days Duncan found Debbie passed out in the middle of the floor, facedown with her backside in the air as if she had been on the move but suddenly lost power. Even then, the couple had yet to graduate to OxyContin. It was their eldest son, Brian, who first brought it home.

Brian worked in the mines and had fallen into his father's way with pills to cope with the strains of the job. Willis warned him off and was shocked at how fast his son went downhill. Brian ballooned to four hundred pounds on OxyContin prescriptions topped up with pills bought on the street. "I tried to talk to him, but he'd got to that point where he thought he already knew everything, which most people do when they get on them," Willis said.

He was on a job in Texas one Christmas Eve in the mid-2000s when he got a call from Debbie. "She said, they've broken into the house and took everything in there that weren't tied down," said Willis. "I had an RCA big screen. I had a Panasonic surround sound. I had a tuner scanner. I could pick up anybody around. I had three guns that was probably worth about thirty-five hundred. I had my boy's knife collection that I was putting together for him."

Willis put the word out, looking to see if anyone was trying to sell his stuff locally. "Came to found out who done it. My son. Brian robbed his own house to buy drugs. Sure did. It was a heartbreaking situation."

The profits were reaped by Williamson's doctors and pharmacists. Diane Shafer and Katherine Hoover were making thousands of dollars a day in cash payments. Shafer's clinic was taking in around a million dollars a year from the early 2000s. There was so much money she ran out of places to stash it.

What the doctors ordered, the drugstores supplied. Month on month, the orders of hydrocodone and OxyContin escalated. The drug makers and distributors delivered without question.

Years later, Wilbert Hatcher wondered why. "This is spit town. How many pills were they selling? Enough for a major city. This is ridiculous."

CHAPTER 4

The Sales Pitch

I N 2000, DR. Rajan Masih uprooted his family from Texas, where he worked as an emergency room physician and as a doctor in a federal prison, for the fifteen-hundred-mile journey to West Virginia's eastern panhandle, that part of the state orphaned on the other side of the Monongahela National Forest.

Masih settled with his wife, a police officer born in El Paso, and children in Petersburg, an undistinguished town of a couple of thousand people. The job at a hospital in Grant County wasn't so different from Texas. Perhaps not so many gunshot wounds. But after a while, Masih encountered a new phenomenon, the OxyContin salesman.

Drug company representatives are a way of life for doctors. Masih usually heard them out, as they were often the best way to learn about a new medicine. The reps might pull out a medical study or two to back up their case for why it was better than drugs already on the market. It was an odd situation. The salespeople had no medical training, but chances were they knew more about the nuts and bolts of the medicines they were selling than the primary care doctors they were trying to win over. Or at the least they had the scientific papers to hand out and a ready supply of answers to questions about side effects physicians might be seeing in their patients.

But it quickly became apparent to Masih that the rep from Purdue was something different, and so was the drug he was selling. Masih remembers the salesman banging on the office door, loaded down with glossy brochures and bearing pizza.

The pitch began conventionally enough, with all the ways in which Purdue said OxyContin was better than the painkillers already on the market. The key selling point was its claim to provide twelve hours of relief. Masih recalls the rep explaining how OxyContin overcame the problem of prescribing regular painkillers taken every four hours. They created peaks and troughs, and patients were hit by an initial high dose of the narcotic but then had to endure rising pain again as the drug wore off and they waited for time to elapse before they could take the next pill. "He had a graph showing exactly that, comparing OxyContin with the peaks and troughs of Vicodin and Percocet," said Masih. "And he had the *New England Journal of Medicine* article saying that people don't get addicted. If they have legitimate pain, they won't get addicted. That got handed out to every doctor."

In time the pressure stepped up. Masih was surprised to be presented with the prescribing patterns of other doctors he knew around that part of West Virginia. The Purdue rep chastised him for not prescribing more. "He'd come saying, 'This person writes more than anyone. Doc, we really need to get you on board here.' It was aggressive," said Masih. "In order to get into our office, you had to get in with the front desk. He's bringing pizza. He's got mugs, pens, all this kind of stuff for all the girls that work in the office. It's not subtle."

Masih had never known such high-pressure selling from a drug rep before. He was not alone. Purdue had unleashed the biggest drug-marketing push anyone could remember using data to target its selling in a way that had never been done before and sending hundreds of sales reps to sweet-talk and cajole tens of thousands of doctors into prescribing OxyContin. Doctors reported Purdue's sales staff trying a range of tactics from implying they were not good physicians if they weren't prescribing opioids on demand to implicit threats of every doctor's nightmare, the malpractice lawsuit. But years later, the parts physicians remember most clearly are what proved to be very persuasive lies.

PURDUE'S AGGRESSIVE SALES strategy grew out of the hurdles the company faced as it submitted its application for approval of OxyContin to the FDA back in December 1994. The company saw no great problem in getting permission to sell the drug. It was pretty similar to opioids already on the market, only stronger. The narcotic at its core, oxycodone, was known and approved for use in other painkillers, including Vicodin.

One challenge lay in persuading the FDA to approve this supercharged pill for as wide a use as possible in spite of its high dosage of oxycodone. There was little doubt the agency would endorse the drug for treatment of severe pain, but that was a short-term market mostly limited to patients just out of an operation or injured in an accident or who were dying from cancer. Approval to sell OxyContin for moderate pain was the big earner. Those patients, people living with damaged backs or chronic diseases such as arthritis, would keep coming back for years, providing a never-ending stream of buyers.

All this would be spelled out on what is known in the industry as "the label," a long set of instructions and warnings inserted into each package of drugs to guide prescribing doctors and patients. Purdue would be permitted to market OxyContin only within the parameters set down by the label: the wording would make or break the drug.

Purdue's other challenge was to distinguish OxyContin from other opioids already on the market. The company was keen to have the label endorse the properties of its slow-release mechanism, the drug's unique selling point. Getting a decent night's sleep is a huge challenge for people in pain, and the sales department wanted to be able to tell doctors it was better than rival opioids because they lasted for only three or four hours, until patients were woken by the return of pain and had to take another pill. OxyContin's system of storing a large amount of narcotic to be bled slowly into the system meant people would be able to sleep through the night.

But three months after the company submitted its application, the marketing office circulated an alarming memo. A focus group of about forty doctors put up resistance to prescribing OxyContin because they were worried the high dosage of oxycodone would make it attractive to those with a drug habit.

The report on this insightful focus group recommended Purdue do clinical trials to demonstrate the benefits of OxyContin over the pain-killers it was trying to displace, such as Percocet and Vicodin. One way was to show that "there might be any reductions in the side effects that one might get when compared with combination opioids." Combination opioids, including Percocet and Vicodin, mixed the narcotic with acetaminophen, or Paracetamol, to help with the pain as the narcotic wore off. But acetaminophen causes liver damage and sometimes death when taken long term. OxyContin was pure narcotic.

The sales department also thought it would be even better if tests could show that OxyContin's delayed-release mechanism made it harder for people to misuse than drugs taken more frequently, known as instant-release, or IR, painkillers. "If the product was proven to have a lower abuse potential than IR oxycodone it would improve the likelihood of usage for non-cancer pain," the memo said.

A draft label already in the works at the FDA made no mention of either benefit. A few months later, it had been reworded. "Delayed absorption, as provided by OxyContin tablets, is believed to reduce the abuse liability of a drug," the new label said.

In one sentence Purdue had a marketing device and a means of reassuring doctors suspicious of opioids. Not only that, but the company could point to OxyContin as the only opioid to make such a claim on its label. That neither the claim the drug was more effective nor the assertion it was safer was true did not hold back Purdue.

The wording should have been a warning in itself. Its master-ful avoidance of specifics in claiming only a belief that slow release discouraged misuse reflected an absence of evidence. Purdue officials later testified that the company had not done any clinical studies to test the potential for abuse. The claim was supposition based on weak research papers purporting to show that drug abusers preferred immediate-release painkillers because they gave a quicker hit.

The label made other claims that proved to be demonstrably false, including an assertion that addiction is rare when opioids are taken under a doctor's care.

Even its promise of a good night's sleep was open to question. The company's own documentation to the FDA included a graph showing that tests on its controlled-release oxycodone gave patients an initial surge of the drug, peaking at around three hours, and then the impact fell rapidly, so that after twelve hours the concentration of narcotic in the blood was less than one-third of its height. Once it was on the market, some patients reported OxyContin wore off after eight or nine hours.

The FDA has the whip hand in deciding what goes on a drug's label. What appeared eventually on the OxyContin label mirrored the company's sales pitch. Purdue later insisted that the FDA alone decided the wording, and the agency confirmed that. But even if the drug maker did not dictate the text of the label, there is little doubt that it effectively decided the wording because the FDA had nothing more to go on than Purdue's claims for its own drug. Those claims were in turn effectively scripted by the marketing department.

The FDA official who oversaw the OxyContin approval process was Curtis Wright. In 1993, as OxyContin was in development, an agency toxicologist told Purdue to conduct a clinical trial, a standard addiction and overdose test, by grinding the drug down and injecting it into animals. The company balked, saying there was already plenty of information available about oxycodone when in fact studies of the long-term effects of opioids were extremely limited. Purdue was as reluctant then as it was later on to discover the real impact of its drug. Wright sided with the company, and no test was done.

As it turned out, Wright was not particularly impressed by the claims for the new drug. He noted in his assessment that OxyContin was as good as any other on the market, but its only real advantage was that it did not have to be taken as often. The FDA report said the effects of the drug would be like those for other opioids, that its side effects were also similar, and that dependence was possible. Wright also recommended that Purdue should not be permitted to claim that OxyContin was better than other opioids, and he issued an explicit warning that "care should be taken to limit competitive promotion" of the drug, a swipe at some of the grand claims made for it by the manufacturer.

Yet ultimately, Wright did approve OxyContin for wide use. He deemed it an appropriate remedy for moderate to severe pain—a departure from the FDA's usual practice. Shortly afterward he left the FDA. Within two years he was working at Purdue.

If the claims for OxyContin's reduced abuse potential were highly misleading, another part of the label approved by the FDA was only too accurate. Technically, it was a warning, but it served more as a blueprint. "Tablets are to be swallowed whole, and are not to be broken, chewed or crushed. Taking broken, chewed or crushed OxyContin tablets could lead to the rapid release and absorption of a potentially toxic dose of oxycodone," the label read.

In the weeks before the final approval for the drug came through, Purdue's marketing team was mapping out its sales strategy. At its heart was a push to sell the drug as widely as possible. "It was reinforced that we do not want to niche OxyContin just for cancer pain," the minutes of a 1995 launch-team meeting said.

Sales reps were instructed to tell physicians there was no need to try a lower-dose pill first; they could go straight to OxyContin because it was safer. The drug was pushed as "the opioid to start with" and the "opioid to stay with." A drug for life. A perpetual payout for Purdue.

Above all, the convenience of twelve-hour dosing "was emphasized as the most important benefit." The promotional literature pushed the notion that twice-a-day OxyContin was "the easy way" against the "hard way" of more regular doses of Vicodin and Percocet.

Purdue launched OxyContin with an announcement touting it as "New hope for millions of Americans," positioning the drug as a valuable weapon in the war on untreated pain. Millions of people, it said, lived in agony because of "unwarranted fears of uncontrollable side effects and/or addiction by physicians and patients alike." The company said the fear of addiction was exaggerated and largely unfounded.

Purdue had done its bit to promote the case for a "pain epidemic" to justify mass prescribing. Its marketing strategists adopted one of Arthur Sackler's old tricks with an opinion poll to highlight "the prevalence and problems of chronic pain."

The company called the pill a significant advance in the treatment of persistent pain and suggested it was effective for arthritis, lower back pain, injuries, and cancer. It claimed that unlike other drugs, OxyContin offered "smooth and sustained pain control all day and all night" and said side effects from opioids "diminished over time, even as daily doses increased." None of this was true.

Arthur's lessons were well learned. OxyContin was pushed onto the market with an intense advertising campaign targeted at doctors as the gateway to mass prescribing. The salesmen Purdue sent out weren't doctors, but they were well armed with talking points and medical literature, not least Russell Portenoy's claims about a less than 1 percent addiction rate.

The sales message was not unlike the one Arthur pushed for Valium. OxyContin was the new drug for everyone. The FDA's label encompassed just about anything within its definition of "moderate to severe pain."

Purdue turned the label it had in effect drafted into one of its leading sales tools. The marketing department told reps to present it to doctors as evidence of independent approval of the claims made for the drug.

As the marketing plan kicked in, Purdue hosted conferences in resorts from Florida to California, paying more than five thousand doctors, pharmacists, and nurses to train as speakers to tour the country promoting opioid painkillers. They were then dispatched to spread the message at hospitals, medical conferences, and anywhere else doctors would listen.

But if Purdue was to break beyond the cancer market, it also needed to reach the primary care doctors prescribing the instant-release painkillers whose market the company was hoping to poach.

Patient privacy effectively ends with a person's name. Once identity is removed from medical records, everything else about a patient is up for sale. Their conditions, treatments, and the drugs they are taking, even the names of prescribing doctors, are traded. Pharmacies sell the data on which physicians are prescribing what drugs, and the pharmaceutical companies pay handsomely for it.

Purdue bought up the stats on where Vicodin, Percocet, and other instant-release opioids were dispensed and which doctors were the most common prescribers and pointed its sales reps in that direction. First they looked for the physicians prescribing the most opioids and worked on getting them to switch from Vicodin or Percocet to OxyContin. Then the reps put the squeeze on other physicians in the same area by suggesting they were letting their patients down by not prescribing narcotics at the same rate as their colleagues down the road.

One of the reps unleashed on unsuspecting doctors was Sean Thatcher, a Purdue salesman in Montana. He carried a list of about a hundred practitioners who were "priority targets for the sales team" based on their prescribing histories because they were regarded as "potentially high prescribers" of OxyContin.

Three or four times a year, Thatcher hosted talks by speakers paid by Purdue to which he invited doctors. He said his focus was on selling OxyContin. It earned him bigger bonuses than other drugs.

One tactic Thatcher picked up at Purdue training sessions was to ask doctors and medical staff to flag the charts of patients who would be "good candidates" for OxyContin. Typically, these would be people on opioids made by other companies. Reps would press prescribers to switch them to OxyContin. "The practice of flagging patient charts was among the 'best practices' recommended by managers and discussed by various sales representatives as something that worked well for them in the field."

Sales reps distributed coupons for doctors to give their patients a 30-day free supply of OxyContin to get them started. They also arrived at physicians' offices loaded with free mugs, fishing hats, even a CD: *Get in the Swing With OxyContin*. The Drug Enforcement Administration later said it had never seen anything like it in promoting a narcotic.

For years, doctors have insisted that prescribing is not influenced by such practices, but studies show otherwise. Dr. Rajan Masih found that if he raised concerns about levels of prescribing or that a patient might be addicted, the Purdue rep had a ready answer. "That *New England Journal of Medicine* article saying that people don't get addicted, if they have legitimate pain they won't get addicted, that got handed out to everybody."

Purdue distributed fifteen thousand copies of a video on Oxy-Contin to doctors without first submitting it to the FDA for review. The promotion, called "I got my life back," enlisted an endorsement from a pain specialist, Dr. Alan Spanos. "There's no question that our best, strongest pain medicines is the opioids, but these are the same drugs that have a reputation for causing addiction and other terrible things. Now, in fact, the rate of addiction amongst pain patients who are treated by doctors is much less than 1 percent. They don't wear out; they go on working. They do not have serious medical side effects. And so these drugs, which I repeat are our best, strongest pain medications, should be used much more than they are for patients in pain," he said in the video.

Thatcher was trained to push the same message that OxyContin was more convenient than other opioids because it had to be taken only twice a day. But he said he often heard from prescribers that it did not live up to the claims. "Roughly 30 percent to 40 percent of doctors I called on complained that pain relief from OxyContin did not last twelve hours, as represented, even at high doses," he said. "I was directed to market OxyContin for chronic pain, including lower back pain and pain from arthritis. Some of the doctors I visited had patients who were on OxyContin for a year or more and complained that their patients were developing a tolerance to the product. I was trained to tell doctors that they should titrate up the dose for patients who developed tolerance." Thatcher said he was instructed to tell doctors that what looked like addiction or dependence was really pseudoaddiction.

Purdue threw unprecedented amounts of money into promoting OxyContin, spending several times the advertising budget of rivals. The company had hundreds of its own sales reps pushing the drug but needed more and signed up three hundred from a rival firm, Abbott Laboratories. Abbott insisted on being indemnified by Purdue from lawsuits over OxyContin and then went about selling the drug with gusto. Nearly one thousand reps were pushing it to tens of thousands of doctors across the country.

Abbott rewarded its top sales staff with cash and vacations. Purdue had a generous bonus scheme too, with salaries more than doubled by the boost from sales. A typical Purdue rep was paid $55,000 in 2001 but pulled in bonuses of $71,500. Some went as high as $240,000.

Purdue's marketing was far more successful than it predicted. The company had estimated it would earn $350 million from Oxy-Contin in the first five years. The little opioid pill pulled in more than $2 billion in sales, accounting for 80 percent of Purdue's revenue. The drug maker rushed to expand production.

CHAPTER 5

What They Knew

THE OXYCONTIN SALES reps came knocking on Dr. Art Van Zee's door at the primary health care clinic he ran in rural Virginia. But he was learning fast about the drug in ways Purdue never talked about and about the power of the drug industry when a small-town doctor puts patients before profit.

The Nevada-born physician stumbled across the small Virginia mining town of St. Charles in the mid-1970s as one of a group of student doctors offering free checkups, X-rays, and blood tests to rural communities with limited access to medical care. Van Zee arrived "infused with a sense of social justice and activism that was commonplace then." He ended up staying.

St. Charles sits in Lee County, squeezed into a slither of southwestern Virginia between Kentucky and Tennessee. For decades the town lived and thrived off great mining camps, including the Bonny Blue. Its closure in the 1940s marked the start of the slide. "It's hard to imagine this was the biggest and busiest town in Lee County in those days. There were two thousand men on one shift at Bonny

Blue. Saturday night you couldn't walk through town. It was shoulder to shoulder. They had hotels, grocery stores. It was full of life," said Van Zee.

The community relied on the mine doctor for basic health care. His interest was mainly in keeping men able to work down the pit, but at least he was there. By the 1970s, the nearest medical help was miles away.

Student doctors held health fairs in St. Charles for a few summers, prompting its residents to raise the money to build the clinic Van Zee now runs. The walls are dotted with photographs of the coal camp. Van Zee put them up because patients like spotting their fathers and grandfathers as an affirmation of better times.

After Bonny Blue went out of business, the communities around the mine ebbed away. St. Charles had a population of nearly six hundred people in 1950. It was half of that when Van Zee arrived. By 2016 not much more than one hundred people lived in the town. "There's still one mine up the road. Has a shaft that goes all the way through the mountain into Kentucky. But the town just died when Bonny Blue died," he said. A few of the miners' houses still stand, but the forest has reclaimed much of its territory.

Van Zee saw the first flickers of the coming epidemic in 1999 when patients began telling him about sons, daughters, and grandchildren suddenly hooked on a new drug, OxyContin. Within a year or so, the pill seemed to be everywhere. "I'd probably seen fifteen people who were opioid addicted in twenty-five years, and now there was this tsunami of people addicted to OxyContin. It was hard to find a family that wasn't affected very directly."

Van Zee was used to seeing patients who took Vicodin or Percocet in unsanctioned ways. Middle-aged women to cope with bodies creaking under the strain of the demands of mountain living, younger people as an escape from the mind-numbing boredom of long, foggy winters.

OxyContin was different. It took a hold of people's lives and turned them into thieves who stole from their families and neighbors to meet the cost of feeding an ever-demanding habit. It cost them their jobs, cars, houses, dignity, and sometimes their children. "There had never been anything like that around here. There'd been prescription drug abuse for decades, probably more than in other regions of the country. Young people who would snort Percocet or Lortab at a party, recreationally abuse it, but be able to walk away from it without becoming opiate addicted. But once a high-potency drug like OxyContin that was easy to abuse become highly available, it changed recreational users to addicted individuals in a very short time," said Van Zee.

The drug engulfed parents and their children. In the three years after OxyContin made its appearance, the number of Lee County children placed in foster care was up 300 percent. A survey of students in the county school system in 2000 found that 20 percent of twelfth graders and 9 percent of seventh graders had used OxyContin. "Many of these kids were ones that I had held in my arms when they were babies and had taken care of their parents and their grandparents," said Van Zee.

Overdoses were up. Hepatitis C, a sometimes fatal liver infection transmitted by needles, was escalating as more people sought the power and speed of the high from injecting.

The Virginia state police drug unit had for years worked on a belief that the misuse of Ritalin, a drug mostly prescribed to young people for attention deficit disorder, was the problem of the future. By 2000 the police were focused on OxyContin.

Van Zee was convinced that if Purdue only knew the situation, it would do the right thing. The FDA too. He understood how federal agencies and big pharmaceutical companies might not have their finger on the pulse of rural Appalachia, so he set out to educate them. Van Zee wrote to Purdue and the FDA. His letters went unanswered.

In 2000 an invitation landed for the inaugural meeting of a new organization, the Appalachian Pain Foundation (APF). The founder was a West Virginia doctor, Susan Bertrand, who said she wanted to educate physicians about the benefits of opioids. The money behind the initiative was Purdue's. Company reps approached Bertrand after she gave a talk about pain management in a drugstore in her hometown of Princeton and offered to meet her foundation's costs. Purdue didn't trumpet its sponsorship, but there was a clue in the choice of the main speaker at the APF's launch in West Virginia's capital, Charleston: Dr. David Haddox.

Haddox, the doctor who promoted the theory of pseudoaddiction, was by now on Purdue's payroll and its most public defender of OxyContin in the face of increasing numbers of newspaper stories about overdoses and addiction. Haddox developed a line in dismissing the articles as scaremongering and ill-informed. He bandied about the false 1 percent addiction-risk claim, questioned whether the dead had really been killed by OxyContin, and asserted that addiction and overdose were nothing compared to the national epidemic of untreated pain.

At the core of Haddox's defense of OxyContin was a variation on the National Rifle Association's claim that guns don't kill people; people kill people. It was not the drugs causing the addiction and overdoses but the users. The problem was the people, not the pills.

Van Zee decided he needed to talk to Haddox. He spotted that the Purdue executive was addressing the Appalachian Pain Foundation's second meeting, a couple of hours drive from St. Charles. After Haddox had spoken with his usual enthusiasm about what a godsend prescription opioids were in liberating the afflicted from pain, Van Zee took the opportunity of questions to describe what OxyContin was doing to Lee County. After the meeting, he approached Haddox and pleaded for Purdue to rein in its marketing, saying the company was pushing the drug much too widely. Haddox said that wasn't his department and left.

Van Zee continued to make a nuisance of himself, writing letters, rounding up support among other doctors, and organizing public meetings. He wrote to Purdue, comparing the catastrophe gripping parts of Appalachia to the "sentinel areas" of New York and San Francisco at the beginning of the HIV/AIDS epidemic.

The company was worried enough by this small-town doctor to invite him to dinner with Haddox and a group of Purdue's medical researchers. Van Zee told his dinner companions OxyContin was creating a "medical, social, legal, and societal catastrophe," and he presented Haddox with a list of actions he wanted Purdue to take. These included warning letters to doctors across the country, alerting them to the rising levels of OxyContin abuse and addiction in Appalachia, and to end the marketing of the drug for chronic noncancer pain, including the sponsorship of seminars. He also wanted Purdue to use the extensive data it collected to examine whether there was a connection between marketing and higher levels of addiction and overdoses. The last item on the list was to remake OxyContin to include an inhibitor to suppress addiction.

Haddox could not have been happy. Van Zee's evidence flew in the face of his contention that the problem was with the users not the drug and undermined his claim that if there was an epidemic in the country, it was of untreated pain, not addiction to opioids.

Van Zee thought Purdue was being willfully blind. He sent off for copies of the company's application for OxyContin's approval by the FDA and saw from it that when the drug was pulverized in a test, two-thirds of the oxycodone could be extracted for snorting or injecting. "I looked at that and thought there was ample warning right there that this could be a highly abusable drug. Just the opposite of what they were saying," he said.

In reviewing Purdue's sales materials, Van Zee noted a systematic effort to play down the risk of addiction. The company's "Partners Against Pain" website for doctors, its videos, and literature all falsely claimed the risk of patients becoming hooked was extremely small. He saw that sales reps pushed the "less than 1 percent" risk of addiction line based on the spurious interpretation of the Porter and Jick letter, which by then had already come under scrutiny.

The misrepresentation of the letter had attracted the attention of Dr. Steven Passik, whose interest in pain treatment started when he worked with Russell Portenoy and Katherine Foley at Sloan Kettering. He was paid by Purdue as a consultant, but in 2001 in a letter to the *Journal of Pain* he raised concerns about the claims made for the Porter and Jick study. "In our zeal to improve access to opioids and relieve patient suffering, pain specialists have understated the problem, drawing faulty conclusions from very limited data. In effect, we have told primary care doctors and other prescribers that the risk was so low that they essentially could ignore the possibility of addiction," he wrote.

"The more I read from a lot of the thought leaders quoting these studies, the more I thought it is ridiculous evidence," said Van Zee. "Portenoy later admitted he was just trying to change mind-sets. He admitted they were just trying to get people to be more willing to use opioids more liberally. At that time, there were egregious things where people were dying from cancer and were in terrible pain, and their doctors would give them pitiful amounts of opioids. It was inhumane. There were very definitely mind-sets to change about prescribing opioids. But they went about it the wrong way."

By 2001 the situation was so bad in Lee County that Van Zee organized a town hall meeting in St. Charles and began a petition to the FDA to have OxyContin withdrawn from sale. People came from across the county. "There were eight hundred people in our little high school auditorium over the OxyContin problem because it was painful; it was acute. There was nobody untouched."

VAN ZEE WAS getting nowhere with Purdue, but he thought the FDA might be more reasonable. The agency had not been idle. The steady drip of reports from coroners, police departments, the Drug Enforcement Administration, and in local newspapers finally forced the FDA to face up to its calamitous mistake in approving OxyContin's original label falsely claiming the drug reduced the risk of addiction.

But rather than the FDA using its authority as a regulator to impose a new label, it got into negotiations with Purdue that dragged on for four months in 2001. Company executives were alarmed at the message any change would send. Would it scare off doctors from prescribing OxyContin? Would it be read as a confirmation that everything Van Zee and his ilk were saying about the drug was true?

Purdue also feared the legal ramifications of being "singled out" in this way. The company was already facing a raft of lawsuits over

OxyContin as the death toll climbed. More than fifty-five hundred people died of prescription opioid painkillers in 2001. That same year, five years after the drug came onto the market, the FDA and the company agreed on a new label, dropping the claim that the time-release formula reduced the risk of abuse and replacing it with a statement that OxyContin was just as much a risk as any other opioid, legal or illicit. Purdue was obliged to put a black box around its warning as an alert to prescribing doctors. It also sent a notice to hundreds of thousands of physicians, drawing attention to the new label.

The change was a stunning admission of incompetence by the FDA. It had been bamboozled by Purdue's unsubstantiated claims, cooked up in the marketing department, into endorsing its highly addictive drug as safer than less dangerous alternatives on the basis of no real data or investigation.

Van Zee was pleased at the change to the label but the damage had been done. Prescribing of OxyContin continued to climb rapidly. Van Zee was pressing for a more radical response. He wanted Purdue to end its marketing and the FDA to restrict the drug to treatment of severe pain and end the mass prescribing for chronic conditions.

The mess obliged the FDA to cast a more critical eye over the broader issue of opioid prescribing and the claims made for painkillers. The agency has a number of advisory committees made up of its own officials and outside experts who take testimony from the medical and scientific community, as well as interested members of the public, to recommend policy and practices.

In 2002 the FDA called a meeting of its Advisory Committee for the Anesthesia, Critical Care, and Addiction Products Division to consider whether opioids should be prescribed less widely and whether additional studies were required before approving new narcotic drugs.

The hearing alarmed the manufacturers and not only Purdue, although it had the most at stake. By then OxyContin was earning the company more than $1.5 billion a year. Sales of other opioids were escalating, too. Demand for the weaker instant-release hydrocodone pills doubled between the mid-1990s and 2002 to 86 million prescriptions, worth close to a half-billion dollars a year. Drug makers were eager for a slice of this growing market and didn't want to see the FDA make it harder to get new opioid painkillers into pharmacies.

The advisory committee meeting was scheduled for September 2001, but the 9/11 attacks pushed it back to the following January. The hearing was chaired by Dr. Nathaniel Katz, a pain specialist who believed there was a role for opioids but had his own concerns about the lack of data on the risks and rewards. He was instructed by the FDA not to allow the meeting to become focused on OxyContin. Purdue didn't want its drug singled out, even though it was the reason the hearing was called.

It was Katz's first time as chair of an FDA hearing, and he was a little in awe of the giants of the pain-care world around him. Russell Portenoy was testifying. So was the other heavyweight pain specialist from Sloan Kettering, Katherine Foley. Bob Rappaport, deputy head of the division the hearing was advising, was there for the FDA. Haddox was selected to speak for the pharmaceutical industry. Even though the FDA did not want OxyContin to become the focus of the hearing, the drug's defenders were all over the gathering. Van Zee sat in the public gallery.

Before speaking, participants were obliged to list any of their financial backers. Portenoy had contracts and grants with sixteen pharmaceutical companies, including Purdue, Abbott, and Endo, another big opioid maker. Van Zee thought he detected a sense of pride in Portenoy as he ticked off the list. Foley said she was on Purdue's speaker's bureau.

Portenoy gave a presentation in which he acknowledged the escalation of opioid addiction and admitted that pain specialists and the drug industry had been singing from the same hymn sheet on opioids. He also conceded there had been a reluctance "to discuss the legitimate risk associated with opioid toxicity and abuse addiction because of the concern that if we opened up Pandora's box and talked about addiction and abuse, all of the progress that has been made during the past ten years would be lost."

Portenoy added that there was real fear that focusing on "the OxyContin problem" would undermine the "progress that has been made in destigmatizing opioid therapy." He continued, "Because of that concern, in my estimation, there has been a bit of a tacit under-standing that we won't talk about this too much. And now pain spe-cialists, I think, are recognizing that this has been a problem. We do need to talk about it. We need to address it in a proactive way, and based on the science." It was a frank admission that the opioid evan-gelists had ignored the evidence that didn't suit them.

Portenoy conceded something else, too. He acknowledged there was little data to back up his assertion that opioid therapy was effec-tive for all types of pain. But what he gave with one hand, he took with the other. Whatever the advisory committee decided, he said that nothing should be done to delay getting new opioids onto the market when "everybody in the community knows it's safe and effective."

One member of the FDA panel, Dr. Steven Passik, who the pre-vious year had flagged his concerns about the use of the Porter and Jick letter to claim a minimal risk of addiction, again spoke up about it. He said he was concerned about the "paucity of real outcomes data" on dependency and addiction. "There was a lot of data that was cited to help allay fears of addiction that probably didn't have that much to do with what the real risk was," he said.

Van Zee got to make his case at the part of the FDA meeting where the public was permitted to speak, but he left with the sense no one was paying much attention. By the end of the two-day hearing, it was clear to him that there was no sense of urgency on the part of the FDA. He felt like he was running around pushing alarms and that the people with the power to change policy were pretending there wasn't a fire. "If the FDA had got on a bus and come down to central Appalachia or gone up to Maine and spent a couple of days talking to people in communities about what was going on, maybe they would have understood more. They just didn't understand the scope and the tragedy of it," he said.

"There are many many people that were thought leaders that are bright guys that could be good doctors, but they're so tied to the industry in terms of shared interests, in terms of currying favor for funding for their career or their research, that they can't be unbiased about things, and they would overlook or minimize the problems at the beginning of this opioid tragedy."

Van Zee got Portenoy aside after the meeting. "I talked to him about this terrible tragedy we were having over the use of OxyContin. By that time I had these maps that showed state by state what OxyContin prescribing was nationally. In our region, West Virginia, eastern Kentucky, prescribing was 300 to 600 percent higher than the national average."

Van Zee laid out the maps for Portenoy and pointed to the numbers. There was a direct correlation between prescribing rates for OxyContin and addiction and overdoses. "Up to that point, it was very unclear: Why are we having such huge problems? Why is it central Appalachia? Until you look at the numbers and see the obvious. I said, 'We've got 300 percent higher prescribing. This is what's happening to the families of good people,'" said Van Zee.

"Portenoy's response was, 'That's good.' Meaning it's good that there is that much more opioids out there. Good because we need to have a lot more liberalized prescribing. We need to have a lot more opioids out there so people could get fairly treated for their pain."

Van Zee tried to explain that he wasn't unsympathetic to people in pain, but OxyContin was doing way more harm than good. It was a catastrophe for Lee County and a lot of other places besides. "I said, 'You've got to really understand what a tragedy it is.' He was arrogant and just kind of brushed me off. It was upsetting because his position was such that he could have a lot of influence on things."

The FDA advisory panel recommended the agency set new standards for the approval of opioids, including a requirement for manufacturers to test whether their drugs were effective for long-term use and much tighter oversight of whether prescription narcotics were ending up in the hands of the wrong people. But it was no surprise to Van Zee when the FDA did not do anything to address the immediate crisis. "If you've got people like Portenoy getting up and talking to the FDA, and you got some little country doctor that you never heard of that doesn't have any letters behind his name talking, who are you going to listen to?" he said.

If the FDA wouldn't listen, perhaps Congress would. Committees of both houses held a series of hearings in the early 2000s that suggested the legislature might finally be taking notice of the burgeoning crisis. Van Zee's warnings had not gone unnoticed on Capitol Hill, and he was called to a Senate committee hearing a few months after speaking to the FDA. "There has never been anything to compare to the epidemic of drug abuse and addiction that we have seen the last three years with OxyContin," he told the senators.

Van Zee again accused Purdue of overstating the benefits and playing down the risks of its drug. He was already describing the crisis as an epidemic and laid out the causes. He ticked off overprescribing by doctors and Purdue's busy sales force. With his customary foresight, he warned that as OxyContin use spread, it was driving an increasingly profitable black market that would be hard to rein in. "The recall of OxyContin is not a recall of opioids. OxyContin is unique and its abuse unprecedented. The economics of OxyContin diversion and abuse will now perpetuate this disaster, regardless of the full array of measures taken to stem the tide," Van Zee told Congress.

Purdue's head of research and development, Paul Goldenheim, one of the four men along with Richard Sackler who had mapped out the future of OxyContin, spoke for the company. Goldenheim's strategy was to spread the blame and absolve the drug. He assured the senators Purdue had made a "corporate priority" of addressing the addiction crisis and said there was no more important tool than education. "Educating teenagers about the risks and dangers of prescription drug abuse is critical, and we have initiated an important program that we are calling Painfully Obvious," he said. "All of this material is designed to help capture the attention of teenagers and convey the message that abusing drugs is not cool." Painfully Obvious remained unknown to hordes of American teenagers even as overdoses climbed.

Goldenheim also pulled a trick the company was to keep up for years. Autopsies of the overdosed usually showed the dead with an array of drugs in their system. Often opioids but also marijuana, cocaine, and alcohol. That, said Goldenheim, went to show that the issue wasn't OxyContin but the broad misuse of drugs. "Knowledgeable law enforcement officers have said that if OxyContin were not available, those abusing and diverting drugs would not stop their behavior, but would simply transfer to other legal and illegal drugs," he told the committee. "OxyContin is a part of this larger problem."

This was disingenuous. It was undoubtedly true that people getting high on OxyContin would switch to other drugs if it weren't available. After all, many of them came to it from other narcotics. But they were weaker and therefore less risky than OxyContin. Its strength was tipping people over the edge. It was only when Oxy-Contin came on the scene that the death toll surged to the heights then being seen.

Goldenheim's performance was a mix of feigned outrage at Purdue being picked on and persistent misdirection. He falsely claimed Purdue's sales force encouraged doctors to use OxyContin only if other drugs were not effective, when reps were telling physicians to switch because the pill was better. Goldenheim claimed Purdue focused its marketing on patients with a history of taking opioids. That wasn't true, either. The sales force was telling doctors OxyContin was the drug to begin with and stay with.

Purdue was desperate to make sure that prescribing of OxyContin was not limited to trained pain specialists. It was profiting hugely from wide prescribing by primary care doctors.

The company's headquarters is in Connecticut, at the time represented by Senator Christopher Dodd, an influential Democrat who sat in the Senate for thirty years. Dodd praised Van Zee for his dedication and reassured his fellow senators that he would show Purdue no favor. Then he lobbed a few softball questions at Goldenheim, allowing him to expand unchallenged on how dedicated the company was to combating the crisis, before settling on his target: Van Zee.

Dodd skimmed over OxyContin's toll to zero in on the "serious, serious problem" of "this exaggerated fear of addiction" in prescribing opioids.

The senator sidestepped questions about the lack of evidence for claims that there was little risk of addiction to demand Van Zee produce evidence for his assertion that Purdue's marketing was driving the rising number of overdoses. The doctor said there was an old adage in medical circles that if a drug is widely available, it will be widely abused.

Dodd sneered at him: "Another one of those Appalachian things?"

No, said Van Zee. He started to back up his view. Take a look at a map of OxyContin consumption across the United States. Dodd cut him off. The senator said he could see no connection between marketing and the illicit consumption of the drug.

Van Zee tried again, but Dodd wasn't listening. By the end, the senator was parroting Purdue's line that the problem was society, not OxyContin. "There is something far more profound going on here than just the availability through legal channels of a painkiller," he said.

Van Zee wasn't going to let Dodd get away with that. "If you have an area of the country, and perhaps that is our area, that has high prescribers of controlled prescription drugs or opioids and you have a pharmaceutical company that finds out which physicians are most liberal prescribers of opioids, and if you couple that with the sales representative force that has lucrative incentives to increase the OxyContin sales or whatever other drug is involved in their territory, I think it is a recipe for commercial success and public health problems," the doctor fired back.

Van Zee said that Purdue's pushing of the 1 percent mantra was wrong. Addiction rates were far higher, somewhere between 5 and 12 percent. Even at that lower rate, the toll would be devastating if OxyContin continued to be prescribed so easily and widely. "If it is

5 percent and you have a million people on OxyContin, that means you have iatrogenically addicted fifty thousand people and not only destroyed their lives but much of their family," the doctor explained to the committee. "Over the next decade we will find out that there has been a lot of unfortunate errors made about how much we have done with how little knowledge we have had to do it."

Van Zee could feel the opportunities to change the course of the crisis slipping through his fingers. He was among the first doctors to raise the alarm, but he struggled to be taken seriously against the arrayed forces of the opioid makers' money, a Congress unwilling to challenge the industry, and a federal medical establishment that showed little interest in addressing its wider responsibilities to the public health.

AS IT HAPPENED, Dr. Nathaniel Katz, the chair of the FDA advisory committee, was not entirely persuaded by the big names testifying at the hearing. He was a true believer in the benefits of opioids and an early enthusiast for much wider prescribing of narcotics. But it disturbed him that it was impossible to get an answer to the most basic questions about their effects. No one could even say what proportion of patients prescribed opioids became addicted or whether they worked for long-term treatment.

Katz couldn't see how it was possible to make informed decisions without data. Looking back, he said that OxyContin should never have been approved in the absence of better information on the effectiveness and the consequences of narcotics. "Why did we take the scraps of inadequate data that we had at that time and allow ourselves to go so far with allowing shifts in prescribing policy based on such inadequate data?" he wondered. "It occurred to me at that time that we would never tolerate this in relation to any other drug. These are the questions we always ask. You put acetaminophen on the market. What percentage of people end up needing a liver transplant? It's the standard question about any drug-related complication." But not about opioids, because the twin wings of the prescribing movement—Portenoy leading the doctors and Purdue at the head of the drug makers—said the question had already been answered by history.

By the early 2000s, there was a growing body of evidence calling into question the claims made for opioids. A study in the *Medical Letter on Drugs and Therapeutics* concluded that OxyContin held no advantage either in effectiveness or in safety over other opioids. Other studies showed the risk of addiction was considerably higher than the claims being made for OxyContin.

At the FDA hearing, Katz asked Haddox what the industry thought about "pursuing an aggressive program of clinical research to better understand what is it exactly that we are talking about here."

Haddox dismissed the idea that it was necessary to study whether opioids were effective. "We are dealing with compounds that are not exactly new. Oxycodone, for instance, has been synthesized since 1917, [and] has been continuously marketed in the world since. Morphine, of course, was isolated in the 1800s. So I don't think we're talking about new issues," he said.

It was to become a familiar argument. Opiates had been around for thousands of years. Their effectiveness was not in question. But that long history also presented compelling evidence of the addictive qualities of those same drugs. Haddox acknowledged there was a need to study opioid addiction but questioned whether it was the pharmaceutical industry's duty to fund it, knowing well that if the drug companies didn't, then it probably wouldn't happen. The narcotics manufacturers had no interest in exploring whether their drugs really worked as well as they claimed or in research that might expose the true risk of addiction.

The drug makers recognized that this was dangerous territory for them. The opioid industry needed to move the focus away from questions about the worth of its drugs. There was too much talk about the addicted and the overdosed as victims. The opioid evangelists and the narcotics manufacturers embraced a strategy to shift the attention to those they said were the real victims—the millions of people in chronic pain whose access to painkillers should not be impeded by the sins of others. At the same time, it would blame the addicted for their condition. One phrase kept spilling from the mouths of industry executives and the painkiller enthusiasts: *balanced approach*. Katz had used it himself in summing up the hearing, saying that the FDA should "balance maximal availability to patients" that need opioids while trying to stem addiction and misuse.

But it was soon clear that the industry's insistence on a balanced approach meant there should be no restrictions on the prescribing of narcotics to "good patients" who should not be made to suffer because of a few bad apples who became hooked. The strategy separated the addicted from the patient, when in many cases one was becoming the other. It kept the blame on the user, not the pill. Above all, it pushed aside questions about whether opioids worked as the drug makers claimed.

Katz came to hate the term *balanced approach* because he realized it was not about balance at all: "The concept of balance was a linguistic weapon. It was a concept that was weaponized in favor of unbridled opioid prescribing while at the same time sounding so socially responsible."

CHAPTER 6

Investigation

IN 2001 THE West Virginia Bureau of Criminal Investigation (BCI) asked Mike Smith to go undercover to work drug busts. Smith was a first sergeant in the state police, stationed just south of the capital, Charleston. He grew up in West Virginia with ambitions to escape to Washington and become a Secret Service agent. So he worked his way through a criminal justice degree and then took off for DC to sit the Secret Service exam. But Smith so disliked the city, he came back home and joined the West Virginia state police.

The BCI told him there was a growing problem with pills. Coroners were reporting ever-larger numbers of deaths from painkiller overdoses. This was all new to Smith. Until then, hunting drug traffickers mostly meant finding dope growers.

At first Smith approached the pill problem the same way he did marijuana. Work your way along the chain from the user to the dealer to the producer, using the fear of long prison sentences and the lure of plea deals to extract information about the next link. Smith started buying opioids on the street. The easiest drugs to find were

Vicodin and Percocet, but there was OxyContin, too. He had no problem finding users or people willing to sell him pills. He thought the hard part would be to discover where the pills were coming from, but there was no secret. The sellers said all Smith had to do was get himself to a small town on the border with Kentucky. Williamson. Pilliamson they called it. "I quickly learned that when I asked for hydrocodone, people would say, 'All you got to do is go down to Williamson Wellness and see a Dr. Hoover down there, and you are good to go.'"

Smith went to Williamson and observed. He parked himself outside the Wellness Center, a nondescript converted feed store near the railroad line cutting through the town. Each morning the crowd outside the clinic started to gather an hour or more before it opened, and the line at the door rarely diminished until it shut. Around the corner, he saw the same thing outside Dr. Diane Shafer's office.

Smith wasn't sure what was going on. These were doctors writing prescriptions. What would be illegal about that? This was virgin territory for a cop used to busting illegal drugs. He began to educate himself on the legal responsibilities of a doctor prescribing narcotics.

Smith sent an undercover officer into the clinic to buy pills. He paid $250 in cash for a first consultation to diagnose a condition requiring an opioid prescription. When the undercover officer went back a month later and asked to see the doctor again, he was kept waiting for hours. People willing just to slap down cash were given a new prescription by the receptionist and were out of the door in minutes. "It was pretty obvious that people didn't want to see the doctor and the doctor didn't want to see them," said Smith.

The policeman struggled to understand what he was looking at. One rogue doctor churning out pills? Smith knew the human cost of addiction. Opioids stole people's jobs and homes and tore their families apart. The addicted clogged hospital emergency rooms and jails. Children missed school because their parents were too out of it to get them there.

The epidemic sapped the energy and time of police departments and social services. West Virginia calculated it cost the public purse hundreds of millions of dollars a year.

Smith talked to the users. It became clear to him that many didn't understand the power of opioids, particularly OxyContin, until it was too late. "I don't know how many people I've spoken to who wouldn't touch drugs for nothing and got injured and went to doctor and first thing doctor did was write oxycodone.

"OxyContin became the moonshine, the drug of choice. It ended up being lucrative because the doctors figured out really quick, 'These guys are wanting pain pills. If I just write a script, they leave. They're happy, I'm happy.'"

Smith continued to watch. Henry Vinson loomed ever larger as a presence. The policeman concluded the ex-con was pulling the strings at Williamson Wellness and Diane Shafer's clinic. The office staff in both places answered to him. Far from being rivals, the two clinics appeared to be working in tandem, with Vinson as the common denominator. They used the same five drugstores to dispense prescriptions. Both clinics steered people away from the Walmart pharmacy, five minutes' drive from the center of Williamson, on the other side of the Kentucky border.

Smith was working with an agent of the Federal Bureau of Investigation (FBI), Joe Ciccarelli. Ciccarelli arrived from a posting in Florida but knew West Virginia well because in the early 1980s he'd been a police officer in the university town of Huntington, up on the border with Ohio. Back then there were a few people illegally using Dilaudid, an opioid typically prescribed for end-of-life care. "These junkies would forge prescriptions, and back in the precomputer days I can remember standing in pharmacies going through prescriptions going, 'That's a junkie. That's a junkie. These are false scripts,'" said Ciccarelli.

"The rest of the time we spent driving around the parking lots of bars at night trying to catch people smoking marijuana. That was our drug problem. To compare that with what we are faced with now is going from here to Mars and back."

Ciccarelli left Huntington to join the FBI in 1984. Then he was posted to Miami at the height of its notoriety as the cocaine-delivery capital of America. "We're talking shiploads of cocaine. Freighter loads. Planeloads. And we were making significant cases, but you knew that it was a drop in the bucket compared to what was sitting in Colombia, waiting to come."

In 1999 the FBI sent him back to West Virginia as part of its drug task force. This was a different world from chasing international cartels. Ciccarelli was based in Huntington. There was a lot of crack and meth amphetamine dealing there, but increasingly his attention was drawn to the southwestern part of the state. In all his years on the drug squad, it was the first time he confronted painkiller addiction and dealing. Like Smith, he wasn't sure what he was looking at.

Smith and Ciccarelli worked together on the investigation as part of a state and federal task force. They thought the scale of prescribing couldn't be legal but struggled to get the Drug Enforcement Administration interested, and the various state regulatory boards seemed to regard any investigation of the behavior of doctors and pharmacists as an unwarranted intrusion on their fiefdoms. Nailing doctors for too many prescriptions was complicated: How do you prove they didn't believe the patients were in pain or needed drugs?

The FBI began sniffing around Williamson, talking to some of the staff at the clinics. April Sparks worked as an assistant to one of the doctors recruited by Vinson, Dr. Armando Acosta. She told the FBI it was widely known in the office and among patients that Acosta offered those who could not afford the cost of a consultation an alternative means of payment. The doctor exchanged opioid prescriptions for sex.

The investigators wanted evidence. Could Sparks prove this? She confessed that Acosta had prescribed her OxyContin, that she was hooked, and that he had in effect become her dealer. Sparks said the doctor advised her on how to get the biggest hit from the drug. He suggested snorting or chewing it but also said that people were injecting. When Sparks told Acosta she was having trouble finding a vein, he showed her how to tie off her arm.

He also hit her up for sex. "What are you going to do for me?" he asked when she wanted a prescription.

Acosta asked to see Sparks breasts, and when she bared them he pulled her close and kissed them. She told the FBI she refused his demands for oral sex. When he then cut off her prescriptions, a colleague filled in the names of Sparks and her boyfriend on blank scripts already signed by Acosta for his patients.

Ciccarelli described Acosta as "completely off the reservation."

The doctor was charged in 2001 with illegally distributing controlled substances but eventually reached a plea deal on a single count. A judge described the implications of the doctor presigning blank prescriptions as "truly scary" for public health.

The West Virginia medical board finally paid attention, noting among other things that Acosta's patients "appeared to be writing portions of their own medical records." It stripped him of his license, accusing him of engaging in unprofessional, unethical, and dishonorable conduct. The debarred physician faced up to twenty years in prison. He was lucky to be jailed for a little more than four.

For Smith and Ciccarelli, Acosta's arrest was a window into how the Williamson doctors worked. Sparks's account of piles of cash going through the office every day was brought to the attention of the Internal Revenue Service (IRS), which concluded that Acosta made more than a million dollars writing opioid prescriptions at the Williamson clinic over the two years to 2001 but declared only a fraction of the income.

Vinson handled the money, taking cash from patients and making claims from insurance companies and government health care programs. He paid the doctors in wads of notes or made deposits to a bank just up the street. Vinson also completed some of the physicians' tax forms: it was his signature on a fraudulent return hiding a good chunk of Acosta's income.

Acosta already owed more than $200,000 in unpaid taxes from the early 1990s, and the IRS had an order requiring deductions from his earnings to pay them back. Vinson helped Acosta avoid those payments and to buy property in other people's names as well as underdeclaring his income.

In 2003 Vinson was indicted for conspiracy. He pleaded guilty— he later told me he did so to protect his mother from the government conspiracy to destroy him—and before the year was out he was back in prison, serving another three and a half years.

This might have been a pivotal moment in the story of Mingo County. The workings of the Williamson clinic were laid bare. The overseer, Vinson, was back in prison. The state police and the feds were breathing down the necks of the other doctors, but they struggled to get other agencies and prosecutors interested. The DEA's chief agent in West Virginia brushed them off by saying it wasn't his job to question the medical decisions of doctors. The US attorney for the state was equally unenthused about going up against the medical profession. Even when there was clear evidence of wrongdoing, the regulatory authorities weren't keen to do more than a ticking off.

Ryckman was under scrutiny after a pharmacist reported to the state medical board that the doctor was living in Pennsylvania and phoning in opioid prescriptions to drugstores in West Virginia and Kentucky for patients he had not seen personally. The medical board launched its own investigation and sent a doctor to examine a sample of Ryckman's patient records. The investigator told the board Ryckman was prescribing "astronomical" numbers of opioids with little or no follow-up and with no evidence of X-rays or of tests for the causes of the alleged pain. The board concluded patients were seen each month solely to renew their prescriptions with little or no consultation.

Ryckman tried to talk his way out by saying that the high levels of prescribing were explained by his practice solely treating patients injured at work or in car accidents. He also claimed there was no drug abuse among his patients and that none of them ever complained. This was untrue.

Given the scale of the epidemic then unfolding in West Virginia, it might be thought the medical board would have come down harder, but it settled for ticking Ryckman off for poor record keeping and a warning that his prescribing practices "are below the recognized standard of care." He was sent on a course on how to keep better records and manage controlled drugs. In November 2004, the medical board told Ryckman he had completed his punishment, thanked him for his "cooperation and patience throughout this process," and offered "continued best wishes for success."

Ryckman was free to go on prescribing unmonitored, which he did with vigor. Investigators later calculated that he was taking in $20,000 a day in cash.

With Vinson and Acosta in prison, the other doctors stepped up to the plate. Ryckman moved ownership of the clinic into his name, and Hoover and Shafer took over the administration. They also needed more doctors. The office manager, Myra Miller, recruited her brother, Eric Chico, who was a physician. Miller was also related by marriage to an emergency room doctor at the local hospital, Donald Kiser. She told Kiser he could make good money at the clinic. He knew it was a pill mill but began working part-time between shifts at the emergency room. Kiser soon got a taste for the money—and, as it turned out, other side benefits—and left the hospital to work full-time at Williamson Wellness.

LONNIE HANNAH FACED a different challenge in his attempts to bring rogue doctors to task. Smith and Ciccarelli had to contend with the indifference and what they regarded as the political cowardice of the system. But after Hannah was elected Mingo County sheriff in 2005, he was up against a different beast. Corruption.

Overdose deaths in West Virginia had risen 550 percent since 2000 and even higher in Mingo and the surrounding counties. The state government estimated the crisis was costing it more than a half-billion dollars a year. Hospitals grappled with a growing tide of patients on drugs. Hannah took over a town drowning in the consequences of opioids. "When you had people from Virginia, Kentucky, Ohio coming to this little town, you couldn't hardly get around here, there'd be so many cars. It precipitated a lot of violence, and the court system was clogged up with things that were attributed to drugs. Breaking and entering, domestics, child abuse. Good working people. But when they get on these opioids, and they get on these drugs, then they just can't get away from it."

A patch of ground outside the Wellness clinic served as a dealing site. Many people could make more money trading in pills than they could working full-time. "We saw so many parents getting prescribed OxyContin, selling their prescriptions. Times was hard. It paid the rent. You get ninety OxyContin and could sell them for $100 a piece. That's $9,000. Think about that. Some of them were drawing $650 a month in Social Security, and they can sell their prescription for $9,000," Hannah said.

With that kind of money to be made, some people moved between pill mills. They drove to Virginia, North Carolina, and Ohio. Before long a route opened to Florida that quickly became notorious as one of the easiest places to get multiple prescriptions with few questions.

Hannah was shocked by not only the scale of money to be made but who was dealing. The arrested included a prison guard selling his OxyContin prescription on the street in Williamson, mine superintendents, and truck drivers.

One day a woman walked into Hannah's office. "She had a garbage bag full of prescriptions—empty pill bottles—and set them down. She said these are all my family members, and not one of them has ever saw the doctor," he said.

Hannah picked through the bottles. Every prescription had Dr. Donald Kiser's name on it. The woman listed all the people in her family who were addicted to opioids and said they were getting the prescriptions down at Williamson Wellness Center but had seen the doctor only once, if at all.

Kiser was a popular figure in town because he also worked at the local hospital emergency room. The doctor was not without some important political friends, either. "He had influence. Well, I arrested him. They let him out of jail. Another person came forward, and I went down and arrested him again," Hannah said. "We had a corrupt political system here. Very corrupt."

Ciccarelli noticed. He followed the money and saw that Henry Vinson and Diane Shafer were pouring substantial sums of money, presumably part of the profits from the clinics, into local politics. "Shafer was the cash cow. She was where everybody went to get money to fund their campaigns. So she was a big player in town in a lot of different ways," he said.

The FBI agent concluded that power lay with the county's chief judge, Michael Thornsbury, who had freed Kiser. "The judge controlled every elected office in the courthouse except Hannah. Every one. He became Boss Hogg, in effect," said Ciccarelli.

Hannah said it was impossible to get a conviction against anyone protected by Thornsbury. "They had a revolving door here. They would make bail. They had a racket. On a local level, you couldn't do anything. They were untouchable," he said. "They had the political machine. They had the bail bondsmen. They'd get them out of the jail. 'Get all your big families. You ought to go out and vote against the sheriff for arresting them.'"

The sheriff began to realize that whenever he got a search warrant from the magistrate's office, the target was tipped off by the time he got there. Ciccarelli had similar suspicions.

Kiser could frustrate Hannah, but the state police and DEA were a different matter. The discovery of two empty pill bottles with his name on them in the car of a driver arrested for driving under the influence put him on their radar. He was arrested for distributing a raft of different opioid pills from Percocet to Lortabs and Norcos as well as Xanax over several years.

Investigators discovered that for a while, Kiser was writing significantly more scripts than any other doctor in Mingo County. He pleaded guilty to writing phony prescriptions, was jailed for more than seven years, and lost his license to practice medicine.

Kiser proved a useful source into the workings of the Wellness Center. He told investigators he "observed a money-counting machine at the practice and overheard a conversation between the office manager, Myra Miller, and Dr. Ryckman, where Ryckman commented, 'Why are we paying the accountants if they cannot hide the money?' "

"When we interviewed Donald Kiser, he's telling us they got a money counter," said Smith. "I mean, come on. You don't see a money counter in a legitimate doctor's office."

Ryckman, perhaps suspecting that the rest of the doctors were also under investigation, transferred the clinic out of his name but not the income. He persuaded a nurse practitioner at the Wellness Center, Camille Helsel, to put it under her name but to pay him $25,000 a month from its earnings. In practice, Helsel was no more than a front, as Ryckman sought to put some distance between himself and the business. She had no control over the finances. There was another change, too. The clinic was renamed Mountain Medical. Otherwise, business went on as usual.

Ciccarelli and Smith had been able to go after Acosta and Kiser because they had clearly stepped outside of the normal practice of prescribing, but they struggled to get the DEA and US Attorney's Office in Charleston to look at the bigger picture in Williamson. "It's much easier for us to arrest somebody on a heroin charge," said Ciccarelli.

Early on we were thwarted in a lot of ways. The US Attorney's Office was reluctant to go after physicians. There was a theme from the local DEA diversion people that these are doctors and they have the right to treat people and all this bullshit, and the best you can do is to say they're a bad doctor, not a criminal. We had a DEA diversion investigator here. It was his concept that we can't do anything to these doctors because they're professionals and they're practicing. You basically had to go in and say, "I'm an addict and I need pills, and there's nothing wrong with me." He thought that was the criteria to make a case.

I think the US Attorney's Office is always afraid to tangle with a physician who has the financial wherewithal to hire good counsel.

Smith described the US Attorney's Office as "very timid" in prosecuting doctors. "I knew this case inside and out. I met with a couple of assistant US attorneys at the time. I remember one of them looked at me and said, 'Where did you go to medical school?' I said I didn't go to medical school. He sat down and was condescending and said, 'Mike, the reason these people go to medical school is so that way they can make money. There is no crime against making money.'"

Smith vented his frustration over the hesitation of prosecutors to go after these doctors at Booth Goodwin, then an assistant prosecutor who later became US attorney in West Virginia. Goodwin was sympathetic but said prosecuting doctors was not as easy as Smith thought. "It was very frustrating to the special agents who would come to me and the prosecutors in my office and say, 'For God's sakes, we've got people lined up out the door. They're just handing out scripts to anybody who comes in the door and says they've got back pain.' Exactly. They say they've got back pain. He's a doctor. He's got prescription-writing privileges. For us to prosecute him, we've got to bring in an expert and by virtue of bringing in that expert it's built in reasonable doubt," said Goodwin.

"I said, 'You find me a doctor who is literally just handing out scripts. Not conducting any examinations. Not asking any questions or any kind of care, and we'll prosecute them as a drug dealer. But you're not going to find that, for goodness' sakes.'"

WILLIAMSON WELLNESS, A.K.A. Mountain Medical, was certainly making money. Investigators calculated that in 2009 alone, the clinic pulled in $4.6 million in a town with a population of little more than three thousand people. Business was booming for the pharmacies, too. The lines at Hurley's were as long as at the clinic itself. It was the same across the river, just inside Kentucky, at Family Pharmacy, owned by Larry Ray Barnett. Barnett knew the Williamson doctors well. One day Hoover arrived with Ryckman at her side, introducing him as a doctor at the clinic.

Years later, Barnett claimed not to know that Williamson Wellness had a list of acceptable pharmacies and that his was on it. He also said that he had never heard the clinic described as a pill mill, even though that's pretty much what everyone else in town was calling it. Neither had he heard that Kiser was nicknamed Pill Billy. Even after the doctor's arrest, which filled the front of the local newspaper, Barnett managed to miss the description of Kiser as "a danger to the community because he prescribed thousands of addictive pills without legitimate purpose."

It seems Barnett wasn't curious about very much at all. The extremely large number of prescriptions arriving under Hoover's signature rang no alarm bells, even though DEA bulletins for pharmacists regularly flagged warnings about overprescription of opioids. Barnett was equally vague on whether he remembered similar warnings from the Kentucky medical board. He said he saw no red flags even as the prescriptions poured in by fax and phone.

With business booming, a new drugstore popped up in town. Within a couple of years, Tug Valley Pharmacy was dispensing more pain pills than any other in Williamson. In 2009 the pharmacist, Randy Ballengee, ordered 3 million hydrocodone pills from the distribution company, McKesson. The Walmart on the other side of the river dispensed only a few thousand.

"Let's call this whole thing what it is. It's pretty much a cartel. It was a DTO, a drug trafficking organization," said Sergeant Mike Smith. "Then right in the middle of this drug trafficking organization, you have a little pharmacy that pops up and everybody's okay with it. I think that they needed another pharmacy because the other pharmacies couldn't keep up with the amount of pills they were doing, and they needed to bring somebody in. I'm sitting here looking at this. It's hard to believe that was allowed."

The Wellness Center put a notice in its reception area: "Tug Valley Pharmacy will be seeing our patients."

Ballengee later claimed to have no idea the clinic was widely spoken of locally as a "pill mill." He even claimed not to be sure where it was, even though it was two blocks from his pharmacy and there were long lines outside almost every day.

The clinics streamlined the system further. Faxing or calling in individual prescriptions is time-consuming. Helsel, the nurse practitioner at the clinic, took to writing lists of names on a sheet of paper alongside dosages. When the sheet was full, she faxed it to one of the five pharmacies. That in itself was illegal. Prescriptions have to be written and signed individually by a doctor.

Almost every prescription was for thirty, sixty, or ninety milligrams. Investigators discovered that some of the pharmacies had bottles prefilled with set amounts of pills ready to move off the shelf. "The list comes in, you print out the name, slap a tag on the bottle. There you go," said Smith.

The state policeman went to the US Attorney's Office with the evidence about the illegal lists of prescriptions. "I thought what the clinics were doing fell under the definition of wire fraud because it was an illegal act taking place through electronic communication, so I tried to get them to prosecute them as a drug house, as a house of ill repute, same statute as a crack house. They wouldn't go for it. I tried to use the wire fraud to get everybody, the pharmacies and the doctors. They didn't go for that."

Frustrated at the federal prosecutor's unwillingness to file charges, Smith went to the West Virginia Board of Pharmacy: "They said I was right in what I was alleging. However, what they did is they talked to the pharmacists and told them they couldn't do that anymore," he said.

The whole thing was a game, a scam. Everyone was going along with it. The doctors, the pharmacists, even the city of Williamson. It brought a lot of money in from out of town.

The businesses did good. You had pharmacies that were doing really good. You had a state senator's office that was right between the two clinics, and he didn't say anything. He's right in the center of these pharmacies and the doctors' offices. I went down there, and it looked like a carnival. There's no way people down there didn't know what was going on. There was a lot of money being made. That was the big thing, was the amount of money that was coming in.

Smith nonetheless found it hard to understand why doctors would contribute to such misery. "These doctors, they're smart people. They can make a living doing other things. They know, or should have known. They read the papers, watch TV. They know what was going on in these communities. They were making money, but there was a price. There was a lady giving her baby a bath in Mingo County, and she left the hot water on to get the water warm and ended up passing out on pills. The baby stayed in that hot water as it kept running hot. It cooked the baby alive. That's the consequences."

CHAPTER 7

Vital Sign

J UST AS OXYCONTIN was taking off, Americans noticed a new addition to the nightly television news. Commercials for pills to combat everything from arthritis to high cholesterol flooded their screens after the Food and Drug Administration loosened advertising regulations.

The FDA obliges narrators to reel off side effects and "major risks" for prescription drugs. Advertisers attempt to distract from the warnings with scenes of good-looking, newly revived elderly people engaging in public foreplay while a soothing voice warns about four-hour erections.

One of the most advertised drugs on television is Lyrica, a medicine for nerve and muscle pain. Its commercials caution that it can cause "serious, even life-threatening, allergic reactions." Users are warned that if their face, mouth, or neck swells up, or they develop hives, or they suddenly have trouble breathing, they should find the nearest emergency room. The narrator drops in that there is also a risk of suicide. All the while, the ad shows a happy couple off to the movies, hand in hand.

This approach works well enough that pharmaceutical companies spend more than $5 billion a year pushing their products on television in the only country that permits medical advertising other than New Zealand. Most viewers now spend far more time watching drug ads than seeing their doctors. The target audience is older Americans planted in front of the evening news or *General Hospital*. More than 70 percent of commercial breaks on the *CBS Evening News* show at least one drug ad.

Pharma pressed the FDA to permit television advertising on the grounds that people have the right to be better informed about the medicines they are taking and to know their choices. The medical profession was suspicious. It preferred patients to leave it to doctors to diagnose and decide the appropriate medication. A shifting culture and legal rulings worked in the drug companies' favor, as Americans, less trusting of institutions as the years passed, became more assertive about their health care.

But drug ads do not leave viewers particularly well informed. Their tone and pictures often suggest pills are the only path to better health and that they will magically wash away debilitating conditions, even if the voice-over says otherwise. A study in the *Annals of Family Medicine* said ads portray people who "have lost control over their social, emotional, or physical lives without the medication." It described drug commercials as deliberately ambiguous about who might need the advertised medicine and accused them of trying to keep people living in fear of being afflicted by whatever the drug claimed to combat.

Doctors have grown used to patients who associate every ache and creak of aging with some condition they have never heard of until it popped up on their screen. They arrive for consultations armed with a self-diagnosis from the television and Internet to demand a prescription for instant relief. Some physicians respond by giving patients what they want, whether it will do them any good or not, just to get them out the door. But a poll of doctors revealed that more than 60 percent would prescribe a more innocuous drug or even a placebo if a patient didn't need what they were asking for.

Television advertising is one block in the construction of what doctors regard as the "pill for every ill" mentality that has increasingly gotten a grip on the United States, reflecting a wider change in the relationship between physician and patient. As medicine has felt less like a service and more like an industry, with insurance premiums climbing and doctors under pressure to cycle through more consultations faster, patients increasingly regard themselves as customers. As customers, they expect to get what they ask for, and more often what they want is a pill, not a lecture on diet and exercise. So it proved as opioid painkillers washed across America.

To Jane Ballantyne this was a strange and alien patient culture. Ballantyne trained as a doctor at the Royal Free Hospital School of Medicine in London and then in anesthesiology at a hospital in Oxford. For a few years, she worked in the United Kingdom's socialized and popular National Health Service.

Ballantyne moved to Massachusetts General Hospital (MGH) at Harvard University in 1990, where she began to specialize in pain treatment and adjust to a very different system of health care. She rose to head the hospital's Division of Pain Medicine, one of the most prestigious positions in the specialty. Her colleagues call her "a giant in her field." At least, some do.

As an anesthesiologist, Ballantyne saw the pill culture evolve on the operating table. Patients about to go under the knife are required to list the prescription drugs they are on to ensure there is no conflict with the anesthesia. In the early 1990s, they typically listed two or three medications at most. "Now, when they do tell you what medications they're on because they know it might compromise their care, they're on as much as thirty or thirty-five medications because it seems everybody's on everything," she said.

Ballantyne took up pain medicine just as the credo on treatment and opiates was taking hold. She listened to the evangelists promoting opioids and saw the possibilities.

> Our message was a message of hope. Our peers were people like Russ Portenoy, and we believed we could make

people's lives better using these drugs. We were teaching that
we shouldn't withhold opiates from people suffering from
chronic pain and that the risks of addiction were pretty low
because that was the teaching we'd received.

Those were the days when Purdue Pharma was very
active in going around hospitals, and persuading everybody
that opiates were great and we were part of that. We were
very much part of that enthusiasm because we thought, as
everybody did to begin with, that this was a way we could
help people. We were sucked into that whole thing. We went
off teaching the value of opiates in our textbooks until we
realized that this wasn't helping.

Purdue Pharma came knocking. In 2002 the hospital announced
a $3 million donation from the drug maker to sponsor education in
the latest pain-management techniques in return for renaming Ballantyne's department the "MGH Purdue Pharma Pain Center." But
by then, the hospital had grown wary of the company's claims for
its drug and in its opioid educational programs, and was backing
away. "Once things did start changing—and they changed very rapidly once Purdue Pharma started promoting OxyContin—we began
to feel the effects of more and more difficult patients, difficult and
demanding patients. And you began to think these numbers aren't
right."

Ballantyne, like Van Zee at his clinic in St. Charles, found that
experience wasn't matching theory. Doctors were told they could
repeatedly ratchet up the dosage of narcotics and switch to the powerful extended-release drugs without endangering the patient because
the pain in effect canceled out the risk of addiction. But Ballantyne
saw that her patients were not better off and were showing signs of
dependence. "What we began to observe is that people who were
on high doses of opiates were always in a huge amount of pain and
always ill. Very ill. They just weren't doing well."

Among those patients on high doses over months and years, Ballantyne heard from one after another that the more drugs they took,

the worse their pain became, but if they tried to stop or cut back on the pills, their pain also worsened. They were trapped. "You had never seen people in such agony as these people on high doses of opiates, and we thought it's not just because of the underlying pain; it's to do with the medication."

Ballantyne's misgivings grew as she listened to relatives of her patients disturbed at how much the drugs had changed them. Husbands spoke of wives as if a part of them were lost. Mothers complained that children had become sullen and distant, their judgment gone, their personality warped, their character altered. None of this should have been happening. Pain relief was supposed to free the patient, not imprison them.

The Harvard specialist began recording her findings.

BALLANTYNE'S DOUBTS ABOUT the promise of opioids as the holy grail of pain medicine settled in just as the drug industry was seeing the fruits of its push to force the hand of doctors. The American Pain Society, a body partially funded by pharmaceutical companies, had for several years promoted the concept of pain as the "fifth vital sign," alongside other measures of health such as heart rate and blood pressure. "Vital signs are taken seriously," said its president, James Campbell, in a speech to the society. "If pain were assessed with the same zeal as other vital signs are, it would have a much better chance of being treated properly. We need to train doctors and nurses to treat pain as a vital sign." The society even copyrighted the phrase: "Pain: the 5th Vital Sign."

Its first success was with the Veterans Administration (VA) health system, which in late 2000 issued a "Pain as the 5th Vital Sign Toolkit" for its hospitals. As doctors had no means to measure pain, unlike heart rate or blood pressure, patients were required to offer their own assessment. To facilitate this, the VA used color-coded smiley faces to represent a rising scale of pain from zero to ten.

Getting the Veterans Administration on board was a big step forward for the opioid lobby, but it wanted to see the fifth vital sign adopted in all of the nation's hospitals. The key to that was to win over the Joint Commission for Accreditation of Healthcare Organizations, which certifies around twenty thousand hospitals and clinics in the United States. Its stamp of approval is the gateway for medical facilities to tap into the huge pot of federal money paying for the elderly, disabled, and poor insured under the government's Medicare and Medicaid programs. Hospitals are careful not to get on the wrong side of the Joint Commission's "best practices" or to fail the regular performance reviews.

So when the commission issued new standards for pain care in 2001 in response to what it called "the national outcry about the widespread problem of undertreatment," hospital administrators picked over the document to ensure they understood exactly what was required.

The commission later tried to back away from its handiwork and deny it was endorsing mass prescribing of opioids, but its standards reinforced the claims made by Portenoy, Haddox, and their colleagues. It repeated without scrutiny the assertion that 50 million Americans were suffering from chronic pain, a figure based on industry's distorted reading of drug company–funded surveys. The commission embraced the claim that opioids carry a low risk of addiction when used to treat pain, while promoting the dubious concept of pseudoaddiction.

The new standards laid out how hospitals were expected to respond. Every patient was to be asked about their pain levels even if pain had nothing to do with why they were seeing a medic. Hospitals adopted the VA's smiley charts, which suddenly popped up on walls in emergency rooms and consulting clinics across the country. They came in several forms, but typical was one in which a big green smile symbolized a lack of pain, while a grim red face represented "unimaginable, unspeakable" levels. The commission ruled that anybody identifying as a five—a yellow neutral face described as "very distressing"—or above was to be was to be referred for a pain consultation.

The assessment was routinely referred to in hospital instructions and by medical staff as the fifth vital sign, but it was no more than an estimation by each patient that physicians could do little to verify or challenge.

The Joint Commission told hospitals they would be expected to meet the new standards for pain management at the next accreditation survey. Purdue Pharma was waiting in the wings. It stepped up with an array of material to educate doctors in pain management. The company offered to supply and distribute it for free in return for virtually exclusive rights to effectively indoctrinate medical staff. It was of little surprise then when the training video declared that some clinicians had "inaccurate and exaggerated concerns about addiction, tolerance, and risk of death" when prescribing narcotics. The video asserted that there is "no evidence that addiction is a significant issue when persons are given opioids for pain control." Neither claim was true.

Purdue funded more than twenty thousand pain-related educational programs. Some doctors came to regard them as little more than a sales pitch for OxyContin. The videos and manuals were the principal pain education many medics received as opioids came on to the market in a big way. Some doctors were skeptical about the value of patient self-assessment, but the Joint Commission's regulations soon came to be viewed as a rigid standard. In time, pain as the fifth vital sign worked its way into hospital culture. New generations of nurses, steeped in the opioid orthodoxy, sometimes came to see pain as more important than other health indicators.

The Joint Commission needed a way to judge whether its edict on pain was being adhered to and latched on to patient satisfaction surveys used to determine Medicare and Medicaid payments to hospitals. A question was added to the surveys about whether patients were satisfied with their treatment for pain.

Dr. Roger Chou, a pain specialist at Oregon Health and Science University who has made long-term studies of the effectiveness of opioid painkillers and helped shape the policy of the Centers for

Disease Control and Prevention (CDC) on the epidemic, said the focus on pain caused patients to give it greater weight than made sense. "When you start asking people, 'How much pain are you having?' every time they come into the hospital, then people start thinking, 'Well, maybe I shouldn't be having this little ache I've been having. Maybe there's something wrong.' You're medicalizing what's a normal part of life. You're looking for something when there may not be anything there."

One consequence was that people with relatively minor pain were increasingly directed toward medicinal treatment, while consideration of safer and more effective alternatives were marginalized. Another, said Chou, was the increased expectation that pain can be eliminated. "In the vast majority of people, you can't make their pain go away. So this idea about checking their pain score every time and trying to get their pain to go away has you cranking up the opioid dose because you keep chasing that pain score."

Chou said that chasing the lowest score on the pain chart often came at the expense of quality of life as opioid doses increased. "It's better to have a little bit of pain and be functional than to have no pain and be completely unfunctional."

Health insurance companies piled yet more pressure on doctors to follow the path of least resistance by cutting consultation times and payments for more costly forms of pain treatment, such as physiotherapy. It took a determined doctor to resist. Physicians could spend a half hour pressing a person to take more responsibility for their own health—eat better, exercise more, drink less, find ways to deal with stress—only to watch an unhappy patient make their views known on the satisfaction survey. Or they could quickly do what the patient came in for: give them a pill and get full marks. "This is more like a business model. What's your customer satisfaction?" said Dr. Jennifer Plumb, a hospital emergency room and urgent care doctor in Salt Lake City. "People want antibiotics and they want pain killers, and if you don't give them what they want, guess what happens to the patient satisfaction scores. Physicians face a choice. They can do what's easy and sign the prescription. The patients are happy. The hospital system is happy. Or they can do what's hard. I'll tell you, that's a challenging discussion to have."

IN DETROIT, DR. Charles Lucas's three decades of experience as a surgeon told him to do what was hard.

Lucas grew up in the city and stuck with it through its most troubled years. He was a young surgeon at Detroit Receiving Hospital during the riots and white flight of the 1960s. A decade later, Lucas was chief of its Emergency Surgical Service. His specialty was trauma surgery. Gunshot wounds and car accidents mostly. He was instrumental in establishing the publicly owned hospital as the highest-level trauma center in Michigan and one of the first top-tier centers in the country.

Detroit Receiving Hospital trains more than half the doctors in Michigan, and Lucas, as a professor of surgery, has seen many of his protégés rise. "It's fair to say that doctors wanting to try something other than opiates didn't get encouragement from the hospital, the insurance companies, or the patients. They were on their own," he lamented.

On the wards, nurses routinely oversaw the administering of pain medication. In theory they were supposed to do a thorough consultation before increasing a patient's dosage, but the demands of the job often made that impractical. "The nurses are too damned busy to spend a lot of time talking with somebody, so they just increase the medicine. Nurses don't have the time to have long discussions with everybody," said Lucas.

One unforeseen consequence of the pain scale was that the smiley face chosen by a patient too often determined the size of the dosage prescribed, even though there was not supposed to be a correlation. Higher levels of pain did not necessarily require larger amounts of narcotics. Medical staff called it "dosing to numbers."

Emergency departments faced the same pressures. They soon became a beacon for the addicted, who quickly learned to game the system. They turned up feigning pain, knowing harassed medical staff under time pressures and the cudgel of the Joint Commission's guidelines were likely to prescribe narcotics and move on without too many questions. Emergency rooms rarely checked whether a walk-in patient already had an opioid prescription.

"Some of the old-time nurses, they have that jaundiced look in their eye and say 'So-and-so's complaining of pain.' You can tell by the look in their eye that they don't think it's justified that they get any more medicine. The younger nurses, they say we have to treat this pain because they've been indoctrinated—they've got to get rid of the pain. God forbid you don't get rid of the pain. That would be like a mortal sin not getting rid of the pain, even though it might kill the patient," said Lucas with a rebellious snort.

The surgeon was to discover the price of dissent. Lucas was knocked back in surprise, and then infuriated, to be summonsed to appear before his hospital's ethics committee after a nurse reported him for failing to provide adequate pain treatment.

Lucas's long-standing patients include Gail Purton, the wife of a well-known Michigan radio personality, Dick Purton. Lucas operated on Purton a few times, and she was back for surgery after ovarian cancer spread. "It was a big operation. Cut off all sorts of cancer."

The next day a nurse asked Purton if she was in pain. Purton said she was. The nurse reported Lucas for failing to properly address a patient's pain. That prompted the hospital ethics committee to summon the surgeon. "I got reported because I wasn't giving her enough pain medicine. She had a big cut from here to here," Lucas said, running his finger across the front of his shirt.

The surgeon responded with a five-page letter to the ethics committee chairman, whom he happened to have trained, challenging the questioning of his professional judgment. Gail Purton wrote her own letter, praising Lucas's care and saying that she never expected not to have pain after a major operation.

The case was dropped, but it was not an isolated incident. Lucas has worked closely with another surgeon, Anna Ledgerwood, since 1972. She too was hauled before the ethics committee on more than one occasion on the same charge. One of the investigations, for alleged inadequate pain management after a hernia operation, went all the way up to the state medical board. It cleared Ledgerwood, but Lucas said more junior surgeons buckled to the pressure to administer opioids just to stay out of trouble. "If they will give me a hard time, then they will surely give a young resident a much harder time," he said. "I tend to be a fighter. That's my nature. But somebody who just wants to take care of patients, they want to be a professional physician, they don't want to put up with all this crap; they're intimidated. They're also frustrated by it. The medical community knows that too many pain medicines are being written. Doctors talk about it among themselves. They're not in a position to challenge the system. But they know."

Lucas regarded the new pain orthodoxy as a growing tyranny, and he thought it was killing patients. He too began to collect data.

AS THE JOINT Commission was pushing out its new guidelines, a parallel effort was under way to influence the prescribing habits of doctors in small clinics and private practices across the country. Many were still hesitant to prescribe narcotics in part because of fear of legal liability for overdose or addiction.

The American Pain Society and Purdue Pharma's David Haddox were instrumental in writing a policy document reassuring doctors they would not face disciplinary action for prescribing narcotics even in large quantities. State governments regulate the practice of medicine, and so the industry latched on to the Federation of State Medical Boards as the vehicle for its ambitions.

With more than a little financial incentive, the FSMB drew up new guidelines for pain treatment that sounded many of the same themes as the Joint Commission. The document picked up on Haddox's theories that what looked like addiction was not addiction at all. "Physicians should recognize that tolerance and physical dependence are normal consequences of sustained use of opioid analgesics and are not synonymous with addiction," it said.

Haddox would go further later on and engineer a call by the federation for doctors to be punished for failing to adequately treat pain. But for now the drug makers settled for breaking down resistance.

The FSMB pressed state medical boards to adopt the guidelines and to reassure doctors that adhering to them would diminish the likelihood of disciplinary action.

In 2001 Purdue Pharma once again stepped up to fund the guidelines' distribution and get them adopted by state medical boards. Other drug companies paid too, but Purdue led the way, with grants totaling $672,400. Over the following decade, the FSMB took close to $2 million from the drug industry, which mostly went to promote the guidelines and to finance a book, *Responsible Opioid Prescribing*, written with the oversight and advice of a clutch of doctors who were strong advocates of wider use of prescription narcotics. The book was sold to state medical boards and health departments for distribution to physicians, clinics, and hospitals. The drug industry paid for the publication, but the FSMB kept the $270,000 profit from sales.

Within a few years, the model guidelines were adopted in full or in part by thirty-five states. Some went further. California led the way with a law effectively giving doctors immunity from prosecution for prescribing opioids except in the most blatantly criminal way. It also required medics to screen patients for pain. Doctors had already gotten the message from legal actions such as a 1998 case in which a jury awarded $1.5 million against a medical center for allegedly failing to provide adequate pain treatment. Purdue made sure physicians were acquainted with the cases.

Years later, the FSMB told a Senate investigation that it wasn't promoting opioids; it was merely offering advice to doctors on how to prescribe responsibly if they chose to do so. But the overall tone of the document was to reassure doctors that opioids were safe and to firmly suggest that hesitation to prescribe them was based on ignorance and prejudice at the expense of the patient. "Millions of Americans suffer from debilitating pain—a condition that, for some, can be relieved through the use of opioids. Studies have concluded that both acute pain and chronic pain are often under-treated in the United States, creating serious repercussions that include the loss of productivity and quality of life," it said.

BY THE TIME the FSMB guidelines were landing in doctors' in-boxes, Jane Ballantyne had reached her own conclusions about the impact of escalating opioid use. In 2003 she coauthored an article in the *New England Journal of Medicine*, as prestigious a publication as it gets in the medical field, challenging a central pillar of the new thinking on painkillers. Ballantyne noted the dearth of comprehensive trials, saying that two important questions remained unanswered even as mass prescribing of opioids took off. Do they work long term? Are higher doses safe to take year after year? Purdue and the opioid evangelists said yes, but where was the evidence for it?

Ballantyne wrote that there was evidence that putting some patients on serial prescriptions of strong opioids has the opposite of the intended effect. High doses not only build up a tolerance to the drug but cause increased sensitivity to pain. Opioids were actually making things worse while becoming less effective. The drugs were defeating themselves.

Her conclusion seemed to warn that if there was an epidemic of pain, it was partly driven by the cure. On top of that, there was evidence that the drugs were toxic. Then came the conclusion that stuck a dagger into the heart of the campaign for wider opioid prescribing. "Whereas it was previously thought that unlimited dose escalation was at least safe, evidence now suggests that prolonged, high-dose opioid therapy may be neither safe nor effective," she wrote.

Ballantyne thought the article would be a welcome if uncomfortable revelation to doctors grappling to help patients who never seemed to get on top of their pain no matter how many opioids they took. She assumed it would at least cause her profession and the drug industry to take stock of the impact of mass prescribing. By the time the article appeared, the registered death toll from prescription opioids had risen to nearly eight thousand a year.

"When the 2003 *New England Journal* article came out, I thought it was going to make the medical community sit up and say, 'Wow. These drugs that we've been thinking are helping people are not. We have a real problem.' But the medical community didn't at all say, 'Wow,'" Ballantyne said with half a laugh fifteen years later. "In my naïveté I thought that Purdue was our friend and they'd be interested in that too. That they didn't want to harm people any more than we wanted to see people harmed and that they would work with us to come up with better solutions."

With Ballantyne's paper, MGH's attitude toward Purdue cooled. In the end, the hospital saw only $1 million of the promised donation, and it was directed away from MGH and to a Harvard educational fund. No more was heard about renaming Ballantyne's pain center after Purdue Pharma. "We didn't want the money by then because we'd realized what the game was," she said.

Ballantyne faced considerable pushback against her warnings led by other pain doctors who did not want to hear challenges to the new policies they were so heavily invested in. "People in my field who had been, like me, taught we have to do this—people who'd been lobbying to try and increase opiate use, like the palliative care physicians—said, 'What are you doing? We worked so hard to get to this point, and now you're going to turn it all round,'" she said. "They become so rattled when you suggest you shouldn't give the opiates—and it's partly in the pain field and especially people in pharma—because it's big business."

Ballantyne is restrained. Other doctors say she was subject to hurtful abuse by opioid advocates angry that someone in such a prominent position should have challenged them.

She was also increasingly aware that the "less than 1 percent become addicted" mantra—a notion she openly scoffed at when I raised it—was false. Quantifying addiction and who is vulnerable is notoriously difficult. The numbers for who might become hooked are all over the place. Ballantyne, like a lot of doctors, estimated that between 10 and 15 percent of the population is vulnerable but that it depends on the substance and circumstances. What she was certain of was that OxyContin had been a game changer. "The long-acting opiates suddenly put much higher doses into people's hands and much more of it, and taking it around the clock made them dependent on it."

Ballantyne concluded that OxyContin supercharged what was already widespread dependence on lower levels of hydrocodone and oxycodone by drawing a new group of people into the "at risk" category. The drug was so powerful that it widened the circle of those vulnerable to addiction to suck in users of Percocet and Vicodin who had not allowed those drugs to take over their lives and who were not immediately at risk of overdose. OxyContin had found a fertile bed to burrow into. "Giving long-acting opiates captured a whole population that wouldn't have got into trouble with opiates if they hadn't been prescribed and become dependent on a drug it would never have occurred to them to take," she said.

The danger was compounded by OxyContin's failure to live up to its promise of holding pain at bay for twelve hours. For some patients it wore off after eight hours. That caused them to take three pills a day instead of two, greatly increasing their overall dose of narcotic and with it the risk of addiction.

LUCAS AND LEDGERWOOD had their own study on the impact of opioids in the works. They had come to believe the tyranny of the smiley faces was costing lives because the policy was used to override the judgment of surgeons. "If I operate upon you, if I cut on your belly, I expect you to be up walking in the hallway that evening. I expect you to be taking deep breaths because I don't want you getting pneumonia. I don't want you getting in trouble. Those things are painful. We're pushing you to do the things that are painful. Why? Because we want to get you better," Lucas said.

Years of surgery have given Lucas a healthy respect for pain as a tool for recovery. To suppress it was dangerous. But as large doses of opioids became the norm, the surgeon noted an increasing number of incidents of patients struggling to breathe after routine operations and being moved to intensive care. "Narcotic depresses the respiratory center. You don't breathe well. You get into trouble. You go to the ICU. Next thing you know you're incubated and you're on a ventilator for a couple of days. These things are happening because of the ingrained system we have regarding treatment of pain in the medical profession. These are things that don't have to happen," said Lucas.

Lucas and Ledgerwood visited trauma centers to collect data on deaths, mostly from vehicle accidents and falls, before and after the Joint Commission regulations on pain treatment. In 2007 the two doctors published their findings. Before the commission's dictum, 0.7 percent of trauma center patients died from "excess administration of pain medicines." The death toll rose fivefold to 3.6 percent after the commission's policies kicked in. "In each case, administration of sedation led to a change in vital signs or a deterioration in the respiratory status requiring some type of intervention which, in turn, led to a cascade of events resulting in death," the paper said.

Those were only the deaths in which there was little doubt opioids were responsible. The toll may have been considerably higher, given that a number of others were not included because, while the indicators suggested that painkillers were the cause, there was room for doubt. "Overmedication with sedatives/narcotics...clearly contributed to deaths," the study concluded.

The doctors called their paper "Kindness Kills." "I'm convinced that because of the pressures brought to bear by the Joint Commission, we are killing people. Just like the title of that paper says, kindness kills," said Lucas.

The study said the perception among medical staff that the Joint Commission was the ultimate authority created "great psychological pressure on caregivers" to use narcotics. Lucas and Ledgerwood concluded that doctors were intimidated into administering opioids and that nurses lived in fear of a black mark in their personnel file if they failed to address pain.

In a damning critique, the paper said that the commission's reliance on pain scales to guide treatment had created an "excessive emphasis on undermedication at the same time ignoring overmedica-tion." The obsession with ensuring people were not in pain was at the expense of ignoring the dangers of giving large amounts of opioids to people recovering from surgery or serious injury. The drugs may kill the pain, but they also risked killing the patient.

The two doctors made no secret of who they blamed for "this preventable cause of death and disability": the Joint Commission. "It's about money. Money has influence, and it influenced the Joint Commission," said Lucas.

The surgeon presented the paper to a meeting of the Central Surgical Association and saw it published by the *Journal of the American College of Surgeons* under the headline "Kindness Kills: The Negative Impact of Pain as the Fifth Vital Sign."

Lucas said he got a stream of letters and emails from doctors who recognized the problem. But, unlike Ballantyne, he wasn't surprised when the policy remained the same. "Did I expect a change? No. It is too ingrained into the medical profession. It's become financial just like the drug industry is financial. It's nothing to do with right or wrong. It's about how the money flows," he said. "When you write a paper you want there to be unemotional data out there. You want that unemotional data to be analyzed and interpreted in one way or the other, but you don't expect the Renaissance."

YEARS AFTER JANE Ballantyne's warning about the dangers of mass prescribing opioids as a quick fix for pain were published in the *New England Journal of Medicine*, a renowned British pain specialist, Cathy Stannard, called the doctor's paper "a distant warning bell," challenging the opening of the floodgates to strong opioids.

Ballantyne did not stop sounding the bell. She continued to collect data and to publish ever more detailed insights into the impact of painkillers. A less rapacious drug industry might have paused in its headlong charge to sell opioids, and less blinkered and compliant regulators might have determined that this was the moment to weigh the claims made in favor of permitting such widespread prescribing.

Instead, Ballantyne, like Art Van Zee and later Charles Lucas and anyone else who challenged the new orthodoxy, was subject to sustained personal attacks coordinated by the industry through its various fronts. They were dismissed as cranks and extremists.

The three doctors did not deny that pain was inadequately treated, but their wide experience told them that opioids were not the answer. Van Zee saw the devastation of addiction from overprescribing; Ballantyne recognized the harm caused by ever-escalating doses, Lucas witnessed the dangers of pain management in hospitals. They were not alone. Studies emerged from the United States and Europe backing their conclusions.

Each warning was a missed opportunity. Any of the bells sounded by Van Zee and Ballantyne might have served as the moment to stop a crisis becoming an epidemic. But the refusal to hear ensured the devastation ran unchecked for another decade before it was taken seriously.

ACT II
HOOKED

CHAPTER 8

A Loaded Gun in the Suicide Ward

T HE MEMBER FOR Kentucky's Fifth Congressional District
came to appreciate the scale of the catastrophe engulfing his
part of Appalachia only when he read about it in a local newspaper.
"This thing sneaked up on me," said Harold "Hal" Rogers, a Republican whose constituency sprawls the length of eastern Kentucky's
highlands and forests. "The *Lexington Herald-Leader* newspaper in
2003 came out with a big banner headline dubbing eastern Kentucky
as the painkiller capital of the world, which completely shocked me. I
had no idea. We were ground zero."

Over several weeks, the paper laid bare the toll of opioids in
general and OxyContin in particular on the people Rogers has
represented for nearly four decades. "Nearly half a ton of narcotics
reached six small mountain counties from 1998 to 2001—the equivalent of three quarters of a pound for every adult who lives there,"
the paper reported. That worked out at around two hundred opioid pills per person. "All the drugs were legal, but they didn't stay
that way."

OxyContin was remaking one of the poorest societies in the country. A region already grappling with economic and social decline was ill-prepared to cope with the wave of opioids. The toll of addiction was measured in overdoses, crime, and the number of children taken into care. Opioids proved as hard a blow to mountain communities across eastern Kentucky as the collapse of mining and rise of unemployment, fracturing a society already struggling for survival.

Rogers was stunned. He knew about the infiltration of OxyContin into his district—"hillbilly heroin," they were calling it by then—and the congressman was already making noise about the way Purdue was pushing the drug to doctors. A year earlier, he used his position as a subcommittee chair to call a hearing about the dangers of opioid overprescribing. Rogers brought a constituent to testify. A miner turned Pentecostal pastor, the Reverend Donnie Coots sat with his son, Joshua, who was dressed in an electric-blue suit and not saying a word. Joshua was hooked on OxyContin after a car accident. The father told how his son "would do anything to get the drug—steal, cheat, lie."

"I will never forget the sight because two or three months later, the young man overdosed and died," said Rogers.

For all that, the *Lexington Herald-Leader*'s stories were a revelation to him. "I didn't know what to do, if anything. What can a congressman do? But if not me, who?" he said.

There was a lot for Rogers to understand. The congressman struggled to get his head around not only how the drugs worked their way into the fabric of the communities he represented but why. What was it about eastern Kentucky?

ROGERS WAS A public prosecutor before he was a politician, and so his first instinct after reading the *Lexington Herald-Leader* series was to treat it as he had the waves of the crack and meth amphetamine and round up support from county governments for thirty-five undercover agents to sweep through eastern Kentucky, chasing down dealers. Several thousand people were arrested, and prosecutors had a nearly perfect conviction rate. But it did little to hold back the opioid tide, and arrests created their own challenges. "At first I thought this is really just a law enforcement problem, and we treated it like that for a while. But then we realized we had an army of kids left by these parents we sent off to jail or who died. An army of kids that were a product of the problem. Unintended victims."

Rogers joined Drs. Van Zee and Ballantyne in urging the Food and Drug Administration to narrow the circumstances in which OxyContin could be dispensed. In 2003 the congressman addressed an FDA hearing on the issue—the second advisory committee meeting chaired by Dr. Nathaniel Katz.

As he spoke, Rogers struggled to remember who in Greek mythology was lashed to a ship's mast so he could listen to the Sirens' call without being lured onto the rocks. Someone piped up that it was Ulysses. In that case, said Rogers, OxyContin is as enticing as the Sirens, and, like Ulysses, people need tying to the mast for their own protection. As the congressman saw it, that was the job of the federal regulator, the FDA. He pleaded with the agency to curb prescribing by restricting the use of OxyContin to the dying and those in the most severe pain. "So long as the FDA endorses the practice of prescribing this insidious but alluring addictive drug for a broken finger, we will have this problem," he said. "It has got to be fought at the source. The flood is too great for us to deal with down there. It has got to be dealt with where the huge amounts of these drugs are being allowed to flow. You must restrict—tie us to the mast."

Rogers is a conservative Republican. He voted against gun control and for repeal of Obamacare. He has consistently backed measures to curtail abortion rights and supported a constitutional ban on same-sex marriage. On the whole, Rogers is a friend of big corporations, but for him Purdue Pharma was beyond the pale. He blames it for an epidemic "driven by greed, not need," and he accuses the company of pushing "a big lie" that its drug was not addictive. "We want to believe that our pharmaceutical manufacturers do the right thing all the time. There is a real question here about the practices of overselling, overpromoting the use of OxyContin to doctors, to pharmacies, to the public," he told the FDA.

Rogers said that if the agency needed more evidence of the destruction wrought by OxyContin, it should look at the corruption of the medical profession. Take the doctor who wrote 800 opioid prescriptions a month—one every ten minutes of the working day. "What is most appalling in this case is that the doctor actually expressed concern to his colleagues about the amount of OxyContin he was prescribing. Who else did he express his concern to? His Purdue Pharma sales rep—who told the doctor, who happened to be a very top client of his, that he was doing the right thing."

The congressman had other examples: a Kentucky doctor who prescribed more than 2 million pills to 4,000 patients over 101 days, and the physician who saw 133 patients in a day in an office without electricity and was prescribing OxyContin and Viagra to teenage boys until the feds locked him up for twenty years.

"Frankly, this is the most devastating thing that I have seen in my more than twenty-two years now in the US Congress in my district. I have never seen anything like this. This drug is tearing apart families, it is ruining lives, it is stretching the resources of law enforcement and social service agencies to the absolute limit, and it has actually reached epidemic proportions in my district," Rogers said. "Unless you stop this now, it will cause many more deaths and renderings of families."

Another congressman, Frank Wolf, spoke of OxyContin "leaving a trail of broken lives, murder, suicide, grieving families, and growing law enforcement problems" in his Virginia district. He reminded the FDA that it had moved quickly to regulate the sale of dietary supplements containing the natural compound ephedrine after it was blamed for the death of Baltimore Orioles pitcher Steve Bechler earlier in 2003. Why, he wondered, was there such swift action over Bechler when the authorities were so hesitant to take action to prevent more deaths like that of Joshua Coots? "Who represents the poor and the suffering and the Joshuas and the people like that who can't hire the big firms from New York and Washington to come in and have direct access to the prominent people who make decisions in this town?" he asked. "Ephedra, they moved quickly. Big-time ballplayer, everybody knows his name, they moved. The Joshuas, they do absolutely nothing for."

Wolf told the hearing that the FDA's decisions that day would decide how many more people died and how many families were destroyed.

The FDA continued to allow OxyContin to be widely prescribed for moderate pain.

"We were ignored," Congressman Rogers told me. "They just listened to us, smiled, waved good-bye."

HAL ROGERS WAS not deterred. In the following years he did as much as any member of Congress to draw attention to the opioid crisis and hunt for solutions even if he was thwarted by his own colleagues on Capitol Hill and the pernicious influence of pharmaceutical company money over legislation, just as he had been brushed off by the FDA.

Rogers founded a group, Operation Unite, that was ahead of its time in searching for ways to combat the opioid scourge in eastern Kentucky. It offered vouchers to people who were addicted and poor to get treatment at facilities in other states because there were not enough in the region. It brought together coalitions to provide counseling and created clubs for young people as an alternative to seeking entertainment in opioids. It helped established drug courts in every county when there had been just one in the entire region.

This recognition of addiction as a condition requiring treatment and understanding was a long way from the establishment's reaction to the crack epidemic, and it would not go unnoticed in the African American communities still living with the legacy of mass criminalization and incarceration for low-level drug offenses. But Rogers struggled to break through prejudices toward underprivileged white people who it seemed to him were too often blamed for their situation and the addiction crisis.

The congressman introduced one piece of legislation after another to curb opioid prescribing, but most of it failed. He was reminded repeatedly of the limits of an individual legislator's influence in the face of corporate financial and political muscle and of who wields power in the institution to which he was elected.

Through it all, Rogers struggled to understand the forces that drove his district into the Sirens' arms. He concluded that the region was a "perfect mix for an epidemic" because of its aging population of war veterans and retirees, tough foresters and miners, living with above-average unemployment and below-average access to health care and medical information. "My district is one of the most unhealthy in the country. We're way above everybody else on heart disease, diabetes, obesity, cancer. We've got a lot of elderly, sick, which made this pain relief so attractive," he said. "Along comes the pharmaceuticals saying, 'Hey, we've got a perfect answer for you. Just take this little pill. It's like taking a pill for a stomachache or whatever. This is non-addictive.' But it gave relief and joy in often desperate people."

For all that, Rogers thought there was something deeper at work, what he called "a societal thing." "A lot of that has to do with lack of hope. Despair," he said.

His was a region once romanticized in tales of rugged self-sufficient frontiersmen and the fabled birthplace of bluegrass exemplifying the iconic story America tells about itself. Perhaps no legend was more powerful than that of Daniel Boone, the coon-hat-wearing frontiersman who carved his way into what is now Kentucky. The myths were so enduring that in the early 1960s, the Boone story was made into television series. But by then a different image of the region also had a hold—that of the antimodern, moonshine-swilling, gun-toting, backward "hillbilly." Far better watched than the Boone series was *The Beverly Hillbillies*, a sitcom in which unsophisticated mountain folk find oil on their land, get rich, and move to live among

California's millionaires. It was never quite clear to people in Appalachia what it was the rest of the country was laughing at.

In 1963 the rest of America was offered a different insight into eastern Kentucky by Harry Caudill, a lawyer and three-term state legislator from the southeastern coalfields who sought to explain the region's exploitation by some of the country's biggest corporations in a book described as changing Appalachia forever, *Night Comes to the Cumberlands: A Biography of a Depressed Area.* Caudill recounted the "greed and cunning" of the coal and timber magnates who stripped the area of its resources, ravaged its landscape, and then abandoned its people to near destitution.

The big corporations bought up the land and even the right to minerals on other people's land. West Virginia and eastern Kentucky were in effect colonized, and their people had little choice but to work for businesses that kept them in perpetual debt by paying in chits that could be used only at the company store. The profits from coal built mansions in Manhattan, while miners lived without electricity or running water. "From the beginning, the coal and timber companies insisted on keeping all, or nearly all, the wealth they produced," wrote Caudill. "They were unwilling to plough more than a tiny part of the money they earned back into schools, libraries, health facilities and other institutions essential to a balanced, pleasant, productive and civilized society. The knowledge and guile of their managers enabled them to corrupt and cozen all too many of the region's elected public officials and to thwart the legitimate aspirations of the people."

Caudill was later accused of exaggeration and inaccuracy, but the book had an impact. President John Kennedy was shocked by the depth of poverty he encountered campaigning in neighboring West Virginia. He ordered his staff to read *Night Comes* and come up with a plan. Reporters arrived from around the country, and ordinary Americans responded to their accounts by shipping clothes and food as if to some foreign disaster.

Kennedy's assassination left it to the new president, Lyndon Johnson, to visit eastern Kentucky to launch his War on Poverty in

1964. The president's helicopter put down on an abandoned min-iature golf course in Inez, a town of a few hundred people, twenty minutes' drive from the West Virginia border.

Johnson knew all too well the hardships of grinding poverty from his childhood in the Texas Hill Country. His set piece for the cameras was staged on the porch of the log-cabin home of Tommy Fletcher, a thirty-eight-year-old former sawmill worker who was struggling to feed eight children on just $400 a year, less than one-tenth of the average family income in the United States.

The president promised "not only to relieve the symptoms of pov-erty, but to cure it and, above all, to prevent it." Billions of dollars were poured into the War on Poverty, and they ate deep into want. Food stamps, Medicare and Medicaid, and educational programs alleviated some of the worst of the deprivations Johnson encountered, but they did not overcome its causes. The War on Poverty did not create jobs, and the region could not unhitch itself from its depen-dence on coal.

Hal Rogers's district enjoyed a fleeting boom in the 1970s as demand for coal surged on the back of the international oil crisis and gas shortages. The city of Beattyville rode the wave. Its three new car dealerships were a badge of prosperity. Two decades later, they were all closed as the mines retreated once again. For a while, people clung to the belief that the city would bounce back once it found a new source of wealth to tap into. There was a glimmer of hope in a new private prison just outside of town and a clothing factory. But they closed, too. Before long, the school system was the biggest employer in the county. As incomes fell in real terms, more than half of the residents were dependent on food stamps and disability payments.

By the 2000s, a typical household in Beattyville survived on an income less than one quarter that of the national median. A US cen-sus survey recorded it as the poorest white town—98 percent of its seventeen hundred residents were white—in the country. One-third of teenagers dropped out of high school or left without graduating. Few of the minority who made it to college moved back.

People in Beattyville got a fair idea of what other parts of the country thought about them from the arrival of Christian missionaries of the Divide Methodist Protestant church in the run-up to Christmas 2012 with deliveries of food and clothes. One of the missionaries was Jane Boyd, an accountant's assistant. "They're just real poor. You hear about crime and drugs and people breaking into houses when people go out to work. There's nothing here. I don't think there's a lot of hope. I don't know why people stay. It breaks your heart. I wish we could do more for them," she said.

The role of welfare in the plight of rural America remains a contested and raw issue. Steve Mays, the county judge-executive, an antiquated title that carries political and administrative power but no judicial authority, was born and lives in Beattyville. As a Republican, he's politically against a system its critics say has created a culture of dependence and disincentive to work. As a resident of Beattyville, he sees it as a lifeboat for his and other communities that would have sunk into destitution or even disappeared. If welfare has proved more a salve than a solution to the region's long-term problems, it is also true that public assistance shores up the economy of eastern Kentucky, home to five of the ten poorest counties in the United States. Even many of those who work are still dependent on food stamps. Three decades after Johnson's visit, Tommy Fletcher still didn't have a job, but he did have a means of just about surviving thanks to LBJ—disability benefits.

INTO THIS WALKED a new corporate plunderer. The drug manufacturers, like the mine barons before them, would make vast profits on the backs of broken people and communities, give little in return, not even to undo the damage, and then walk away to bank their vast profits far from the destruction.

When opioids landed in Beattyville, they served several needs. There was their intended function of relieving pain. Aside from the miners and loggers, there were no shortage of patients looking for relief from the demands of hard rural living. Opioids also served as a balm for the stress of struggling to pay the bills, keeping a job, dealing with the worry of an uncertain future without a pension. But as the numbers of pills reached critical mass thanks to overprescribing, and OxyContin upped the stakes, word spread of their potential as entertainment, particularly among the young. The pills were too often readily to hand at home. As Hal Rogers put it, "Our medicine cabinets are more dangerous than our cars."

Steve Mays was a policeman for sixteen years, half of them as police chief, before he became the judge-executive. "We don't have a lot of jobs here. Some people look for a way out. They haven't accomplished what they wanted to, and they're just looking for that escape. They get that high, and once it gets a hold of you, they have a hard time getting away from it. They don't think the future looks good for them, or they don't feel there's any hope, so they continue to stay on that drug. It's people of all ages. You feel sorry for them. Good people. It takes their lives over. They do things you wouldn't normally think they'd do. Stealing, writing bad checks, younger girls prostitute themselves out for drugs."

As OxyContin supercharged the demand for narcotics, dealing in prescription painkillers emerged as a means of economic survival and even prosperity that paid better than many jobs in eastern Kentucky, as it had in neighboring Mingo County. A trade grew up in which food stamps were exchanged for soft drinks, which were in turn sold for opioids. Elderly people in Beattyville, where retirement income was one-third of the national average, sold their prescription drugs to dealers to pay the rent.

No family was immune from the threat. Opioids worked their way into every part of the city. Poor or prosperous. Employed or not.

Mays, the county judge-executive, feels the sting all the more acutely because his daughter was convicted of illegally obtaining drugs from a local pharmacy where she worked. "I feel like the drug problem is our biggest issue. Not only does it destroy lives but the economic situation. If a company's not going to come in because they don't have a lot of workforce to choose from, or don't feel like they do, there's your jobs gone. And then people move out of here. A lot of people move out of here to bigger places to find jobs. So your population starts going down even more. I don't know how to change that. I'm not smart enough to say how to do it," he said.

There are many ways to measure the cost. Part of the price is paid by Beattyville's children. The local primary school runs a support group for grandparents raising their grandchildren. Forty percent of children are not living with parents because of drugs. The cost can also be measured in the breakdown of trust.

"For me, this was a place where people pretty much never locked the door. Everybody kind of operated without this intense concern about security," said Dee Davis, founder of the Center for Rural Strategies, an eastern Kentucky grassroots advocacy group aimed at improving conditions in rural Appalachia, who lives in Whitesburg, where Caudill once lived. "And then in a short fashion it was like, if your niece came over to the house, you're afraid of her going to the bathroom because she'll start riffling through the medicine cabinet."

Davis came to see OxyContin's impact on his region as a wave of destruction to rival the plunder of the coal barons. "Purdue Pharma introduced this. They changed the game. They changed the culture. They changed the communities. All of a sudden you've got kids having to live with their grandparents. You've got schoolteachers using their own money to make sandwiches to send home with kids to make sure they had something to eat when they weren't in school. The kind of damage they did to a resilient, culturally strong set of mountain communities is unconscionable. Places like Appalachia were just sacrifice zones to greed and perfidy," Davis said. "Those of us living in communities with expendable people have had to pay the price. It's happened in my family. I can go down the street where I live and point out what's happened there. I can go to my parents' house in Hazard, and I can go up and down the street there and say it happened in this house and it happened in this house. It's not abstract. It's a visceral understanding to what addiction does to communities that we all share now as part of this culture."

The flow of opioids into communities across Appalachia was having another effect, less immediately visible at the time. At around the turn of the century, the death rate for middle-aged white Americans began to rise in a stark reversal of decades of health gains. It went unnoticed at first because other categories of people continued to live longer, and so overall life expectancy went on rising for a few more years. It also took time for the statistics to reveal that those most likely to have their lives cut short were living in eastern Kentucky, West Virginia, and the other communities at the heart of the opioid crisis.

The mortality rate for Americans aged forty-five to fifty-four plummeted through the twentieth century, falling by more than two-thirds. The United States was so successful at combating killers such as heart disease that by 1990 the death rate among white middle-aged Americans was lower than in France and Germany. Over the next two decades it continued to fall in the Europe Union's two most populous nations. But the gains made in the United States stalled and then reversed, as mortality climbed again until it was significantly higher than in France or Germany.

Two Princeton academics, Anne Case and Angus Deaton, calculated that the increase represented about a half-million lives cut short since 2000. The reversal was not matched by any other developed country. In the United Kingdom, for instance, the mortality rate for middle-aged people dropped by one-third over the same period.

Opioids were the big driver, but Case and Deaton said they could not have been seen in isolation. Drugs were part of a stable of killers adding up to "deaths of despair." For years, lung cancer and heart disease were the leading causes of death until the decline in smoking helped bring them down. Now deaths from drugs pushed into first place, trailed by alcohol. Suicides also increased sharply and were a close third. When Case and Deaton went looking for what underpinned these numbers, one indicator leaped out: education.

In 1990 the mortality rate from drugs, alcohol, and suicide was low across the country. Then a gap opened up between Americans with a college degree and those who did not make it past high school. At first the divergence is gradual, but by the late 1990s the death rate among less-well-educated whites takes off. Among men it doubled. For women it doubled and then doubled again, although in absolute terms it remained half of that for men. In contrast, the mortality rate for people with a college degree largely held steady. Twenty years after the gap started to open up, a white American whose education stopped at high school was six times more likely to die of drugs, alcohol, or suicide than a person who made it through college.

The instinctive conclusion from Case and Deaton's findings is that deaths of despair are linked to poverty. Poorly educated people tend to earn less and are more likely to work in insecure jobs with the stress of struggling to make ends meet each month. In the midst of this surge in deaths from drugs, alcohol, and suicide, the country was hit by the most severe economic recession anyone but the very old had known.

But that was not the whole story. African Americans have long endured similar or worse financial insecurity and economic hardships, yet their death rates continued to decline. For decades, black Americans were far likelier to die younger than their white compatriots. But as the life expectancy of less-educated whites fell and African Americans lived longer, the mortality rates flipped between the two groups. Neither were Europeans, who were hit as hard and sometimes harder by the Great Recession, dying significantly younger, whatever their level of education. So there was something else going on.

Deaton saw the numbers in the context of a long-term decline for less-educated Americans driven by the "destruction of a way of life of the working class." He tied that to a breakdown of the implicit social contract between labor and capital built from the 1940s until the 1980s. Those four decades had been marked not only by a drop in wages in real terms but also by a decline in job security. The weakening of labor unions eroded pay and other benefits and undercut social life and a means of local and national influence. That in turn led to an increasing sense of marginalization.

As people without a higher education fell behind, Case and Deaton said they built up a "cumulative disadvantage," affecting the likelihood they would marry and stay married and shaping the future of their children, their health, their retirement.

Deaton likened the devastation of economic and social decline in parts of America to the impact of the arrival of Europeans on the way of life of the Plains Indians. "The story is rooted in the labor market, but involves many aspects of life, including health in childhood, marriage, child rearing, and religion," he said.

The Appalachian Regional Commission, a product of the War on Poverty that now covers 25 million people in all of West Virginia and parts of twelve other states, picked up on Case and Deaton's work and did its own study. The findings in *Appalachian Diseases of Despair* suggested the region was the main driver in the increasing numbers of Americans whose lives were cut short. In 1999 the mortality rate from drugs, alcohol, and suicide was slightly lower in Appalachia than the rest of the country. Five years later, with the spread of opioids, deaths had surged in the Appalachian region to 24 percent above other parts of the United States. By 2015 the gap was even wider.

When applied to all types of deaths, the numbers were even more stark. During the same period, the mortality rate for working-age Americans outside of Appalachia fell by 10 percent. Within the region it *increased* by 5 percent.

Overdoses drove the rising numbers of premature deaths, running 65 percent higher in Appalachia than the rest of the nation. But there were big disparities within the region. West Virginia and eastern Kentucky had the highest mortality rates for diseases of despair in general and overdose deaths in particular. They were 80 percent above southern parts of Appalachia.

Dee Davis flinches at the term *deaths of despair* as an implicit judgment of the communities he serves. He also regards it as diminishing the unique impact of opioids and particularly OxyContin. Prescription painkillers were not just another contributor on the road of decline but were in themselves a cause of devastation. A poison that not only killed but wrecked the existence of the living. The pills destroyed families and communities on a scale that alcohol and suicide never did. "It's easy to put a template over it and say these people are full of despair. 'What is their hope? Who are they?' But it was a business decision to introduce these drugs to this community. It was somebody figuring out how to have a good quarter and a better year. They made some choices. They decided which people are valuable and which ones are expendable."

CHAPTER 9

Paying to Play

AS THE TOLL of expendables rose, the Food and Drug Administration circled the wagons.

The FDA was forced to admit its blunder in allowing OxyContin to be sold as safer and more effective than other opioids when the label for the drug was changed in 2001 to withdraw the claims. The agency attempted to spin the move as evidence it was taking "aggressive steps" to confront addiction. But to critics such as Congressman Hal Rogers and Dr. Art Van Zee, it was further confirmation of the FDA's complicity in the crisis, and they stepped up pressure on the agency to rein in the spread of prescription opioids.

This might have been a moment for the FDA to take stock and rethink the policy of ever-expanding access to narcotic painkillers. The agency didn't deny that OxyContin had unleashed a thirst for powerful opioids that had taken hold in some of the most marginalized and vulnerable parts of the country and was beginning to spread to other communities. But increasingly vocal criticism of the agency's role in letting loose the epidemic had the opposite of the intended effect. Former FDA officials describe an increasing sense of siege within the divisions dealing with drug approvals and narcotics, and a determination not to change direction.

The debacle over OxyContin's label was an embarrassment. The agency had been bamboozled by Purdue's unsubstantiated claims for the drug—cooked up in the marketing department—into endorsing a highly addictive narcotic pill as safer than other opioids on the basis of no real data or investigation. The FDA missed the opportunity to require Purdue to test OxyContin when one of the agency's junior officials asked for clinical trials but was overruled. One failure piled on another.

Five years too late, the FDA finally pulled the false claims that OxyContin's time-release formula reduced its potential for getting high and replaced it with a statement that the drug was just as much a risk as any other opioid, legal or illicit.

Dr. John Jenkins, the director of the Office of New Drugs, put on a bullish face to the outside world in an appearance before Congress in 2002. He said tamely that at the time OxyContin was approved, the agency could not have known it would be at the heart of an addiction crisis.

Now the FDA was patting itself on the back for righting the wrongs in OxyContin's label. Jenkins said the changes were the result of his agency "working closely with Purdue to strengthen the warnings." This might have left the impression that Purdue was doing its best to ensure its drug was carefully prescribed even as it continued to push OxyContin as a default treatment for pain.

The FDA had warned Purdue in 2000 that it was falsely advertising OxyContin as having been tested as a treatment for all types of arthritis and for claiming it could be used as the first-line medication for osteoarthritis. It wasn't true, and Purdue left out important information about the limitations and risks involved. The company was allowed to pull the ad without further sanction. The FDA declared the matter "resolved with the cooperation of the sponsor."

This was what the FDA's critics found so frustrating. Here was Purdue once again lying about OxyContin and pushing it for a use for which it was not approved, yet the regulator did no more than seek its "cooperation." It looked from the outside as if Purdue spent its time exploring illegitimate ways to sell OxyContin. Meanwhile, the company's executives were telling the FDA how committed the drug maker was to fighting addiction.

The FDA wasn't the only one to drop the ball. A clutch of federal agencies with long names have responsibility for combating drug addiction and overdoses. Any one of them—the Substance Abuse and Mental Health Services Administration (SAMSHA), the National Institute on Drug Abuse (NIDA), and the Office of National Drug Control Policy, popularly known as the "White House drug czar"—could have taken the lead if they had been alert or interested enough. Each decided the people dying of prescription opioids weren't a priority. But it was to the FDA that Congressman Rogers and others looked to lead the way because it determined which drugs were approved and for what use.

The agency remained locked in its view that OxyContin was good for those it was prescribed for, even if that claim was open to challenge. John Jenkins warned Congress that "imposing restrictions on use of opioids could have substantial likelihood of hurting legitimate patients and reversing the tremendous progress that has been achieved in the appropriate treatment of pain."

Some of the strongest resistance to limiting access to OxyContin came from the FDA's drug approval division, where officials opposed factoring addiction in to the process of approving opioid painkillers. They stuck to the mantra: if the drug was misused, then the problem was the user, not the pill.

Within drug approvals, the analgesics division handled opioids. Its deputy chief, Dr. Bob Rappaport, was wedded to keeping open access to narcotics for people with chronic pain. Officials who dealt with Rappaport and members of his staff such as Dr. Sharon Hertz, a medical officer, in the 2000s found a division solidly on board with the industry's notion of an untreated pain epidemic. The agency dismissed the growing body of critics of its handling of prescription painkillers as ill-informed, stuck in the past, or, in the case of Hal Rogers, as a political grandstander.

As Rogers saw it, the FDA had been captured by the drug industry.

IT WAS ALL a far cry from the FDA's glory days.

If Americans think about the role of the Food and Drug Administration in their lives at all, it is probably to imagine the agency as Frances Oldham Kelsey saw it more than a half century ago. Kelsey's name isn't widely recognized today, but in her time she was a national hero for standing fast as a "bureaucratic nitpicker" against a company attempting to sweep a dangerous drug onto the market.

Kelsey was new to the job of reviewing requests for drug licensing at the FDA when an application for approval of a sedative to treat pregnant women for morning sickness landed on her desk in September 1960. Thalidomide was already on sale across Europe, and there was no reason to think its approval in the United States under the brand name Kevadon was anything but a formality.

Then Kelsey took a look. The US manufacturer, William Merrell of Cincinnati, dumped a mass of paperwork on the FDA. As Kelsey waded through, she was struck less by what she was told than what she wasn't. Where were the studies she knew raised concerns about the drug? She rejected the application and asked Merrell for more data. The company sent reams, but it didn't satisfy Kelsey and she kept asking for more detail. She later said of Merrell that she had the feeling "they were at no time being wholly frank with me."

Kelsey told the *Washington Post* in 1962 she thought thalidomide a "peculiar drug." For a start, experiments on animals had not replicated the effect it was supposed to have on humans by making them sleepy.

Kelsey, working with a chemist and a pharmacologist, decided that the evidence for thalidomide's safety was "incomplete in many respects." Besides, there were plenty of other sedatives on the market, so why rush into approving another one?

For Merrell, the urgency was to get tons of the drug it had already manufactured out of warehouses and making money in pharmacies. The company wrote letters, made phone calls, and sent its representatives to pressure Kelsey at her office. It even tried insults, calling her stupid. The firm did an end run around Kelsey by complaining to her bosses that she was being unnecessarily pedantic. The FDA stood by its official and later criticized "excessive contacts" made by pharmaceutical companies trying to win faster approval for drugs.

The tussle of wills dragged on for more than a year, with Kelsey refusing to move the application forward until the manufacturer demonstrated thalidomide was safe. The dispute was settled as the horror of the drug's toll on thousands of babies born with life-changing deformities unfolded in Europe. Merrell pulled its application.

Kelsey was hailed as a hero. President John F. Kennedy praised her "exceptional judgment" and gave her a medal. So did Congress, which wrote legislation tightening pharmaceutical safety laws and requiring full disclosure by manufacturers of side effects and safety issues. The FDA set up its own drug testing branch. Kelsey was its first director.

The near miss with thalidomide put the FDA firmly in charge of the pharmaceutical approval process. It trod with care, following the example set by Kelsey. Drug makers didn't like what they regarded as unnecessarily lengthy and thorough clinical trials or the slow pace of approvals, but for a long time they were helpless to challenge them.

The charge for reform came from an unexpected direction. The outbreak of the HIV/AIDS epidemic in the eighties generated an urgency to find medicines to fight the disease. As the death toll rose into the thousands and then tens of thousands, activists grew increasingly frustrated at what they saw as the FDA's dawdling over new drugs to tackle HIV and associated cancer. A presidential advisory panel said delays cost thousands of lives and that people who were dying anyway were prepared to accept the risks of taking experimental medicines that had not been fully tested. AIDS activists held mass protests outside the FDA's headquarters, their anger fueled by a view that the agency's sluggish response to the epidemic was representative of the indifference of the government and American society in general to a disease afflicting some of the most stigmatized in society—gay men and intravenous drug users.

The agency relented and created mechanisms to get medicines more quickly into the hands of those who needed them.

Drug manufacturers seized the moment. Lobbyists worked their way through Congress, complaining that months of delay in the approval of new drugs cost them tens of millions of dollars and accusing the FDA of asking for more data than was legally required before approving a drug. The FDA said it didn't have the staff to move faster because Congress wouldn't pay.

The result was the 1992 Prescription Drug User Fee Act. From then on, drug manufacturers would pay fees to fund approval of their new medicines. The drug companies were hesitant when they saw the draft legislation, fearing the new law might be no more than a revenue-raising measure without any speeding up of the approval process. A deal was struck. The new money would be used to hire more FDA officials, not cut the government's contribution to the agency. The law also mandated tighter schedules for drug approvals. On the face of it, it made sense to make the user of the service meet the cost. The head of the FDA's Center for Drug Evaluation, Dr. Carl Peck, was concerned that the new setup shifted at least some power from the agency to the drug companies, but his warnings were ignored. Five years later, Congress set even shorter approval times, and legislators continued to tinker with the law every few years. The effect was to halve the time it took to get a new drug onto the market.

As the fees rose through the 2000s, the FDA pulled in hundreds of millions of dollars a year and became ever more reliant on pharmaceutical company payments to fund the drug testing division. FDA commissioners have spent years denying that money buys influence over the agency. Certainly, the industry still regards the FDA as too slow and fussy in approving new drugs. The well-financed pharmaceutical lobby continued to mobilize members of Congress to cajole the agency to speed up the approval of new medicines. The FDA insists it sticks rigidly to the protocols without favor, but the opioid epidemic only strengthened the increasingly pervasive view that the regulator and big pharma are too close.

Former officials say a culture developed inside the agency of avoiding conflict with an industry only too ready to let loose the lobbyists on Capitol Hill. Trade groups influenced the divvying up of the FDA's budget. Some officials worried about a growing culture in which drug companies were regarded as clients to be satisfied and that the FDA at times behaved less like a regulator than a business partner.

In the 1990s, the FDA faced accusations of covering for the drug industry over the danger of antidepressants inducing suicide, particularly in teenagers. The agency was caught withholding a report that appeared to provide evidence in support of the claims. When the move was exposed, the FDA said the study wasn't complete and needed confirmation. But the failure even to mention the report's existence, and the agency's refusal to let the author speak publicly about its findings, again opened the FDA to accusations of putting the interests of drug manufacturers before the public health.

THE PERSISTENT COMPLAINTS about the speed of the drug approval process underpinned a move by two professors in 2002 who spotted an opening to influence FDA policies on pain medicines and perhaps get drug companies to pay for a few days at the beach at the same time.

Robert Dworkin, director of the anesthesiology clinical research center at the University of Rochester School of Medicine, and Dennis Turk, professor of anesthesiology and pain research of the University of Washington, latched on to frustration within the drug industry over the FDA's rules on the testing of new opioids. Pharmaceutical companies and pain specialists thought clinical trial procedures inefficient and said the resulting delays in the release of new painkillers caused unnecessary suffering. The process also happened to hold up the plans of some manufacturers to jump into the booming opioid market.

In 2002, Dworkin and Turk began to plan a conference to shape how the FDA approved new opioids and spent several months kicking around ideas on email. They would invite officials responsible for overseeing approvals and a group of top medical specialists. Then they would ask the big pharmaceutical companies to pay for the meeting in return for a seat at the table.

There was nothing unusual about asking drug firms to sponsor conferences. Pharmaceutical company profits course through the veins of the medical profession. Neither was it unreasonable to bring FDA officials and the manufacturers together. Most of the regulators had limited experience of designing drug trials and needed to hear from the scientists as they hammered out the procedures. But what evolved over more than a decade of opaque meetings would come to be seen as a far too cozy world between regulator and regulated when the curtain was suddenly yanked back and the outside world got a look in.

As they planned the first conference, Dworkin and Turk batted about potential sites for the meeting. The Mexican resort of Cancun was an early contender, but, in an email, Dworkin asked Turk for alternatives "with snorkeling."

Turk replied: "Maui, equally good snorkeling."

They agreed on Hawaii.

Dworkin said they should ask six or seven pharmaceutical companies to pay $35,000 each to cover the cost of the conference hotel and travel. The academics drew up a list of potential donors, including Purdue and Endo, the maker of Percocet. The money was to be described as "unrestricted educational grants."

Dworkin also suggested "10K apiece for you and me for preparing materials to distribute in advance, chairing the meeting and preparing the first draft of the article" about the conference.

The two men recognized that key to luring the pharmaceutical firms and their money was the promise of sitting down with the FDA and other government health regulators. The manufacturers were also given a hand in writing the blueprint for regulations governing the clinical trials of their own drugs.

Dworkin liked the way things were shaping up but realized that getting top FDA officials and the drug companies all the way to Hawaii was impractical, so the meeting was shifted to the US East Coast.

After kicking around different ideas for names, they settled on calling the gathering the Initiative on Methods, Measurement, and Pain Assessment in Clinical Trials—IMMPACT for short. Their proposal said up front that the meeting was intended to "collaborate with and inform the FDA/NIH [National Institutes of Health] initiative" for approving new drugs

With the FDA as the lure, Turk and Dworkin quickly found nine drug companies willing to pay $35,000 to attend the first meeting in Baltimore in 2002 with six officials from government agencies, principally the FDA. Among them was Bob Rappaport, deputy chief of its analgesics division.

The conference was deemed a success, and planning for a second one began almost immediately using the same pitch—a seat at the table with the FDA. As the invitations went out, Dworkin wondered in an email "whether this letter should be sent to our FDA friends. will it look odd to them that we are promoting the fact that they are attending???"

Word spread about IMMPACT. Other drug companies wrote asking why they weren't invited to the first meeting. Dworkin was pleased that they getting attention from "one of the real biggies at Merck."

Turk suggested upping the fees for pharma to attend future conferences: "It's like addictive drugs, we gave them a low rate to get them hooked and now we've got them..."

Over time, the two academics made repeated reference to the presence of FDA officials as a key attraction for the manufacturers. One email refers to pharma executives "hobnobbing with the regulators." Another, written by Turk, spoke about how the drug makers regarded the meetings. "Everybody has been very happy with IMMPACT, and they are getting a huge amount for very little money (impact on FDA thinking, exposure to FDA thinking, exposure to academic opinion leaders and their expertise, journal article author-ship, etc.) and they know it."

But in another message, Dworkin was sensitive to how that might be seen by federal officials. "We wouldn't want our FDA friends [to] think that we are suggesting that industry is having an impact on their thinking (but your sentence can be read to mean that IMMPACT has an impact on FDA thinking, which has already been proved to be true)."

As IMMPACT grew, the two academics set up a steering com-mittee that included Rappaport and members of his senior staff at the FDA. Rappaport was also among agency officials named as authors of the papers drawn up from the meetings as guidance on the opioid drug approval process alongside representatives of Purdue, Endo, and Abbot Laboratories.

Other officials were concerned at the blurring of lines between the drug makers and regulators and lack of transparency. A National Institutes of Health official on the steering committee, Ray Dionne, warned of a perception that IMMPACT was "paid for by a few large pharmaceutical firms who are assumed to be influencing outcomes." Dionne proposed that future meetings should be held at the NIH's offices without corporate sponsorship and opened up to "avoid the stigma that this initiative is a 'pay to play' process."

Turk worried to Dworkin that if they changed the way meetings were run, "some FDA folks might opt not to participate and drug companies may withdraw if they don't have the FDA at the table."

Rappaport did not share Dionne's fears. He enthused about the meetings in a talk, "The Impact of IMMPACT," in which he described them as offering "a wealth of opportunity" for communi-cation between the industry and the agency toward "approving new analgesic drug products."

What was going on behind closed doors? Although FDA officials were present, because the meetings were privately organized there was no obligation to keep detailed minutes of the discussions. But from the beginning, IMMPACT billed its mission as improving the clinical trials for opioid painkillers, and its twenty conferences over

fifteen years fulfilled that promise by making a significant impact on
FDA practices. One of the most important changes was the rise of
a process known as "enriched enrollment." Skeptics came to regard
enriched as a euphemism for plucking difficult cases out of the trials.

The bar for new drugs to win approval is not particularly high.
Manufacturers have to show that they are more effective than a placebo in treating a particular disease or condition and that the benefits of the medicine outweigh any risks and side effects. Clinical trials
typically involve comparing a group of patients taking the drug with
a second group given a placebo or a different medicine.

But in designing the trials, manufacturers look only to answer
the core questions set by the FDA: Does the drug work? Is it safe for
those who are prescribed it? As a result, the pill makers are keen to
exclude anyone from the test group whose medical histories create
"noise." In the case of opioids, that means purging those with a history of addiction, even though they are the most likely to become
hooked on the drugs.

Dr. Nathaniel Katz, the pain specialist who chaired early FDA
advisory committee hearings on opioids, was a founding member of
IMMPACT and, as an expert in developing clinical trials, a strong
proponent of enriched enrollment.

> People who have addiction problems make such a mess in
> clinical trials for obvious reasons. If the primary purpose of
> your clinical trial is to answer the question, does this drug
> treat pain better than a placebo? you have to exclude those
> patients. You have to exclude patients who have schizophrenia.
> You have to exclude patients who can't read and write. You
> have to exclude patients who speak Zulu and who don't speak
> English. At the end of the day the study will tell you does the
> drug work better than a placebo. It will not tell you what the
> addiction risk of the drug is in the general population.

The adoption of enriched enrollment made for a faster and
cheaper drug approval process. It got new medicines into pharmacies

quicker, not only helping people who needed treatments for conditions such as cystic fibrosis but also earning pharmaceutical companies back their research costs faster. But it took no account of the dangers of releasing powerful new opioid painkillers in the midst of a drug epidemic. So it proved with one of the most powerful prescription opioids, Opana.

In 2003, Endo, one of the sponsors of IMMPACT, sought FDA approval for Opana, a high-strength version of an oxymorphone drug it had withdrawn from sale two decades earlier because it was so frequently misused. Opana was arguably more dangerous than OxyContin to those who had not built up a tolerance to opioids. The FDA rejected the application after several patients in the clinical trials overdosed. Endo went away and waited.

In the following years the FDA embraced enriched enrollment, permitting Endo to do new tests that weeded out people who showed signs of addiction or misuse early in the trial and to exclude them from the final results. In 2006 the drug maker presented the new data to the FDA, and this time its narcotic pill was approved for sale without any changes to the formula that had been rejected three years earlier.

Endo told the FDA it did not foresee a large market for Opana—just that fraction of pain patients for whom nothing but the strongest opioids worked. But within five years, more than 1 million prescriptions a year were written for the drug, earning the company more than a half-billion dollars. Like OxyContin, it quickly proved a favorite among those sucked in to addiction. Users grasped that the pill was easy to crush and shoot up. Those injecting Opana were blamed for a rise in hepatitis C infections in Kentucky, West Virginia, Tennessee, and Virginia and a leap in HIV infections in southeastern Indiana.

AMONG THOSE WHO fell into Opana's clutches was T. J. Walden, who got hooked on opioids after surgery on a broken arm at the age of eleven and a string of painkiller prescriptions. "Your child is in pain, and you want them to feel better. You don't know there are dangers," said his mother, Emily Walden.

In high school in Kentucky, T. J. experimented with OxyContin and then moved on to Opana. The drug killed him at the age of twenty-two.

Emily Walden wanted to know more about this opioid that took her son's life. When she saw that the same drug that had been rejected in 2003 was approved three years later because of enriched enrollment, she saw a conspiracy. "Opana did not change between 2003 and 2006," she said. "The only thing that changed was the clinical trial. Every opioid since 2006 has used that clinical trial to get approved."

Walden came to regard clinical trials as little more than a pretense at serving the public health. As she saw it, enriched enrollment allowed Endo to discount the risk of addiction or overdose so long as the drug did what the manufacturer claimed when it was used exactly as prescribed in people who were less vulnerable to becoming hooked. That may sound reasonable enough, but it conveniently overlooked several very present realities, not least the vulnerability of a part of the population to addiction, the ardent pursuit of a high by others, and the opioid epidemic surging across the United States.

In 2012, the same year T. J. overdosed and died, Endo made an astonishing admission. The company told the FDA that Opana was killing people because it could easily be crushed, snorted, or injected. It said the drug had become more popular among people addicted to opioids since the changes to OxyContin had made those pills more difficult to break down. Endo said that as a result, Opana was responsible for a "rise in overdoses."

The company told the FDA it had recently pulled the drug from sale "for safety reasons" in order to launch a modified version that, like the newer OxyContin, could not so easily be crushed. But Endo's move was less about protecting the public than shoring up profits.

The company's patent was expiring, and it was keen to keep rival generic versions of Opana off the market. It told the FDA the generics were too dangerous to go on sale, even though they were exactly the drug Endo had been selling for years.

The FDA's judgment was stinging. It said the new, supposedly crush-resistant version of Opana did not work well and that it could still be "subjected to other forms of manipulation, such as cutting, grinding, or chewing, followed by swallowing." As the coup de grâce, the agency said that an investigation raised the troubling possibility that the allegedly safer version of Opana was more frequently injected than the original formulation.

After that, Endo tried a different tactic of paying other drug makers not to make generic versions of Opana. The company was charged with violating antitrust laws for making $250 million in payments and incentives to its rivals to keep their pills off the market, an illegal practice known as "pay to delay." Endo settled the case by agreeing to independent monitoring of its marketing practices.

ENDO HAD IN effect admitted Opana should never have been approved in the first place, and it probably would not have been without enriched enrollment, a process now routinely used as part of clinical trials for opioids. Dworkin and Turk said the IMMPACT meetings were not responsible for the switch to using enriched enrollment in the testing of Opana. They said that the first meeting to deal directly with the issue was not until 2006 and that by then, the FDA was already adopting the measure based on decisions the agency made at least two years earlier.

But others involved say that the process was not so clearly divided. Several people who were part of the broader push for enriched enrollment that benefited Opana were also instrumental in the IMMPACT meetings, among them Nathaniel Katz. Discussion about the process may not have been formally on the agenda in the early conferences, but some participants say there was plenty of talk on the sidelines because it was such a hot topic. Katz acknowledges that the time line is blurry and there was crossover.

Dr. Jane Ballantyne was invited to participate in an IMMPACT meeting after enriched enrollment was formally on the agenda. "I was very struck by the fact that this was all about designing studies so that you could make drugs look good and that you were there to design studies for the benefit of pharma so they could get their studies conducted as quickly as possible and with favorable results," she said. "All this business about positive selection, enriched enrollment—that's what they're sitting around the table trying to cook up."

Katz defends enriched enrollment as an improvement of the process for answering the core question about whether a drug works, particularly in targeting treatments that benefit only a small proportion of patients with some diseases, such as a recent medicine for a subset of people with cystic fibrosis. But he acknowledges that in deliberately excluding people considered vulnerable to addiction, the trials avoid a question made all the more crucial by the opioid epidemic. "It turns out the FDA doesn't care about the risk of addiction in the general population. That's why they continue to accept very highly focused designs that answer the questions that they have to answer. Now you might ask the question, well, is that right? Shouldn't the FDA be concerned about that? I think the answer to that question is yes, but that's not how the FDA works right now."

The IMMPACT emails were exposed by a freedom-of-information request at the behest of Dr. Andrew Kolodny, an addiction specialist who emerged as one of the most strident and influential critics of the FDA's handling of the opioid epidemic. He first tried to get the messages from the FDA itself, but when the documents arrived after a lengthy wait, large parts were blacked out, ostensibly on privacy grounds. Kolodny got a fuller version with an FOIA request to the University of Washington, a public institution where Turk was a professor.

It wasn't difficult to see why the FDA did not want the emails made public in full. After reading them, Senator Joe Manchin of West Virginia accused the agency of allowing itself to be part of "pay to play" meetings, giving pharmaceutical companies "undue

influence over FDA's approval process for prescription painkillers."
Manchin asked if the IMMPACT meetings had contributed to the
"FDA's failure to protect and promote public health through the reg-
ulation and supervision of prescription painkillers."

Congressman Hal Rogers said they were further evidence that
"the pharmaceuticals had a lot of sway with FDA and the policies
they put forward."

Katz, as a founding member of IMMPACT, said the backlash
to the emails was overblown. "I was involved in those meetings from
the very beginning. All of those conspiracy theories and accusations
are all absolute nonsense and have nothing to do with reality that
goes on the inside," he said.

> Thank God the IMMPACT group came together where you
> can actually sit around in a room, close the door, nobody's
> watching, nobody's listening, and you can actually have an
> honest and open discussion about how should we design
> these studies, how should we develop better drugs? You can't
> do that without industry being present because nobody at
> the FDA has ever designed a clinical trial unless they hap-
> pened to have done it before they got to the FDA. Nobody in
> the FDA has sat in the trenches and managed patients with
> chronic pain. You need different perspectives in order to fig-
> ure out the best way forward.

Katz said that without the industry at the table, "all you're going to
come up with is puffs of air."

Dworkin and Turk declined to answer specific questions about
their actions but deny their handling of the meetings breached legal
or ethical boundaries. Dworkin acknowledged to me that his email
exchanges with Turk were "too glib and were easily misunderstood,
but nothing in these emails describes or reflects any improper behavior that actually occurred."

After obtaining the emails, Kolodny made a formal request
to the FDA to investigate whether Rappaport and other officials

breached ethics rules through their involvement with IMMPACT. The Department of Health and Human Service's Inspector General's Office concluded that they did not, in part because there was no requirement to report their close workings with the outside private group, including membership of its steering committee.

Although the official judgment was that there was no impropriety, the tone of the emails and their characterization of the relationship between FDA officials and big pharma rocked the agency. Dr. Peter Lurie, a former senior FDA official in the commissioner's office responsible for public health strategy and analysis, told me the revelations about IMMPACT were "deeply embarrassing."

> People very close to me worked on it. It's a symbolic thing. It shouldn't have happened the way it did, and I'm not certain that the agency is clear enough on how to prevent it in the future. I think it was mishandled. Quite honestly, they continue to deal with those people even today, and I just think that's not a good judgment either. I think they should have cut them off. Those people revealed themselves to be really kind of craven and we should have been done with them, but they didn't want to do it. They valued the scientific expertise that they brought to the table.

The then FDA commissioner, Dr. Margaret Hamburg, told me she objected to both the way the IMMPACT meetings were conducted and the role of her officials, if not their goal. "We did put much more stringent requirements and oversight over the project once we became aware. I was disturbed and I got actively involved," she said.

In late 2014, Dworkin and Turk gave a written assurance to Hamburg that they and others involved with IMMPACT and a successor program, ACCTION, "will not represent or suggest in written or oral statements than an industry participant will gain special access to or influence on FDA officials in exchange for industry funds or fees."

In the end, the real impact of the exposure of IMMPACT was the political fallout. It proved another blow to the FDA's credibility as it struggled to reassure skeptical members of Congress and bereaved parents such as Emily Walden that it was fulfilling its proper function as a drug regulator.

Perhaps more than anything, IMMPACT revealed the priorities of the FDA's drug approval division. It appeared to be less interested in how to combat the opioid epidemic it had helped unleash than in how to get more narcotics onto the market quicker. That was at least in part as a result of the strong attachment of Rappaport and others in the division to keeping open wide access to opioids.

It was all a long way from Frances Oldham Kelsey.

Lurie dismisses those critics who see the FDA as simply bought off by the drug makers. But he concedes that does not mean the pharmaccutical industry's money is without influence over the agency in more subtle ways, including access. He said there is so much drug company money swirling around the FDA and other federal agencies that too often officials are numbed to its effect. "If you're a fish in a fish bowl, do you realize that you're swimming in water? It's so around you, can you even notice it anymore?"

CHAPTER 10

Pursuit

ROBERT BYRD WAS the longest-serving member of the US Senate in history when he died in 2010. He spent more than a half century on Capitol Hill representing West Virginia and by the end of the twentieth century had considerable clout in an institution steeped in respect for longevity. Byrd used his influence to direct billions of dollars to building federal facilities in his state to replace some of the jobs lost by the coal industry's retreat. Besides the routine pork-barrel projects of roads and bridges, West Virginia has been blessed with a giant radio telescope, the FBI's fingerprint division, and the Coast Guard's National Maritime Center in a state with no coast.

Byrd also saw to it that West Virginia got more than its fair share of federal prisons in the age of mass incarceration. The guard jobs were particularly welcome because they did not require higher levels of education or specific skills. Prison workers really only needed two things: not to have a criminal record and to be able to pass a drug test.

It was that last requirement that inadvertently drew the attention of West Virginia's attorney general Darrell McGraw to the encroachment of OxyContin. A member of the state legislature mentioned to McGraw in the early 2000s that one of the federal prisons was having to send a bus to pick up guards out of state because it couldn't find enough people locally who were clean.

McGraw soon learned that this was not an issue confined to prisons. Call centers, delivery firms recruiting drivers, and factories were turning away significant numbers of applicants—sometimes as many as one in four—because they failed drug screening or walked out the door when they were told they had to do a urine test.

From there, West Virginia's attorney general got a rapid education in what OxyContin was doing to his state. As he examined Purdue Pharma's actions, it began to look an awful lot like the company was behaving in the same way as another powerful industry—big tobacco. McGraw had just emerged from a legal battle with the cigarette companies as part of a nationwide lawsuit by states demanding compensation for the cost of health care for smokers. It was clear to McGraw that Purdue was targeting people in his state because they were vulnerable, just as the cigarette companies directed their advertising at the young and minorities. The drug maker's efforts to play down the negative impact of its pills also smacked of the tobacco industry's years of concealing evidence of the dangers of smoking.

McGraw filed a lawsuit against Purdue Pharma in June 2001, the first against the company by a state attorney general. The legal battle with big tobacco provided the road map.

McGraw had been a cigarette salesman in his youth, working as a rep for Philip Morris, the largest US tobacco company. He knew the workings from the inside and had been more than willing to join the national lawsuit against the cigarette makers. Although the litigation was a national effort, each state had to file its case locally. Fighting the tobacco industry in a state like West Virginia was a lonely task. McGraw knew there was no enthusiasm among the state's politicians for funding a lawsuit against a major corporation. They thought it sent out the wrong message to big business. "If I had gone to the state legislature and said I want you to appropriate $2 million for me to sue the tobacco companies, that would have been more than half of any amount of money that they had ever appropriated. If I had done that, there are people out here who would still be laughing about McGraw coming and saying he wanted $2 million to sue the tobacco companies," he said, still amused at the thought two decades later.

So he latched on to an innovation made fashionable by the now disgraced New York attorney general Eliot Spitzer. McGraw found the authority to appoint a private law firm working on a contingency fee, which saved having to ask the legislature for funds. If the state won, the law firm got paid from the financial settlement. If McGraw lost, it didn't cost the West Virginia taxpayer a cent. He saw it as a win-win and, above all, politically feasible.

The tobacco companies eventually paid out $206 billion in the largest civil settlement in US history. West Virginia's slice was $1.8 billion. With the money came the model for McGraw to go after Purdue Pharma.

As state investigators dug into the company's marketing methods, McGraw was increasingly reminded of his days as a cigarette salesman. "Purdue reps operated in much the way I did when I represented Philip Morris in the tobacco business," he said.

McGraw's investigators piled up evidence that the drug maker was making claims for OxyContin's effectiveness and safety that weren't true. He also knew from his own doctor how Purdue sales staff played on the medical profession's ever-present fear of being sued.

In suing the tobacco companies, US states sought to recoup the huge costs of caring for those diseased by cigarettes. McGraw saw Purdue in the same way: OxyContin was costing West Virginia dearly not only in wrecked lives but also in the escalating demands of caring for orphaned children, running treatment programs, and the demands of overdoses on emergency services.

Judges told McGraw they were alarmed at the growing number of children taken into care because their parents were hooked on drugs and neglecting them. McGraw's brother was a circuit court judge in Wyoming County. "My brother described this phenomena he sees in his own courtroom which he never saw before. The first one or two benches are filled with children who the welfare department wants the judge to take away because the mother's abusing drugs, because the mother's not capable of taking care of the child." In parts of West Virginia and eastern Kentucky, ever-increasing numbers of children were cared for by grandparents because their parents were incapable, incarcerated, or dead.

McGraw had not even filed the lawsuit before his office received a call from Purdue asking for a meeting. The company sent a delegation of five or six people. McGraw said most of them, lobbyists and lawyers, were forgettable. But one man made his mark, Dr. David Haddox. Haddox quickly made it known he was a fellow West Virginian. For McGraw, that necessitated a particular show of courtesy out of a kind of tribal respect. But he had no illusions. "In the parlance of the mountains, they were slick fellas," the former attorney general said with a grin.

West Virginia's deputy attorney general (DAG), Fran Hughes, was also in the meeting. "It was their attitude when they came to our office that really pulled us up. They didn't really want to address our questions. Instead, they were focused on showing this PowerPoint presentation. It was all about how effective they work for the treatment of pain," she said.

The company presented a raft of testimonials from patients who said they benefited from OxyContin. Haddox and his colleagues framed it as a medical matter, but McGraw saw them as businessmen and was unpersuaded.

As the discovery process forced Purdue to reveal its ways of working, McGraw became ever more convinced of the rightness of his case. "In law school we were taught that corporations have no heart, no soul. Their sole purpose is to make money, and they're the only legal entity that has eternal life. If Purdue Pharma acts improperly and makes a lot of money off of other people suffering, they would not be unique in that approach."

Lawsuits against companies were generally characterized as an "enforcement action" intended to protect consumers. Businesses and their lobbyists worked hard to ensure that whatever they were accused of, illegal or not, was not branded as a crime. Because it's not called a crime, that creates options. Companies can lobby over civil suits. They can run public relations campaigns. They can bring outside pressure to bear and even work to get the lawsuit dropped in a way that is more complicated with criminal charges. "We file a lawsuit, and they go to the next meeting of the national association of big pharma and say, 'We can't let with this kind of thing get started in this country. We've got this screwball down here that's a zealot of some kind, and we've got to do something about that. So what we have to do is we all have to stick together,'" said McGraw.

It's common to hear opioid manufacturers and their executives denounced on the streets of West Virginia these days as no better than Mexican cartels. As drug dealers in Armani suits. McGraw paused at the thought. "When I represented Philip Morris, was I a tobacco pusher? Yes, they're drug pushers. Of course they are."

So why didn't McGraw push for criminal charges? "Now you're back into politics again."

The attorney general of West Virginia is the state's chief legal officer, but his powers had been whittled down over the years when they came into conflict with stronger political interests. McGraw said the governor's office, under pressure from business groups and segments of the press, opposed criminal charges against Purdue. McGraw circles the touchiest political question. At the time, West Virginia's governor was Joe Manchin. He is now one of the state's senators in Washington, where he has been an energetic and forthright critic of opioid manufacturers and distributors and the federal institutions that have facilitated them. But that is not the politician McGraw recognizes.

The former state attorney general said Manchin sent his representatives to tell McGraw not to prosecute Purdue on criminal charges. "You go to court, and all of a sudden your lawsuit suddenly lands in the court of the only person that that governor appointed. And then you're before that court, and guess who chose to talk to the judge? One of the governor's helpers. In that scenario, guess what would happen? They threw us out," he said.

McGraw won on appeal. "This is the kind of thing you have to deal with. It doesn't make any difference whether it's tobacco or whether it's pharmaceuticals or whatever it may be. It may be insurance companies or finance companies. But those are the kind of things that you have to know you're going to be dealing with when you go up against corporations," he said.

The case went down to the wire. Eric Holder, later recruited by Barack Obama as attorney general, represented Purdue. The day the case was to come to court in November 2004, Holder agreed to a settlement requiring the drug manufacturer to pay West Virginia $10 million without admitting liability. It was a pittance compared to the hundreds of millions of dollars a year Purdue was pulling in from OxyContin. The company was also able ensure that the court sealed the records documenting its criminality. Purdue wanted the details to remain hidden from public gaze and the regulatory authorities. For all that, McGraw could claim to have held OxyContin's manufacturer to some sort of account

AS MCGRAW WAS pushing his state investigation, the US attorney for the Western District of Virginia, John Brownlee, was also casting an eye over Purdue. After Brownlee took over in 2001, the new federal prosecutor was bothered by the fact that no matter how many pill mills or doctors or pharmacists or dealers his office put out of business, overdoses kept rising. So he looked further up the pipeline. Brownlee wondered where the drugs were coming from. "Who sells this stuff? How does it get in there? And it really became one company, Purdue Pharma. And so the question was, why are we seeing an explosion of areas like southwestern Virginia and rural Kentucky and West Virginia?" he said.

Brownlee, a former paratrooper, was in some ways an unusual prosecutor to take on a major corporation. His office had just twenty-four lawyers covering more than fifty counties across western Virginia, and corporate malfeasance on a national scale was usually the purview of Washington or New York. Instead, the investigation began in the small town of Abingdon. As subpoenaed documents rolled in and investigators conducted hundreds of interviews, Brownlee's office found itself wading through several million of Purdue's internal memos, marketing plans, and notes from sales reps. The mounting evidence convinced Brownlee that Purdue knew it was selling a lie in OxyContin. "This was the magic pill, right? This was a long-acting pill that the addicts wouldn't like and you couldn't get dependent on, and that is the magic bullet. The reality is it just wasn't true," he said. "It was highly deceptive, and then they trained their sales force to go out and to push that deception on physicians."

The evidence showed that Purdue marketed OxyContin by making claims that were not in its submission to the FDA for approval. The company's persistent assertions that OxyContin was a superior drug looked to be little better than a marketing scam.

Brownlee's investigators also found documents from a 1999 study provided to Purdue by its UK partner showing that osteoarthritis patients using OxyContin had symptoms of opioid withdrawal after they were no longer given the drug. That was a clear challenge to Purdue's claim that people in pain did not become dependent on the drug.

In 2000 Purdue's medical department alerted the management to increasing numbers of patients reporting they had become hooked on OxyContin. The Purdue employee responsible asked if they should write up the study, "or would this add to the current negative press and should be deferred?" The supervisor said not to write it up.

"This case was really built on notes," said Brownlee.

A salesperson would go into a doctor's office and tell them about their product, OxyContin, and then they would come out and type in notes about visit. Then that visit was sent up to the main database. So we said, where in the United States were they marketing the drug in the ways that we found to be illegal? It was all fifty states. There was at least one instance of a note that showed an illegal marketing effort in every state in the country. So you knew at that point this is a culture. This was intentional.

Brownlee's office came across training videos in which reps acted out selling OxyContin using the false claims. "This was pushed by the company to be marketed in an illegal way, pushed from the highest levels of the company, so that in my view made them a criminal enterprise that needed to be dealt with," he said.

Almost immediately after Purdue learned it was under investigation, the company dispatched a heavyweight lawyer with pull in Washington, DC, to deal with this young prosecutor in rural Virginia. Rudolph Giuliani, later to become President Trump's lawyer, was fresh from finishing his term as mayor of New York, his reputation burnished by his defiant response to the 9/11 attacks. A worshipful press dubbed him "America's mayor."

Brownlee wasn't surprised that a lawyer of Giuliani's standing and influence came knocking. He understood that Purdue would be looking for someone with political clout as well as legal skills. In the end, Brownlee had six conversations with Giuliani. They moved from how to interpret the evidence and questions around discovery to negotiations over the final settlement. Brownlee described Giuliani as "a gentleman." But through it all, the former New York mayor's presence helped ensure there was heightened scrutiny from Washington. The deputy attorney general, James Comey, whose controversial tenure as head of the FBI still lay ahead of him, called about complaints from Purdue's lawyers over the range of company documents Brownlee's office was trying to seize. "The defense lawyers contacted Mr. Comey unbeknownst to us and said those guys down there are crazy," said Brownlee.

The US attorney thought the issue sensitive enough to explain to Comey in person. After Brownlee cleared up the DAG's confusing of Purdue with a chicken processor with a similar sounding name,

Comey signed off on the subpoena policy, and Purdue was forced to hand over the documents.

Brownlee set Purdue a deadline in October 2006 to agree to the plea deal or face a trial. The evening before it was to expire, the federal prosecutor received a call at home from a senior Justice Department official. Michael Elston was chief of staff to the new deputy attorney general, Paul McNulty.

Elston asked about the case. Brownlee was a little surprised, as Elston had never worked on it and had not previously shown an interest.

According to Brownlee, Elston said he received a call from a Purdue defense lawyer and asked why the case against the company was being pushed along so fast. Elston pressed for it to be put on hold.

As Brownlee saw it, lengthy and difficult negotiations had brought Purdue to the brink of admitting it broke the law, and here was an official trying to get him to take the pressure off, possibly jeopardizing the whole case by showing the company that it could influence decisions through its pull in Washington.

Brownlee asked Elston whether he was calling on behalf of McNulty. When Elston said he was not, Brownlee hung up. Purdue accepted the deal that evening.

Eight days later, Elston added Brownlee's name to a list of five US attorneys to be fired by the George W. Bush administration. Brownlee learned about it only later and said he regards all such lists as "inherently political." "The timing on this was always suspicious," he said. "My only interaction with him was that case. It wasn't like we had five cases, and you could have picked one and said that's why I was added to the list. This is the only one I ever had any interaction with him on."

It wasn't unusual for corporate lawyers to try to get leverage with senior Justice Department officials, but Elston's call seemed to Brownlee unusually interventionist. Elston's lawyer has since claimed that his client called Brownlee on instructions from McNulty. Brownlee remains skeptical and describes Elston as "untrustworthy."

Brownlee did not lose his job, but Elston resigned a few months later when the "hit list" of US attorneys who had made themselves unpopular with the Bush administration was revealed.

PURDUE ADMITTED A felony charge of misbranding its products. Three senior executives pleaded guilty to misdemeanors after political pressure staved off more serious charges.

With a criminal conviction, Purdue could no longer hide details of its activities behind sealed court documents. In a sixteen-page statement of facts, the company admitted that "supervisors and employees, with the intent to defraud or mislead, marketed and promoted OxyContin as less addictive, less subject to abuse and diversion, and less likely to cause tolerance and withdrawal than other pain medications."

Purdue admitted to training sales representatives to tell some health care providers it was more difficult to extract the oxycodone from an OxyContin tablet for the purpose of intravenous abuse, even though the company's own study showed that it was a straightforward matter to extract two-thirds of the narcotic from a pill by crushing the tablet. The drug maker also admitted to training sales reps to falsely tell doctors there was less chance of addiction to Oxy-Contin and that patients could stop taking the drug without risk of withdrawal.

Over the years, Purdue had paid out millions of dollars to settle cases in which it did not have to admit to criminal actions or even liability and which kept the records sealed so the evidence of its wrongdoing remained hidden from the American public. There was the settlement with McGraw in 2004, the same year Purdue paid a $2 million fine without any admission of guilt over a DEA investigation into its record keeping. Now Brownlee had exacted an important defeat for the company with a public admission listing its crimes.

"The result of their misrepresentations and crimes sparked one of our nation's greatest prescription drug failures," Brownlee said in hailing his victory. "Purdue's OxyContin never lived up to its hype and never offered a low risk way of reducing pain as promised. Simply put, the genesis of OxyContin was not the result of good science or laboratory experiment. OxyContin was the child of marketers and bottom-line financial decision making."

Purdue agreed to pay a penalty of $600 million, a sum that looks a little less huge when compared to the company's profits. Brownlee wanted to hold company executives to account. According to the New York Times, federal prosecutors were ready to press criminal charges against three senior managers but Purdue's string pulling got them off on misdemeanors. They were familiar as the faces who defended OxyContin at congressional and FDA hearings. Purdue's president, Michael Friedman, its general counsel, Howard Udell, and its chief medical officer, Paul Goldenheim, were fined a total of $34.5 million between them, placed on probation for three years, and each required to perform four hundred hours of community service. The size of the fines reflected just how much the executives were rewarded for pushing OxyContin. It was Goldenheim who a few years earlier had assured Congress that Purdue had made a corporate priority of fighting addiction and had then gone on to mislead it about the company's sales strategy.

Brownlee called the guilty plea a "crushing defeat" for Purdue. Yet he made a significant concession in negotiating it. He agreed that the conviction would be against Purdue Frederick, the company bought by Arthur Sackler back in 1952. But it had since been divided up, and it was Purdue Pharma that was making and selling OxyContin.

It was an important decision because a criminal conviction bars a firm from government contracts. If Purdue Pharma's name was on the conviction, it would probably have forced OxyContin from lucrative public health programs such as Medicaid and Medicare and the Veterans Administration health system, and so diminished its position among private health care providers. Brownlee did not want to be responsible for restricting access to the drug by those who needed it, so the prosecution was targeted at Purdue Frederick, leaving the pharmaceutical wing of the company to continue trading normally.

I didn't feel as a lawyer I could be in a position to bar anyone from getting OxyContin. Faced with that decision, I was just simply not prepared to take it off the market. I didn't feel like that was my role. My role was to address prior criminal conduct. Hold them accountable. Fine them. Make sure the public knew what they did. Put in an inside monitor. But to take that next step, I felt that was a bridge too far for a lawyer. That wasn't my job.

There's a lot of other federal agencies—the FDA, DEA—all these others maybe were better suited to make those judgments than a lawyer in southwestern Virginia. So we pled out Purdue Frederick that did not make or manufacture Oxy-Contin. It was debarred, but that had no impact. I still think that's the right call. But it's a tough one when you've got the kind of conduct that they were pleading to, admittedly.

It was a fateful decision because it left Purdue Pharma to go on ramping up sales of OxyContin.

Purdue's lobbyists quickly went to work on Capitol Hill, accusing Brownlee of grossly misrepresenting the true situation and implying that the company had effectively been blackmailed into the plea agreement. That didn't stop the US Senate from summoning Brownlee to Capitol Hill to explain why no one had gone to jail in the case.

Patrick Leahy, a senator from Vermont, said that as a former prosecutor, he considered "that nothing focuses the mind as much as thinking you are going to be behind bars."

Fines can sometimes become simply a cost of doing business. When you sit behind bars, you think far more about whether you did the right thing. I believe it is fair to ask, in light of Purdue's profits of approximately $2.8 billion between 1996 and 2001, whether the $680 million in penalties they received in this plea agreement will serve as a deterrent to similar future conduct or just simply become part of the cost of doing business. Many are asking why the three executives who pled guilty were not given jail time. As I said before, nothing makes corporate executives think twice about malfeasance more than the prospect of the iron bars slamming shut.

Senator Arlen Specter called fines "expensive licenses for criminal misconduct." "A jail sentence is a deterrent and a fine is not," he said.

As ever, there were senators prepared to speak up for Purdue. Tom Coburn of Oklahoma made an extraordinary intervention just before Brownlee testified in which he essentially asked why everyone was picking on OxyContin. Where was the investigation of other opioids? He then went on to blame the doctors for prescribing OxyContin.

Brownlee told the Senate the sentences would send a strong warning to pharmaceutical companies. A decade later, with tens of thousands more lives claimed by the epidemic kick-started by Oxy-Contin, he is not sure his case had the impact he expected. "I guess as I sit here now, I'm a little surprised that it's the only one of its kind. That with the nature of the abuse and the nature of the problem, that as we sit here that there's no other prosecution out there."

Purdue had dodged another bullet. Its criminal conviction came on top of the growing evidence of the destruction its drug was causing and the increasing skepticism in the medical community about the effectiveness of opioids. But none of it slowed the growth of Oxy-Contin as it began to push deep into those parts of America where the first people heard of the drug was when it ripped into their lives.

CHAPTER 11

The Silence

THE CENTERS FOR Disease Control and Prevention tracks drug overdose deaths by county on color-coded maps. In 1999 a spot of deep red staining southern West Virginia marked the first flaring in a calm sea of blue painted across most of a country oblivious to the early contagion.

Year by year, the red sprawls across the bottom half of West Virginia and eastern Kentucky. The blue gave way to yellows, and yellows darkened to shades of orange as the death rate crept up in the Rust Belt, New England, Florida, and parts of the West. In time, blotches of red erupted across the map even as the deepest hue remained painted over that part of Appalachia where the first warning flicker appeared. But in large parts of the country, if they heard about the crisis at all, they had little sense of the threat it posed. Addiction of that kind was written off as an affliction of others. Hillbillies or African Americans or the homeless. It couldn't happen to them.

The opioid crisis invaded the upscale community of San Ramon, east of San Francisco, on an October day in 2003 after Carmen Pack walked out of her front door with her two young children in search of ice cream. California was enjoying an Indian summer, and, after a hot afternoon in Halloween costumes, seven-year-old Alana was riding her bike and Troy, ten, was on his scooter as they set off down the sidewalk.

Jimena Barreto's gold-colored Mercedes came down the road at about 50 mph, weaving a little. As it drew level with the Packs, the car veered across two lanes and jolted over the curb and into the family. Alana was killed instantly. Troy was barely alive. Their mother was injured. Barreto, a forty-six-year-old nanny who worked for several wealthy families, fled on foot. Troy died in the hospital a few hours later.

Barreto was found in Southern California. She told the police she'd taken at least eight Vicodin pills and muscle relaxants and blacked out at the wheel. Investigators examined her medical records and saw she had several prescriptions for hundreds of opioid pills from six doctors all working in the same Kaiser Permanente hospital. She may also have been drinking vodka.

Barreto was convicted of second-degree murder and sentenced to at least thirty years in prison. The Packs welcomed the sentence, but the more they learned about the circumstances of the case, the more they thought responsibility for the loss of their children lay with more than a driver high on drugs. Barreto had gone from one doctor to another in the same hospital complex, collecting prescriptions for Vicodin and muscle relaxants by faking injuries. "There were six doctors prescribing to her for a long time," said Bob Pack. "They never talked to each other or shared a medical file. She would go in one week, get sixty Vicodin, and a week or two later go in and get another sixty from a different doctor. That can't be. Aren't they required to share medical files so they know what they're doing, or isn't there some kind of computer system where they can look that up or track it? I couldn't believe that there wasn't any of that."

When Bob looked, it turned out there had been a system in place in California for decades requiring pharmacists to report narcotics they dispensed to the state's Justice Department. But the Controlled Substance Utilization Review and Evaluation System, known as CURES, was so backward that drugstores were still sending in their reports by fax. The records were stored and rarely looked at again.

Bob Pack worked in technology. He knew it couldn't be that difficult to turn the system into an electronic database to check that people were not getting multiple prescriptions for opioids.

The grieving father was right about the technology, but he had not counted on the entrenched interests, medical and political, that would turn a simple measure to save lives into a decadelong odyssey. It was a struggle shared by other grieving parents around the country as they determined to find a way to fight back against the epidemic after it ripped into their lives.

BOB PACK'S HOMETOWN, San Ramon, is about as far, geographically and economically, as it is possible to get from West Virginia in the contiguous United States. It has among the highest median incomes in California. As another of its residents, April Rovero, used to see it, whatever may have been going on with drugs in Appalachia was part of another world, just as when heroin and crack hit New York.

Now, just before Christmas each year, April marks the anniversary of the death of her son, Joey, in 2009 by tending a tree in a memorial garden in San Ramon. The tree was bare of leaves as she decorated it with red ornaments for a seventh year. "I keep thinking maybe as the years go by it will get better. What I noticed this year was that I didn't start having that sense of foreboding a week before. It was more two or three days. It is a tough day."

April spent those years putting together the pieces of what happened to Joey and with it an understanding of an epidemic swirling around her but that, like many Americans, she never saw coming. Much of what she found is discomforting. Even now, she doesn't know if her son was actually addicted to oxycodone.

Joey was a senior at Arizona State University, and his mother was expecting him home for Christmas. Instead, she got a call saying he had been found dead in an apartment he shared with two fraternity brothers. A detective told April her son's room was littered with empty medicine bottles. The doctor's name on the labels was Lisa Tseng. Joey died from a mix of oxycodone, Xanax, and alcohol. Through her grief, April struggled to understand how she could have missed such a thing. But there was a clue when Joey was home for Thanksgiving during his first semester at college. He told his mother he thought he had attention deficit/hyperactivity disorder (ADHD). April asked what on earth he was talking about. No teacher in high school had ever said he had a problem concentrating. "He said a friend gave him an Adderall pill, and he was able to study for a test and did really well on it, so he must have ADHD. That told me right there that there is a perception out there that kids think these medicines are safe just because they're prescription."

There are doctors who think the mass prescribing of Adderall helped lay a foundation for the rise of opioids in universities. The number of children said to have ADHD surged over two decades. By 2012, 1 in 10 Americans under the age of seventeen was diagnosed with the disorder, and 3.5 million were being prescribed stimulants to treat it. But Adderall is an amphetamine and over time users develop a tolerance and dependence, and before long it had become the second most illicitly used drug on campuses after marijuana. The drug also proved another step in the conditioning of young Americans to believe that their problems can be solved with a pill.

April learned that Joey and two other men drove six hours to a small clinic in Rowland Heights, California. It was her son's first visit to Dr. Lisa Tseng. Joey cooked up a story about a sprained wrist, anxiety, and aching muscles. Tseng wrote him a prescription for ninety muscle relaxants, thirty of the highest dosage of Xanax, and ninety oxycodone pills.

"What he got was the Holy Trinity. That combination of medication that can absolutely be deadly. It's ridiculous," said April.

She discovered Joey was selling pills to his fraternity brothers. The police found a log in his room listing who owed him money. Joey's roommates were also using opioids. One of them, John, took his own life nine months after Joey's death. "Joey was the first of nine students at Arizona State University in a twelve-month period who passed away from either prescription drug overdose or related to a heroin overdose. They all started with pills," said April.

Once she got past the initial shock, April asked herself why she hadn't heard of this epidemic. This wasn't a small thing. It was everywhere, but she hadn't seen it. Why was no one talking about it?

April had retired as a telecommunications project manager overseeing multimillion-dollar programs across the United States, so she knew how to organize. She founded two campaign groups, one local and one national, to educate and to change policy but quickly discovered that not many in her community wanted to hear about addiction. "Stigma surrounds addiction, surrounds overdose deaths. People don't want to talk about it. Somebody dies, and in the obituary there is rarely any mention. More and more brave people are actually putting stuff in their obituaries, but it used to be zero, and so you don't know about it as a community. You just weren't hearing about it."

April asked the Contra Costa County coroner for numbers. They revealed at least 38 opioid overdose deaths over five years in the three San Ramon valley communities alone, and April hadn't heard about any of them. Morphine. Fentanyl. Hydrocodone. Diazepam and methadone. Heroin. The ages of the victims ranged from the late teens to a seventy-year-old woman killed by several drugs but primarily hydrocodone.

Across the county, 771 people were killed by accidental drug overdoses between 2008 and 2016. About 40 percent of the victims were women, and three-quarters of the deaths involved prescription drugs. Rarely did anyone die with just one drug in their system. April pressed the municipalities in her county to proclaim an annual drug abuse awareness month. She worked with prevention groups, focusing on student athletes who have been particularly susceptible to opioid addiction because of treatment for injuries. But she felt she was swimming against a tide of disbelief and indifference.

In Southern California, Sherrie Rubin faced a similar struggle to get people to wake up to the epidemic around them after her son, Aaron, overdosed. The first she heard about OxyContin was when a nurse asked how long Aaron had been "oxy-dependent." Sherrie had no idea what the medic was talking about but noticed two of her son's friends looking at the floor and not saying a word.

Aaron collapsed after taking an OxyContin pill at a friend's house. The friend had bought the drug illegally in Mexico and delayed calling the emergency services for fear of arrest. By the time Aaron finally arrived at the hospital forty minutes later, he had stopped breathing. A doctor asked what was wrong with him. The friend Aaron had taken the drug with claimed not to know.

Aaron suffered a series of heart attacks and strokes. Doctors told the Rubins their son was going to die. The couple signed a "do not resuscitate" order and called their rabbi about arranging a funeral, but Sherrie noticed a flicker of response when she spoke to her son and insisted doctors keep trying to revive him.

Aaron pulled through, but the delay in getting him to the hospital starved his brain of oxygen. He was left quadriplegic and able to communicate only by using two fingers. One for yes, two for no. Sherrie calls her son's condition "another type of death."

It took time for her to piece together the events of that day, but in time she came to realize that the friend's parents delayed calling an ambulance out of fear the law. They wouldn't tell the doctor Aaron overdosed even as he was dying in front of them. "They offered no information that would help save my son's life because of fear," said Sherrie, her voice breaking.

When she took a step back, Sherrie realized their fear was part of a wider silence running through parts of American society. She began to take notice of what was going on in her community of Poway, near San Diego. "I started hearing about his friends, of these kids dying supposedly because their hearts had just given out. I know these kids in our community. They were healthy, athletic kids. None of them were ill children. I heard something about OxyContin, and then I saw my neighbor, who told me she lost her son Joseph to it," she said.

Sherrie thought she recognized in the disinclination to address reality the same stigma that shrouded AIDS for many years. Her own family had a history of addiction, including an alcoholic and abusive father and siblings using drugs. She talked to her four children about the risks of both, but it never crossed her mind that anyone would take prescription pills unless they had to. "No one even knew what OxyContin was here on the West Coast," she said. "With addiction, people think, society believes, that it's a choice, a personal choice. To some degree the first or second time of a drug, there is a choice. But for a lot of these people, that choice becomes a dependency, and then that dependency becomes a disease, the disease of addiction."

Sherrie set about changing minds. She helped found the San Diego Oxy Task Force, a collective involving bereaved parents and representatives from the district attorney, police, and coroner as well as the DEA. Getting people to listen was a constant struggle. Sherrie gave talks at schools. "The parents just wouldn't come out. A handful of parents would show up, and none of these parents thought that it can happen to their child.... Really, no one wanted to hear it. Kids were dying, but they didn't want it to be acknowledged in the school or in the community."

Even as the death toll escalated, Sherrie struggled to publicize it. "I could see it coming, and I could see a train that was not going to stop, and nobody would listen in the first five years. For me, that was a horrendous crime that nobody wanted to listen. My son's generation was the first that grew up watching pharmaceutical ads on TV. There's an extreme lack of perception of harm about prescription drugs, especially pain pills, created by the pharmaceutical industry. They really had no fear about these drugs, and parents themselves had no understanding. I still see people today taking their Vicodin and having beer and wine. They don't understand the implications of that, that they're both depressant products."

People might be able to disregard the dead, but Aaron was not so easily ignored. Sherrie saw him as the living consequence of a drug overdose and wanted others to see him too. "My son isn't buried in the ground; he's buried aboveground. He's buried inside his own body, fighting every day to break out. It's hard for me every morning to wake up to the son that used to carry me around, dance with me, joke with me, and I have to turn him, I have to change him, I have to feed him. And he can't even say 'Good morning, Mom' verbally."

Aaron made an impression on California legislators as Sherrie successfully campaigned for a Good Samaritan law protecting anyone reporting an overdose from arrest for drug possession. Curbing prescribing was a different matter. Sherrie reserves particular scorn for California's medical board and the state's medical association, which represents doctors. The very people she thought would be at the forefront of protecting the public health appeared interested only in serving the interests of physicians.

Bob Pack ran into the same resistance. Years after his children were killed and his wife injured by a driver high on opioids, he was still struggling to get California to modernize its prescription monitoring program so physicians could instantly check whether a patient was doctor shopping. Bob thought his initiative would be welcomed with open arms because it would save lives. He proposed turning the antiquated CURES prescription monitoring system into an electronic database any doctor or pharmacist could check with a patient still in front of them, much the same way that gun shops carry out background searches in a few minutes. The California Legislature approved the idea, provided it didn't cost the state money, but getting momentum was difficult until former governor Jerry Brown became attorney general in 2007. Brown bought into the idea and appointed Pack as chair of a committee to oversee its development. Then he ran into entrenched interests. "There was resistance from doctors and the California Medical Association [CMA], saying they don't like it because it's too slow and too much trouble," Pack recalled.

The system was slow because it was underfunded after the legislature said it had to be self-sustaining. So Bob pushed for part of the annual license fees paid by doctors and pharmacists to fund CURES. He also wanted its use made mandatory. "The hospitals and the doctors fought it."

Bob won on the funding but lost on the issue of making it compulsory for doctors to consult CURES before prescribing opioids. The California Medical Association, which represents doctors, told the state legislature that its members would in any case sign up in droves, so there was no need for compulsion. "When I met with the CMA, they said in three years 99 percent of doctors will be enrolled in checking CURES. You don't need a mandatory bill to do that," said Bob. "It never happened. The percentage of doctors using the CURES system was really low. It only reached a peak of about 15 percent of doctors in California."

Bob met repeatedly with the CMA to try to get it on board. "They said that checking the CURES system was too interruptive and took too much time for a doctor out of his day. My belief is the real reason is because they're like a hired gun for the pharmaceutical industry, and the doctors and the pharmaceutical industry go hand in hand and there's very big money in opioid prescribing."

Bob Pack was incredulous. California had prescription monitoring before any other state, yet it was being left behind by similar programs in other parts of the country that were clearly effective. Ohio and Kentucky had required doctors to review prescription monitoring data and seen a drop in prescribing. A few years later, New York State would see the same thing, yet California was lagging badly behind.

Others had some success. Judy Rummler helped push through a Good Samaritan law in Minnesota and enabled easier access to an antidote, naloxone, after losing her son, Steve, to an overdose. But when she started pressing for changes to national policy by attending FDA and congressional hearings, Judy ran into the power of the industry lobby, insisting that nothing must be done to restrict mass prescribing of opioids for pain. Like other bereaved parents, she left meetings feeling patronized and dismissed as unreasoned by grief.

Judy Rummler, April Rovero, and others formed a pressure group, Fed Up!, bringing together disparate organizations campaigning for an end to mass prescribing of opioids, many of them run by people who discovered the epidemic only when it hit their families. Some leaders of Fed Up! saw a model in Mothers Against Drunk Driving (MADD), which mobilized popular support for tougher laws against driving under the influence. But MADD had an advantage in that no one judges the victim of a drunk driver. Fed Up! struggled to break past the stigma around addiction. The drug companies exploited it to paint people hooked on opioids as "abusers" who brought their addiction on themselves.

Fed Up! badgered politicians, campaigned against new narcotic drugs, and lobbied for easier access to overdose medicines. The campaigns led to better controls on doctors writing opioid prescriptions and pharmacies filling them, and wider access to overdose antidotes in some states. They also helped break down the stigma around addiction but always ran into the power of the industry.

Dr. Andrew Kolodny was similarly frustrated at what he saw as the complicity of the FDA in the epidemic. With Jane Ballantyne and other doctors, he formed a group, Physicians for Responsible Opioid Prescribing (PROP), in 2010 to throw the authority of the medical profession behind a shift away from mass prescribing and to press for national leadership in combating an epidemic that President Obama had still not said a word about in public.

IN FLORIDA, JANET Colbert was a nurse on a maternity ward in the late 2000s trying to work out why there was a rush of babies born in distress. She had seen a few like this back in the days when cocaine was rampant. Now there was a flood, and she had no idea where it was coming from. "At first, all the nurses were asking, 'What is going on? Why do we have so many of these babies?' Back with the cocaine and all, we would have one once in a while, and this was constant. We were never without. The babies were shaking; they would be screaming; their diaper area was very, very broken down. They had diarrhea. They'd be in such a frenzy, they couldn't even put their mouths around the bottle."

It soon became clear the mothers were hooked on painkillers. Janet Colbert and the other nurses gave these newborns morphine every three hours, but the comfort was temporary. "They slept a little and woke up screaming."

Many were in hospital several months. "One little girl had to get a feeding tube put in her stomach. Maybe at some point later in her life they were able to remove it, but she was discharged after a surgical procedure to put a permanent feeding tube into her stomach because they could not feed her any other way."

Some mothers abandoned their children, apparently having gone in search of a fix. Florida's Department of Families and Children found itself overwhelmed with infants to take care of. Janet worked on a unit with sixty beds for babies: "At any one time we'd have eight to ten who tested for opiates."

But it still wasn't clear why things were so bad in this part of central Florida—Broward County, centered around Fort Lauderdale. Janet spoke to a woman called Renee, who lived at the end of her block. The two women's children played together. One of Renee's sons, Blayne, was hooked on drugs and overdosed. "When she went to the hospital to see him, he told her about the pill mills. How you could just walk in and walk out. Two weeks later, Blayne walked in front of a car and was killed," said Janet.

The two women formed a group, StoppNow, and began holding protests outside the pill mills. As some states, most notably Kentucky, tightened their prescribing practices, and the FBI and police finally made inroads into the indiscriminate dispensing in West Virginia, hundreds of pain clinics popped up around Florida, providing opioid pills to just about anyone who asked. Unlike most states, Florida permitted doctors to dispense as well as prescribe. The clinics were one-stop shops for narcotics.

Among the earliest and biggest pill mills was American Pain, set up in 2007 near Fort Lauderdale by twin brothers Chris and Jeff George, who had no medical training. The pharmacy was run by former strippers, and doctors carried guns under their white coats. The DEA recorded cars with license plates from as far away as Ohio, West

Virginia, Kentucky, and Tennessee in the parking lot. Among the physicians working at American Pain was Dr. Cynthia Cadet. She was eventually charged over the deaths of six patients but convicted only of money laundering. Prosecutors said she made $1.3 million in little more than a year. By the late 2000s, Florida accounted for more opioid prescriptions than any other state.

Janet Colbert led demonstrations outside the clinics to draw public attention, not least the local television news. One of the women who joined the protests wore her daughter's ashes around her neck. Outside the Pain Center of Broward, Colbert spotted the owner, Joel Shumrak, walking around with a Glock gun on his hip. Shumrak found doctors to work at his clinic by advertising on Craigslist.

Janet Colbert's campaign paid off as the state moved against the pain clinics in 2010. The number of opioids prescribed in Florida dropped sharply. But Janet's efforts to get national change were frustrated. She had tried to tell her senator, Marco Rubio, about the pill mills but his office wasn't interested. So she went to Washington in the hopes of seeing him but was rebuffed. Janet kept up the pressure on Rubio to back measures such as mandatory training of doctors prescribing opioids, for prescription monitoring, for anything that would rein in the flood of pills. But it was clear to her that the senator wasn't going to go out on a limb against the drug companies or the medical interests.

Political leadership within Florida wasn't much better. It followed the lead of the Florida Medical Association, which opposed compulsory doctor training or obligatory prescription monitoring, even as the death toll climbed. Janet lost confidence in politicians. "Marco Rubio shouldn't even be a dog catcher in Florida, because as much as I've tried to plead with his office for help to do something for Floridians and for the whole country, he has done nothing."

The George brothers were finally imprisoned on drug charges. Prosecutors said American Pain made $40 million in the short years it operated and took the lives of about fifty people. Before his arrest, Jeff George told the *Palm Beach Post* that he bore no responsibility for the deaths of those who overdosed: "I bought my Lamborghini four years ago. If I wreck it, am I going to hold the Lamborghini dealership responsible?"

THE RED DOTS from the CDC's map found their way to places few would have predicted. The US attorney in Salt Lake City John Huber described "an insatiable appetite in Utah for pain pills and for heroin." The mostly Mormon state was awash in opioids of one kind or another. The dominance of the conservative Church of Latter-day Saints appeared to be a cause of addiction, not a deterrent.

Dan Snarr, a member of the church's high-priest group leadership, struggled to change attitudes within the LDS leadership after his son, Denver, became hooked on painkillers following a rugby injury. He died at the age of twenty-five as he attempted to get himself off the drugs by buying methadone on the street.

Snarr, who is also a former mayor of the small town of Murray in Salt Lake County, said he first realized the scale of the problem when other Mormons came to him after Denver's death to speak about addiction in their own families driven by the church itself. "A lot of people recognize that it's beyond anything to do with pain. It alleviates the stress and pain of this life and the challenges that you face."

Snarr said the culture of the Mormon Church makes "people feel that they should be perfect" and sets up a standard they struggle to live up to. "So they start using prescription painkillers not to address pain, physical pain, but the mental issues that go along with feeling inferior. That you just cannot cope with all the things you're expected to be and to do. When I talk to them, that's what they tell me: 'They make us feel like we're the worst.'"

One of those who struggled was Maline Hairup, a devout Mormon who spurned the stimulants forbidden by her church, including coffee, cigarettes, and alcohol, but was hooked on prescription drugs most of her adult life. She was prescribed opioids in her midtwenties for pancreatitis and migraines. Her sister, Mindy Vincent, reckoned they became a crutch to cope with the pressures of life in a deeply religious society.

> I think my sister found the medication helped with the physical pain, but it also eased emotional pain. In Utah we have a phenomenon known as toxic perfectionism. There's a belief amongst members of the LDS Church that you need to be perfect. That shame you have that you're not good enough drives a lot of people to have a big hole inside of them that they're trying to fill somehow.
>
> Maline never thought she had a problem. She was a firm believer that because the doctor prescribed the pills, it was okay. She didn't see any shame in it. She didn't think she was an addict. It wasn't like taking drugs.

Mindy's aging father, "a superactive member of the LDS Church," and her brother, Stan Hairup, were prescribed opioid painkillers, too—her father to deal with multiple surgeries and Stan to cope with a basketball injury. "Before you knew it, my brother, my dad, and my sister were all sharing pills. They look at that like that's normal and okay because it was prescribed, but the prescriptions weren't for each other," said Mindy.

Maline was good at duping medics in hospital emergency rooms by claiming to be in debilitating pain in order to receive opioid shots. Eventually, her doctor cut her off and put her on a treatment for addiction. By then Stan had moved on to heroin. He gave some to Maline. The first time she used it, it killed her at the age of thirty-eight. "My sister died, and then two more people very close to me died," said Stan. "I was just like, 'I can't do this anymore.' I was so addicted, that's all I ever thought about."

Stan realized he was going to end up dead and checked himself into rehab. Mindy was herself addicted to methamphetamine. Two arrests cost her custody of her son and left her homeless for a time. But ironically, because she was using an illegal drug, she received the help from the system denied her sister hooked on prescription narcotics. A drug court sent Mindy for treatment, and she is now a drug counselor herself. Almost everyone she sees is on opioids. "When you have a dentist sitting in the room with three guys from prison, two veterans, and four guys from the homeless shelter, you realize it affects everybody," she said.

Dan Snarr is still struggling to change attitudes inside his church. "Sometimes it's difficult for the LDS Church to admit there's a problem because they have this personification of worth. If we're the true church, we're perfect. But they need to recognize there's something they need to do."

APRIL ROVERO EVENTUALLY got to see the doctor responsible for Joey's death brought to justice. California prosecutors charged Dr. Lisa Tseng with three counts of murder in the deaths of Joey Rovero and two other men in their twenties who overdosed within a few months of each other. She was also accused of illegally prescribing in the deaths of five other people.

April sat through every day of the eight-week trial. Until Tseng was charged, she had known only about Joey's death. The doctor wrote twenty-seven thousand prescriptions, an average of twenty-five a day, for "crazy, outrageous amounts of medication" and rarely performed a physical exam. One of her patients overdosed in her clinic's bathroom but was saved. When investigators went looking for Tseng's prescribing records, they didn't exist. After California's medical board asked for the files, the doctor forged charts to make it appear she was lowering doses to wean patients off the drugs. Tseng's receptionist testified that she referred to her patients as "druggies."

The prosecution estimated Tseng's practice in a nondescript office on the second floor of a strip mall made $5 million from illegal prescribing. Some of the profits were set aside to buy a new building to expand the clinic and attract new clients.

April was unprepared for what turned out to be the most difficult day of the trial. She was shocked to see a photograph of Joey dead in his bedroom flashed onto the large courtroom screen without warning. "I had never seen that photo. I didn't want to remember him that way, and yet that image is now there," she said.

Seventy-seven witnesses testified. The only one for Tseng was her husband, Gene Tu, who was also a doctor and shared her practice. Two years earlier, Tu faced his own hearing before California's medical board at which he admitted to misprescribing opioids to his wife's former patients after she was barred by the DEA, including to a woman who told him she was addicted and a man who said he needed a refill because his wife took away his medications. The medical board placed Tu on probation for five years and ordered him to attend courses on prescribing practices, medical record keeping, and ethics.

Tu didn't help his wife's case. He was caught out in a lie about their finances, and when prosecutors asked why they hadn't heeded calls from coroners and law enforcement officers about the deaths of more than a dozen patients, Tu said the couple didn't regard them as any big deal.

April wanted to see how Tseng would react at being confronted with the human cost of her greed. "There was zero emotion from day one. I don't know what to think of her. It's so hard for me to understand how somebody could be such a bad person. I don't know anybody else that's so bad that they wouldn't care that they were killing kids," she said.

Nearly six years after Joey Rovero's death, Tseng became the first doctor convicted of murder for prescribing opioids that resulted in overdose deaths. The families of her victims made impact statements a few weeks ahead of the sentencing. April spoke, and listened. "To listen to the downstream impact—one mom having attempted to take her own life after learning her son had died in a horrific kind of way, marriages breaking up—it was just terrible. People six years down the path just still so broken over what happened to their children," she said.

April hoped to hear Tseng express remorse, but still she remained silent. Only at the sentencing did the convicted doctor have something to say. "I'm really terribly sorry," she told the bereaved relatives.

"I have been and forever will be praying for you. May God bless all of you and grant comfort to all who have been affected by my actions."

The judge sentenced Tseng to thirty years to life in prison. The DEA said the conviction "should send a message to doctors who violate the public's trust and engage in what is effectively drug trafficking."

CHAPTER 12

Pushback

A S THE EPIDEMIC coursed from the invisibles of Appalachia and Maine into middle-class communities and onto college campuses, the opioid makers worried that their efforts to blame the addicted and the dead for their condition were slipping out of their hands.

In 2005 the industry launched a new front in its campaign to shift attention back where the drug manufacturers believed it belonged—on the "legitimate patients" and their need for opioids and away from the "abusers."

Burt Rosen, a vice president of government affairs at Purdue Pharma and the company's chief lobbyist in Washington, cofounded the benign-sounding Pain Care Forum, drawing together the industry, patient advocate organizations, academics, and medical interests. Its members included Purdue and Endo, the maker of Opana, and the funding came from the drug manufacturers.

At its first meeting, the forum decided to push for a comprehensive study of Americans in pain to provide statistical legitimacy to its campaign. It organized a briefing on Capitol Hill, "The Epidemic of Pain in America," where members of Congress were told the "appropriate use of opioid medications like oxycodone is safe and effective and unlikely to cause addiction in people who are under the care of a doctor and who have no history of substance abuse." By then, the industry knew that claim was at best a mischaracterization of both the safety and the efficacy of opioids. It also deceptively implied doctors were routinely taking the kind of care in prescribing the drugs that included checking for a history of substance abuse. Many were not because their hospitals or insurance companies wouldn't let them.

The forum urged Congress to back a bill by Representative Mike Rogers and Senator Orrin Hatch, among the principal beneficiaries of pharma's largesse amounting to hundreds of thousands of dollars each to their political coffers, to commission a report on pain by the Institute of Medicine (IOM), a nonprofit that serves as a national adviser on public health. The bill failed. The Pain Care Forum helped Mike Rogers rewrite it, and the legislation was eventually slipped into the Obamacare health reforms.

The IOM published a fat report in 2011 claiming that 116 million Americans, more than one-third of the adult population, were living with chronic pain, costing the country as much as $635 billion a year. The institute quickly admitted it had done its sums wrong and revised the number down to a round 100 million. The committee writing the report called for a "cultural transformation in how the nation understands and approaches pain management and prevention." This included access to a wider range of treatments that avoided drugs. But the industry lobby swung its spotlight onto the headline figure of 100 million people in pain, claiming that this was the "real epidemic," not addiction. The Pain Care Forum wrote to US senators, calling for a hearing on what it said was a report on a "crisis of epidemic proportions." From there it was a small step to the morally loaded question: Why is so much attention being paid to a couple of million addicts when so many decent Americans are living with crippling pain?

The IOM's report was greeted with widespread derision from skeptical specialists because the headline number covered a huge range of pain, some of it transient and a good proportion of which bore no relation to the number of people who needed to see a doctor, let alone be prescribed opioids. Dr. Nathaniel Katz, the pain specialist who chaired FDA advisory committees, called the conclusions "infamous": "That was a political statement. Their methods were all wrong. It is overstated, but it was also another example of compassion for patients with pain translated into a model for opiate prescribing."

The report's credibility was undermined by the tangled associations between some of its authors and the drug companies. Among them was Dr. Myra Christopher, head of the Center for Practical Bioethics, whose endowed chair was established with a $1.5 million grant from Purdue Pharma. She was also a Pain Care Forum participant as well as being financially backed by several corporations that were also members.

Other members of the IOM panel included several researchers and doctors hired as consultants by opioid manufacturers. One of the lead authors, Dr. Sean Mackey, was chief of pain medicine at Stanford University School of Medicine and former president of the American Academy of Pain Medicine when it was receiving large grants from the pharmaceutical industry. He was among the most vigorous defenders of the claim of 100 million Americans in pain, saying in the report, "We recognized that pain management should be a moral imperative and responsibility for all of us who care for persons in pain."

The Pain Care Forum's tentacles reached deep and wide. It spent close to three-quarters of a billion dollars over the decade to 2015 on pushing policies, writing legislation, and funding elected officials in Washington, DC, and across the country to promote opioids and oppose curbs on prescribing. The forum presented itself as representing an array of distinct organizations offering a broad range of opinion with their collective eye firmly on what is best for the patient. Its members included the American Pain Foundation (APF), the American Pain Society, and the American Academy of Pain Medicine. But peel back the covers, and the forum was a web of interwoven corporate interests and specialists in their pay.

Among the most active of the groups was the APF. Ninety percent of its income came from the drug industry. Corporate donors included Purdue, Endo, and Abbott, the company contracted by Purdue to help sell OxyContin. Russell Portenoy was listed in the foundation's accounts as a contributor of up to $10,000 in a single year. Dr. Christopher sat on the foundation's board.

The APF was aggressive in what it described as its mission "to remove barriers to pain care." It ran the Pain Information Center, promoted as a "source of hope to people suffering with pain and their caregivers." The foundation mobilized people to pressure their members of Congress with "action alerts" through the Power Over Pain Action Network that scared pain patients into thinking their drugs would be taken away. It pressed newspapers to print human-interest stories about people living with pain and denounced reporting on opioid addiction.

The APF was quick to defend doctors accused of illegally prescribing opioids, claiming that arrests and curbs on prescribing were driven by "opiophobia." The foundation spent considerable sums pushing what it called "educational guides" promoting prescription narcotics. Purdue Pharma gave it $150,000 to promote the IOM report among members of Congress and federal agencies. FDA commissioner Margaret Hamburg embraced the report's central claim in insisting her agency must balance the risk of addiction with "another major public health priority: managing the pain that affects an estimated one hundred million Americans."

Months after Purdue was handed its criminal conviction in 2007, the chairman and founder of the American Pain Foundation, Dr. James Campbell, the man who as president of the American Pain Society had launched the campaign for recognition of pain as the fifth vital sign, told the US Senate: "I believe Purdue and its management deserve recognition for their contribution to the welfare of these many patients."

In the year the Pain Care Forum was founded and began pushing for the report on pain, close to 11,000 people were killed by an overdose of prescription opioids. Six years later, in 2011, when the report was published, the death toll had escalated to just shy of 17,000 for the year. Purdue's income from OxyContin rose by $1 billion over the same period to more than $3 billion a year.

PHARMACEUTICAL COMPANIES SPEND more than any other industry to buy political influence. Drug makers poured close to $2.5 billion into lobbying and funding members of Congress over the decade to 2016.

Nine out of ten members of the House of Representatives and all but a handful of US senators have taken campaign contributions from drug manufacturers seeking to affect legislation on everything from the cost of drugs to how new medicines are approved. Some of the biggest beneficiaries are, unsurprisingly, those with the greatest influence over new laws, including Paul Ryan, the Speaker of the House of Representatives. Orrin Hatch and Mike Rogers, the authors of the bill setting up the IOM report, each received more than $300,000 in political donations from the industry.

Drug industry lobbyists on Capitol Hill far outnumber members of Congress. Pharmaceutical companies spent $280 million on buying influence in 2017. The industry group Pharmaceutical Research & Manufacturers of America (PhRMA) was among the five biggest spenders on lobbying in Washington that year, allotting more than $25 million to employ 169 lobbyists on Capitol Hill. One hundred and twenty of them had a background in the federal government or Congress as staff or elected officials.

The impact of so much drug company money coursing through Congress is not always visible to the average American, even if it can have an impact on their pockets and lives. In 2003 Congress passed a law largely written by the pharmaceutical industry preventing the federal administration from doing what almost every other government in the developed world does—negotiate prices for drugs paid for with public money. The legislation also threw up barriers to cheaper imports. The result is that federally run programs such as Medicare and Medicaid must pay whatever the drug makers demand.

Manufacturers hide this extortion behind the spurious claim that foreign imports endanger the quality and safety of medicines in the United States. That assertion looks increasingly thin in the face of price gouging, such as the surge in the cost of EpiPen antidotes to allergic reactions. The manufacturer increased the cost to $600 for Americans. In the United Kingdom, the National Health Service negotiated a price of about $70 for the same product.

Attempts by some members of Congress to introduce legislation to bring down the price of prescription medicines or to let people buy them from Canada, where they are often cheaper, failed to make it out of committees where other politicians were regularly heard airing the industry's talking points.

The drug industry's influence over Congress is facilitated by the promise of lucrative second careers in lobbying. Congressman Billy Tauzin played an important role as chair of the Energy and Commerce Committee in shepherding the 2003 legislation limiting price negotiations into law. The following year, Tauzin gave up his seat and, immediately after leaving Congress, took up a $2 million a year post as head of the drug manufacturers trade group PhRMA. He proved so effective that when he left eight years later, Tauzin was the highest-paid health industry lobbyist in the country, earning more than $11 million that year.

Hal Rogers, the representative for eastern Kentucky, was fighting his own battles with the Pain Care Forum in Congress, watching one piece of legislation to curb the mass prescribing of opioids after another whither in the face of big pharma's influence. He found an ally in another Republican member of Congress, Mary Bono.

Bono had not taken notice of the epidemic until her son Chesare with the singer Sonny Bono—half of the sixties pop duo Sonny and Cher—became hooked on opioids after experimenting with drugs as a teenager. Chesare was using OxyContin that Bono believes came from Lisa Tseng, the California doctor convicted of the murder of

Joey Rovero. Chesare ground the drug down and snorted it. He was stealing from his family and selling off his guitars, video games, and even his father's ring to fund his habit. Mary Bono was already acquainted with opioids. Sonny was dependent on Vicodin before his death in a skiing accident.

Chesare eventually made it through rehab. By then Bono had grasped the scale of the epidemic and what was to come. "I watched him go through it all and recognized early on that it was quite obvious that people would have very little choice but to move from prescription opioids to heroin in order to sustain their habit."

Rogers and Bono founded the Congressional Caucus on Prescription Drug Abuse in 2010 to try to generate political support for new laws. Most of them foundered in the face of opposition from the industry or medical profession, or more usually both.

Rogers and Bono drafted legislation requiring the FDA to change the label on OxyContin to limit its use to severe pain. Purdue spent heavily to lobby against the bill, which failed to even come to a vote. The American Academy of Pain Medicine opposed other measures, including Rogers's efforts to have hydrocodone pills moved onto the same more restrictive prescribing schedule as oxycodone.

The American Medical Association (AMA) mobilized against a law sponsored by Rogers and Bono, the Ryan Creedon Act, requiring doctors to be trained to prescribe opioids. "Doctors, God love them, don't like to be told anything about how they practice their trade," said Rogers. "They've been resistant, reluctant to undergo retraining. Especially since for years they have been told by the pharmaceuticals that these pills were nonaddictive and doctors want to stop pain."

The AMA said the legislation would be a burden on physicians and made what Bono called "a massive well-organized effort" to block the measure. The law did not pass. "The AMA refused to admit they were part of a problem," said Bono. "The AMA pushed back on simple ideas like mandatory prescriber education on the highly addictive nature of opioids. I had one doctor specifically tell me he didn't care if people died from the opioid problem. It wasn't his fault. He wasn't doing mandatory education."

Bono called hearings of a trade subcommittee she chaired just to draw the attention of her congressional colleagues to the spreading epidemic. She went to them with newspaper stories about opioid deaths in their districts and flagged warnings from doctors and the police. "If I were to talk to some of my colleagues about this, and even on my committee, they just weren't interested. I would constantly highlight stories about people who were dying in other members' districts, and people just didn't pay attention," she said.

Bono acknowledges that she too didn't see the epidemic until it touched her family. "I was busy focused on other things. Alcohol and marijuana and bad grades. Raising teenagers is hard enough. I certainly didn't think these pills were going to come in and entirely change our lives forever," she said. "Like with all epidemics, you don't care until it hits you smack dab in the face. It's somebody else's problem until it's your problem. It has become everybody's problem."

Bono and Rogers understood that on Capitol Hill, trade associations and lobbyists frequently held sway provided there was no great public interest in an issue. If voters were agitated or mobilized, the lobbyists' power diminished. The drug industry relied on most members of Congress knowing little about medicine and being content to go with the consensus until presented with stark evidence to the contrary, as with the claim of 100 million Americans living in chronic pain.

The lobbyists did not sit idly by as Bono, Rogers, and other members of Congress alarmed at the epidemic tried to better inform their colleagues. "We were getting tremendous pushback from people like Purdue Pharma. Tremendous pushback," said Bono.

The congresswoman didn't win any friends in the industry by characterizing OxyContin as "pharmaceutical grade heroin." Purdue lobbyists paid a visit led by a former congressman, Bill Brewster. Bono said Brewster threatened to cut the company's funding for a drug monitoring program if she kept up her pressure demanding changes to OxyContin and the way it was prescribed. "It wasn't a horse head in my bed, but it was certainly some pressure. The fact is, they were willing to do such things, even though had they listened to me, then it would have improved their company and improved their product. But they were unwilling to listen."

Brewster has denied making the threat, saying his conversation with Bono was "cordial and constructive."

Bono said the lobby was ever present. "We felt it, maybe indirectly at times, but we felt it. We didn't have an awful lot of people lining up to help us. There's passionate advocacy from parents who've lost a loved one, lost a child. But there's not some sort of massive well-organized effort like there was on the other side by the companies," she said.

Part of that well-organized effort was the financial support given to ostensibly grassroots organizations representing pain patients genuinely fearful of losing access to their drugs, regardless of whether opioids were doing them more harm than good. Drug companies spotted a useful vehicle in pain societies. They began funding some in the 1990s, helping them meet the cost of publicity and travel to put forward their case. They directly created others in a campaign with echoes of the tobacco industry's attempts to fight curbs on smoking in the 1980s. The cigarette companies created supposedly grassroots organizations for smokers' rights and backed hospitality groups opposed to limits on smoking in bars and restaurants. The National Smokers Alliance was formed in 1993 with $4 million in seed funding from Philip Morris to push the company's call for a "balanced" approach to smoking: "Smokers and non-smokers; working together to work it out."

In 1998 the US Senate voted down antismoking laws. Senators who opposed the legislation received significantly more in political donations from the tobacco industry than those who supported it. Cigarette companies were behind several "smokers' rights" laws passed in more than half of US states.

Rogers did have some success. He managed to push through a federally funded scheme, the Harold Rogers Prescription Drug Monitoring Program, to help states establish oversight measures to stop doctor shopping for opioids, particularly across state borders.

But the American Society of Interventional Pain Physicians was alarmed that the program fell under the authority of the Justice Department and had a law enforcement component it said would result in witch hunts against doctors. So the group lobbied another congressman from Kentucky, Ed Whitfield, to sponsor a rival program within the Department of Health and Human Services to fund state-run prescription drug monitoring programs without the law looking on.

IN 2009 THE Food and Drug Administration was planning a program to get a better handle on prescribing and the use of opioids by educating doctors and patients alike, known as a Risk Evaluation and Mitigation Strategy (REMS).

The FDA drew up recommendations, including mandatory opioid training for doctors and pharmacists, and the enrollment of patients prescribed higher-strength opioids on a national registry. There was precedent in the registry for a schizophrenia drug.

Dr. Nathaniel Katz pushed hard for the measures, and Dr. Andrew Kolodny thought the recommendations "good stuff" because they limited the number of prescribing doctors and ensured a closer eye was kept on patients. The Pain Care Forum and American Pain Foundation fell back on the tested strategy of claiming that the REMS proposals threatened treatment for millions of people who should not have to suffer because of drug addicts. The forum pushed what it called consensus guidelines that, like the mantra of balanced policies, were intended to ensure not much changed. It gathered thousands of signatures for a petition opposing a patient registry. The American Pain Foundation called on the FDA to "protect the rights of people with pain."

A few months after its initial recommendations, the FDA came out with revised proposals ahead of a public hearing by one of its advisory committees. Drs. Katz and Kolodny were disturbed to see that doctor training would no longer be compulsory and that there would be no registry of patients on opioids. The concessions ripped the heart out of the REMS program.

Katz, the former chair of the same FDA committee, admonished its members: "Since I chaired the first opioid risk management meeting, now eight and a half years ago, somewhere approaching 100,000 people have died of prescription opioid overdoses and related events. What have we been doing all this time?"

Katz dismissed complaints that mandatory training and verification would "excessively burden the health care system" and scorned the proposals for "innumerable forms of voluntary education, monitoring, and surveillance." "Do you really need any more data to tell you that voluntary education does not work? I will remind you of the definition of insanity, attributed to Albert Einstein: doing the same thing over and over again and expecting the results to be different. The days of prescribers not being trained how to safely prescribe the number-one medication in the United States have to be brought to an end by you today," he told the FDA hearing.

Katz also tried a little emotional pressure. "When I bump into you all again after the next eight and a half years, I'd like you to have a clean conscience that you did the right thing," he told the members of the advisory panel.

The drug makers, on the other hand, praised the FDA's retreat under pressure. Industry advocates and their fronts claimed registries would breach patient privacy. They said doctors would opt out of mandatory training and there would not be enough physicians prescribing opioids. The industry argued that the epidemic had very little do to with doctors and patients, and so the restrictions would have little impact on the rising death toll.

The American Pain Foundation's Micke Brown told the hearing that patient registries were punitive and "further stigmatize people with pain, create additional hardships, and erect new barriers to effective pain care."

Brown said there was no reliable data showing that people who follow their prescriptions become addicted to opioids and then start misusing them, even though there was a growing body of medical opinion and evidence pointing to exactly that in many cases. She pleaded with the FDA "to go slowly" in developing REMS.

The advisory committee voted overwhelmingly against the watered-down voluntary measures developed by the FDA, with several members saying they would have little effect on opioid abuse and calling for stronger action. But the FDA is not obliged to follow the advice of its own panel, and so it didn't. Instead, it put in place the voluntary measures anyway, one month after privately briefing the Pain Care Forum on its plans. The FDA justified its decision by saying that compulsory training for doctors would be overly burdensome.

Dr. Jane Ballantyne, who sat on the panel, said the FDA leadership listened to her and other doctors, but she did not think they were being heard. "They listen to pharma and they listen to the pain advocates and they listen to us," she said. "But the FDA are the instrument of pharma.... The FDA puts pharma's interests first."

Hal Rogers spent years pressing the FDA to require doctor training. "We tried to persuade FDA that it had the authority to require additional education requirements for prescribers through the REMS process. But for years, all we heard was no, no, no. Meanwhile, our people were falling prey to addiction, drug abuse, as it became a national problem," he said. "It's clearly the work of the pharmaceuticals. To them, it's more money than anything else. Big time. Billions of dollars just on OxyContin. And they have undue influence at FDA."

In the eight and a half years since Katz testified to the committee, close to 150,000 people died of prescription opioid overdoses according to official figures widely thought to be an underestimate.

The FDA justified its position by reusing a tired formula: it was pursuing a "balanced approach" to opioid painkillers. As Dr. Katz saw it, balance was a cover for inaction. "The concept of balance got used as an excuse for not implementing any kind of policy. It prevented us from bridling opioid prescribing by implying that it deprived deserving patients of their access to opioid therapies. It gave forces that wanted opioid use to be unbridled an excuse to just open it up completely," he said.

In 2012 the American Pain Foundation hurriedly shut its doors after the US Senate Finance Committee announced it was investigating the influence of pharmaceutical company money on supposedly independent advocacy groups. The foundation said it was shutting shop "due to irreparable economic circumstances."

CHAPTER 13

Sounding the Alarm

D R. LEN PAULOZZI'S job at the Centers for Disease Control
and Prevention was to study how people did damage to them
selves in ways other than crashing their cars. He worked in the injury
prevention division on the Home and Recreation Team—a name
that still brings a smile to his face—interpreting statistics on everything from fires and burns to falls, drownings, and suffocation.

In the mid-2000s, Paulozzi thought it would be worth looking
at what progress had been made over the previous two decades with
campaigns to prevent unintentional injuries. He put together graphs
for the twenty years up to the most recent data available, for 2002,
and was pleased to see falling rates of injury in almost every category.

But the graph for accidental drug deaths, classified as unintentional poisonings, left him perplexed. While child poisonings had
been dropping for years because of measures such as childproof medicine containers, the data said older generations were dying of drug
overdoses in ever-increasing numbers.

It didn't make sense to Paulozzi, and initially he thought he'd accidentally flipped the graph: "I thought it's just a mistake. But I checked and rechecked and realized that there were substantial increases that occurred in most age groups for poisoning deaths."

Paulozzi went looking for an explanation. For a start, what kind of poisonings? Digging into the codes used to classify deaths, the numbers showed the increase was almost all accounted for by opiates.

Sporadic reports of increased overdoses had landed on his desk over the past few years but nothing to suggest these weren't local problems. There had been the forensic anthropologist working with the medical examiner in Maine who identified a big increase in oxycodone-related deaths in the state. And something similar from North Carolina. But information was patchy.

Paulozzi had also seen newspaper stories from West Virginia naming OxyContin as the drug driving a surge in overdoses in parts of the state, but there was little hard data and nothing the CDC knew of to suggest an evolving national crisis. Besides, these kind of local outbreaks of drug overdoses happened periodically.

The early data told Paulozzi only so much. Until 1998 the United States used a classification system lumping heroin, morphine, and prescription opiate deaths together. Only after that time did the overdose numbers distinguish between the different kinds of narcotics to reveal the big killer as opioid painkillers. Paulozzi found his way to the Drug Enforcement Administration's records and pulled information on the eight most heavily prescribed opioids, including oxycodone, hydrocodone, and morphine.

Opioids vary in potency, so the data was configured to create a standard measurement of milligrams of oral morphine per pill in order to compare the different drugs. The results shocked Paulozzi. The numbers suggested an epidemic.

In 2006 Paulozzi and two other CDC scientists published the results in the medical journal *Pharmacoepidemiology and Drug Safety* under the headline "Increasing Deaths from Opioid Analgesics in the United States."

The paper said unintentional drug poisoning mortality rates in adults rose a little more than 5 percent a year on average between 1979 and 1990. After that they leaped to more than 18 percent per year. Worst hit were people in their forties, but deaths rose in every age group except the elderly.

In 1999 deaths from cocaine had outpaced prescription opioids. Three years later, that trend was reversed. Legal drugs were for the first time in recent memory killing more people than illegal ones.

Paulozzi's paper said there could be no doubt, the numbers of deaths and prescriptions were rising in parallel. "The increase in deaths generally matched the increase in sales for each type of opioid," it said. The CDC paper sounded the alarm in concluding that "a national epidemic of drug poisoning deaths began in the 1990s."

The CDC tying deaths to prescribing levels certainly alarmed the drug companies that had for so long sought to fog understanding by lumping prescription pill overdoses in with heroin users as "abusers" hardly worthy of bothering with. The separating out of painkillers from heroin made it harder to treat all overdose deaths the same: the evidence proved that mass prescribing was driving the epidemic.

The report gave ammunition to those members of Congress, such as Hal Rogers, pushing for the epidemic to be seen for what it was. But Paulozzi expected the paper to have a wider impact. It had the authority of the CDC's stamp, the agency whose job it was to identify epidemics. Other federal agencies would surely move in and pick up the baton.

Like Ballantyne after she exposed opioid painkillers as not only unsafe but of limited benefit, Paulozzi was to be disappointed. "I guess I was naive. I expected the FDA to do something. I expected the medical community to change their prescribing practices. I expected an attempt to educate patients better about the limitation of benefits and the real risks. That really didn't happen."

Paulozzi said it was obvious that OxyContin was at the heart of the epidemic. He hoped and expected the FDA would pull it from the market. But as far as he could make out, the agency never even discussed the possibility.

The CDC doctor went to a meeting of the FDA's Center for Drug Evaluation and Research to press the case for action. Dr. Doug Throckmorton told him OxyContin already carried a "black box warning" about addiction. But if that was sufficient, why was the epidemic widening?

Paulozzi pressed Throckmorton about mandatory doctor education on the dangers of opioid prescribing but was brushed off by the FDA official. That wasn't going to happen, he said. Any physician who wanted to could volunteer for a course. Not many did.

Paulozzi was shocked at what he regarded as complacency. "There was a resounding silence on the part of the FDA," he said.

The reaction from other federal agencies was little better. The Substance Abuse and Mental Health Services Administration took the view that its job was treatment not prevention. The National Institute on Drug Abuse steered clear of public health policy interventions, preferring to stick to the science of identifying new drugs to treat addiction. It seemed to Paulozzi no one wanted to take responsibility. "We just didn't see policy changes I would say for ten years on the federal level until after the problem became known as a nationally important issue that was killing thousands of people."

Even within the CDC, there was ambivalence. Paulozzi was encouraged to keep up his work, but he got the impression the agency's director, Julie Gerberding, wasn't particularly engaged. She allocated no additional money and no extra staff. "I never had any conversations with Julie Gerberding.... There really was not a heck of a lot of interest in it," he said.

Paulozzi understands some of the hesitation. There was caution about territory. As its name said, it was SAMHSA's job to deal with substance abuse and NIDA's to handle drug abuse. Drug prescribing policy was clearly in the FDA bailiwick. "We didn't really want to step on those toes. At least people above me didn't want to step on those toes, and I was outranked," said Paulozzi.

Within the CDC, there were also issues of jurisdiction. Its National Center for Environmental Health traditionally dealt with drug poisonings involving contaminated methamphetamine or heroin. Still, Paulozzi was free to keep investigating and publishing. He dedicated himself full-time to the task. He fleshed out the initial findings with new research and more recent data. He saw that the biggest increase in the overdose death rate was in West Virginia, where it was up 550 percent since 1999, and that it had doubled in nearly half of US states. He doubled down on the message that prescribing was the problem and pushed for action. "The results suggest that more aggressive regulatory, educational, and treatment measures are necessary to address the increase in fatal drug overdoses," he wrote.

The numbers showed that by 2001, drug deaths had overtaken those from alcohol. Then they surpassed gun deaths. In 2007 Paulozzi offered a prescient warning. "If current rates of increase continue, then drug-induced deaths will surpass deaths related to motor vehicles in more states, and, among Caucasians, may surpass deaths from motor vehicles nationwide by the end of the decade," it said.

Paulozzi identified something else. The number of opioid-related drug deaths had begun in 1990. That backed Ballantyne's view that the push for wider prescribing of narcotics was already taking a toll before OxyContin came on the market, turning a crisis into an epidemic. Paulozzi noted another phenomenon: overdoses were rising more than six times as fast in rural areas as towns and cities. For years, urban areas were far ahead in the rate of total drug poisonings, but by 2004 rural America had caught up.

The CDC has long worked closely with state medical examiners, who are often the first to alert the agency to a surge in deaths from one cause or another. In those cases, state officials can ask the CDC to send officers from its Epidemic Intelligence Service (EIS)— "medical detectives," in popular parlance.

Paulozzi wanted to know what was going on in West Virginia because it was experiencing the biggest increase in drug mortality rates in the country, so he called the state's medical examiner, Jim Kaplan, who was assiduous in documenting the characteristics of death, including patterns of drug use. Kaplan agreed to work with a team of EIS officers to dig into how prescribing was driving the epidemic.

There were a lot of theories floating around about why the situation was so bad in West Virginia. Paulozzi heard the speculation that prescribing was driven by men on the mines, but the stats told him that couldn't be the whole story. "Just as many women were overdosing as men at that time. There weren't very many women who had had a career in coal mines," he said.

Still, he suspected the history of opioid use in the mines had been a factor in Purdue Pharma targeting its marketing on the state with its false reassurances about addiction and effectiveness. "People developed a habit of using drugs and escalated their doses, and 20 percent or so of them had actually moved on to injecting prescription drugs. OxyContin figured commonly in all that," he said.

The results of the research offered a snapshot of the evolving epidemic. Nearly all overdose deaths in West Virginia in 2006 involved prescription drugs. Mostly they were opioids, but nearly half were combined with a benzodiazepines such as Valium, a dangerous mix.

From the research, Paulozzi concluded that the epidemic was initially driven by older people who became hooked while following prescriptions but later started looking for other sources of medicines to feed their addiction, some by doctor shopping, others by buying illegally on the street.

Younger people were more likely to have started using opioids for entertainment and to have obtained them from their family or friends for free. That led researchers to consider that some of the parents who became hooked by accident and found irregular supplies of opioids then became the suppliers, intentionally or not, to their children. "People ultimately were abusing the drugs in all the ways that heroin had been used for fifty years in the United States, including injection and snorting," he said.

As bad as it was, there was worse to come. In 2006 the overdose death rate in West Virginia was 16.2 per 100,000, far above the rest of the country. By 2016 it was more than triple that, and parts of the state were six times higher.

Paulozzi's paper was a documented challenge to the orthodoxy pushed by the drug industry. As the evidence mounted, Paulozzi waited for a response from the system. Even from within the CDC.

SHORTLY AFTER PRESIDENT Obama moved into the White House in 2009, he replaced Gerberding as CDC director with Dr. Tom Frieden, fresh from seven years as New York City's health commissioner. With the city's mayor Michael Bloomberg, he ran an aggressive campaign to curb smoking through taxes, advertising, and a ban on cigarettes in the workplace. Smoking rates fell significantly.

One of the first things Frieden did in his new post was wade through an eight-hundred-page document, *Health Statistics US*. "I was new to the CDC, and so I was looking through it quite carefully. What I was really struck by was that the only thing that was getting worse in America was overdose deaths. That was a striking realization," he said.

Frieden was stunned by the numbers. "AIDS in Africa does that. A war does that. The great influenza pandemic of 1918 does that. But not a lot else. We take for granted that things are at least not getting worse, even if they're not getting better. I'm a data-driven person, so when you see a death rate increasing in this day and age, it's shocking."

As Frieden toured the CDC, getting to know its component parts, he made a point of asking each department if its work had been touched by opioids, and he kept hearing that it was. Frieden was struck not only by the breadth of the impact but also by how little it had penetrated the consciousness of America's medical regulators. "That was my first big realization about the extent of the problem both in its severity and in the many different parts of health it was touching," he said. Then he tried to come up with a plan to tackle it.

Len Paulozzi was surprised to start receiving regular calls from Tom Frieden asking detailed questions about aspects of his research.

"I had never met Julie Gerberding, let alone been called by her. Tom Frieden would call me on my cell phone out of the blue," he said.

Paulozzi felt that at last the epidemic was being taken with the necessary seriousness within his own agency. Some things were immediately clear to Frieden, not least that the crisis was being driven by overprescribing. Less clear was what to do about it. Was this just a few pill mills in West Virginia and Florida? Or was there something deeper going on?

The other issue was where to get the resources to investigate. Congress allocates the CDC's budget to specific areas, in part to make sure the agency does not stray where it is not welcome, such as in monitoring the impact of guns. There wasn't a lot of flexibility to move money around, but Frieden could move personnel. The CDC also looked around for success stories that might provide valuable lessons, such as a promising effort in Washington State to reduce opioid use.

But more than anything, Frieden needed to focus attention on the epidemic. In November 2011, he held a telephone press conference alongside Gil Kerlikowske, director on the Office of National Drug Control Policy, popularly known as the "White House drug czar." Frieden got right to the point he wanted to make. "The topic today is about prescription pain killer overdose, and the unfortunate and, in fact, shocking news is that we are in the midst of an epidemic of prescription drug overdose in this country. It's an epidemic, but it can be stopped," he said.

Frieden noted that fifteen thousand people died from prescription painkiller overdoses in 2010. The CDC director said narcotics were killing forty people a day. "Enough narcotics are prescribed to give every adult in America one month of prescription narcotics. As a result of this large number of prescriptions, there are about one out of every twenty adults who have a history of inappropriately using prescription narcotics. This stems from a few irresponsible doctors, and, in fact, now the burden of dangerous drugs is being created more by a few irresponsible doctors than by drug pushers on the street corners."

Frieden called on state governments to rigorously monitor prescribing, to shut pill mills, and to reduce doctor shopping. He called for physicians to rein in the number of pills they prescribed, giving three days' worth, instead of thirty, as the standard. "Right now, the system is awash in opioids, dangerous drugs that got people hooked and keep them hooked."

Kerlikowske spoke too to claim: "From day one, the Obama administration has been laser focused on responding to this crisis." No one took that seriously, given that the president had yet to say anything about it in public and showed almost no interest in the crisis in private.

At his confirmation hearing two years earlier, Kerlikowske had been asked about numbers showing that prescription drugs were killing more people than gunshot wounds and, in more than one-third of states, more people than in car crashes. The former police chief conceded he did not know that and said that if he was unaware, then so were a lot of Americans. Since then, he said, he had been "shouting this from the rooftops, and the administration has been focused on it."

But that's not how other federal officials saw it, and in the absence of other leadership, Frieden's words—particularly his labeling the rising death toll an epidemic—had an impact. Paulozzi was frustrated that it took Frieden to draw the attention to the crisis. Paulozzi had been calling it an epidemic for five years and that February had given a major presentation on just that theme. But the title of CDC director carries particular weight, and Frieden's words made their mark where it mattered, beginning with Congress.

"Dr. Frieden was the first heavyweight agency head that came out and declared it an epidemic," said Mary Bono. "That was a turning point for us. It was late. Very late. But we had a hard time convincing the DEA, the FDA, and other agencies that there was a problem. We got huge pushback from them. There were up to fifteen federal agencies that had some sort of role in this, and we had to wait for the CDC to say this epidemic was happening. That was absolute government failure."

For bereaved parents working for change, it finally felt as if someone in the federal system was on their side. Frieden rapidly became a hero within activist groups such as Fed Up! For parents such as Pete Jackson, it was what they had been waiting for years to hear. Jackson had been relying on Paulozzi's work in his campaign for reform. "It was CDC that first started cranking out some of those statistics that we were relying on, and I was thinking the FDA's a federal agency, how could they not pay attention to that? You can cast us parents aside and say we're just a bunch of bereaved parents looking for an ax to grind, which I've heard many times. But pay attention to your fellow federal agency. They weren't. It was shocking to us to realize they were on a different page altogether," Jackson said. "There was a lot of opposition to the idea it was an epidemic. CDC began to give it credibility, and I think eventually the medical community overall has had to come along."

Jane Ballantyne credits Paulozzi with building the evidence of an epidemic but said it took Frieden to turn the data into action. "I don't think the CDC even would have done anything if it hadn't been for Tom Frieden because he really had the bit between his teeth. He really thought it was terrible what was going on. If he hadn't have been there, even the CDC wouldn't have taken it up," she said.

The mood in the FDA was suspicious. Some thought Frieden was grandstanding. There was grumbling that he was straying outside of his agency's territory. The pain organizations mobilized to warn that the CDC was planning on taking away everyone's meds.

Frieden acknowledges that the CDC wasn't entirely on solid ground in declaring an epidemic. The agency put together important parts of the puzzle, but there were still gaps in the data and unexplained aspects to the crisis. "Early on we were really attacked for anything we said that suggested that opiates were being overprescribed. The fact is we weren't sure initially. It wasn't immediately apparent what the portion of the prescribing was overprescribing. We have very poor systems to monitor what's going on in health care in this country," he said.

But Frieden looked around, and as far as he could see, no other federal agency was pushing nearly hard enough. He wanted to shake the system out of its inertia and beef up prescription monitoring systems so doctors could check whether patients had prescriptions from other physicians. But Congress allocated only a few hundred thousand dollars to the effort, and it ran into strong opposition in some states from medical associations opposed to any move to oblige doctors to use the system. "The bottom line was the average funding for these programs was $300,000 a year. That's peanuts," said Frieden. "A problem like obesity or opiates that gets worse over a generation doesn't get turned around overnight. And there's interplay between perceptions of a problem and the actions that can be taken. To give you an example from tobacco control, once people understood secondhand smoke was carcinogenic and causes heart attacks, it was easier to get smoke-free laws passed. And getting smoke-free laws passed helped people to understand that secondhand smoke is carcinogenic and causes heart attacks. There's an interplay between a certain understanding and action that has to be taken."

But it still did not have the impact on the White House Frieden hoped for, and he struggled to get traction. The administration was preoccupied with pushing Obama's health care reforms through Congress. The president's advisers Nancy-Ann DeParle and Jeanne Lambrew were widely regarded in the health community as indifferent to public health issues to the point of hostility, an attitude some saw reflected in the priorities of the Affordable Care Act. It didn't help that addiction continued to carry a stigma administration officials were not keen to get tainted by.

Even when the president finally spoke about opioids and the administration promised action, it did not go down well at the CDC that the Obama administration's request for $1 billion from Congress was all for treatment. No money was allocated to education or health programs. It was in stark contrast to the administration's response to Ebola, in which Obama took a personal interest.

In sounding the alarm, Frieden drew attention to something else the CDC had observed. No one took much notice at the time, but they soon would. "We see the ramifications of prescription drug abuse in many, many different ways. So ranging from infants born to mothers who are on opioids and may be at risk of congenital heart disease to infants born to mothers on opioids who are born addicted to opioid medications to increased risky driving in people who are drugged to increases in hepatitis C and potentially HIV among people who started using prescription opioids and then shifted to heroin, either because it cost less or because they needed to get stronger drugs," he said.

"Where we had seen, for more than a decade, steady declines in illnesses associated with injection drug use in several different parts of the country we're beginning to go hear reports of resurgences in the use of injection drug use, specifically heroin."

CHAPTER 14

Kermit

HALF AN HOUR north of Williamson is the small town of Kermit, stretched alongside the Tug Fork river at the northwest tip of Mingo County. Kermit once called itself Lower Burning Creek and then Warfield before settling on the name of President Theodore Roosevelt's son out of gratitude to the government for opening a post office in the town in 1906.

Nearly a thousand people lived in Kermit after World War II, but as jobs melted away, so did the population, until the number of residents slipped below four hundred in the late 1990s. Young people left in search of work, and Kermit felt increasingly like a rustic retirement community. For all that, it retains a special place in West Virginia lore as the lair of the Preece family.

Wilburn and Mary Preece married in 1946 and had fourteen children who came of age as coal's grip on their region slackened. For decades, mining companies owned the local economy and the politics: workers lived in debt to the company store and lined up to vote for the mine owners' anointed politicians. But as Big Coal retreated in the 1970s, the Preeces edged in.

Most of the clan were known around town by nicknames. Wilburn was "Wig"; Mary was "Cooney."

Wig ran a bar where drinkers from dry counties across the river in Kentucky could get a beer or a shot. The illicit gambling upstairs wasn't much of a secret, and everyone in town knew Wig would sell you a bottle outside of legal drinking hours.

One of Wig's sons, Tommy, known as Tomahawk for being born in the back of a taxi in a Kentucky town of that name, was busted for selling marijuana in 1978. It was an embarrassment to the family but also a revelation. Tomakawk's parents quickly recognized the potential, and Cooney began selling dope out of the house. In time her wares expanded to PCP, LSD, and prescription drugs. Valium was popular.

Money bought votes and political influence, and that insulated the Preeces from accountability. Hode Hensley was Kermit police chief until the Preeces took control of that office, too. "I arrested Wig's boy once, and the mother was sitting on the judge's desk as I was getting told I had no case," he told a reporter a few years later.

For a while, Cooney ran the drug business from home, but as word spread and demand surged, she rented a trailer next to city hall and hired a sales assistant to man it for $100 a week. The steady stream of locals turned into a flood of new customers mostly from out of town, traveling from upstate or across the border from Kentucky and Ohio.

Kermit's police station was a hundred yards up a side road and the cops had to pass by the trailer to get to work, but they didn't trouble the business. By then the police chief was David Ramey, husband of one of the Preece daughters, Debbie, and the couple got their cut of the profits. Cooney handed out cash to her children $1,000 at a time.

The whole operation was so open that Cooney kept marijuana in garbage bags next to the trailer. When trash collectors hauled off a load of weed one morning, David Ramey sent his officers to chase down the garbage truck and bring it back.

The family had a sideline in arson. Wig was chief of the Kermit Volunteer Fire Department. The town suffered an astonishing rate of burned-down buildings and an even more unusual degree of failure by the fire department to reach the stricken buildings in time to save them.

Wig knew which fires to go slow on because his daughter Brenda was paid to set them. If the pair got the timing wrong, they suffered the embarrassment of running into each other on the job. Insurance companies paid out handsomely to residents of Kermit.

Mostly the Preeces went untroubled by the law, but occasionally it intruded. Brenda sold PCP to an undercover officer from out of town and faced a trial at the county courthouse in Williamson. Wig saw to it that the school board president, Larry Hamrick, arranged a teaching job for the jury foreman's daughter. Brenda walked.

State police officers posted to Mingo County couldn't believe the impunity enjoyed by the Preeces, but there were enough unhappy people in Kermit tipping off the state and federal authorities that eventually the accusations became impossible to ignore. The FBI put the family under surveillance, and the Internal Revenue Service scrutinized the Preeces' finances. State troopers made undercover drug buys. An assistant US attorney, Joe Savage, led the investigation. "Things happened backwards," Savage said at the time. "The police chief and sheriff weren't doing the arresting, they were selling the drugs. The school board president wasn't teaching children ethics, he was bribing the jurors."

The Preeces took payment for drugs in kind, which encouraged a minor crime spree as users ransacked houses miles away for electronics to swap. Wig told undercover agents posing as drug buyers he wanted a boat and suggested ways they might steal one.

The feds moved a boxcar onto the railroad tracks running along a ridge the other side of the street from city hall to covertly monitor the trailer. Over a single weekend, agents counted more than six hundred people buying drugs. They walked in and out as if they were at any regular store. One day investigators spotted a sign on the door: "Out of drugs: Be back in 30 minutes."

The police estimated the Preeces were selling around twenty-five pounds of marijuana and hundreds of pills a week. Dave Ramey was paid $10,000 a year as police chief, but he and Debbie lived such an opulent lifestyle they were known around town as J. R. and Sue Ellen, after the unscrupulous couple in the glitzy 1980s soap opera *Dallas*.

Federal agents and state police sealed off Kermit shortly after lunch on the last Friday in May 1986. They cut phone lines, blocked the only road in and out, and closed the bridge over the river to Kentucky. A helicopter escorted a line of police cars into town.

Officers went door to door picking up Preeces: Wig and Cooney, seven of their children, including Debbie and her husband, the police chief, and a few other people embraced by the family—twenty in all. Some people turned out to cheer the arrests as the police drove their captives out of town.

Cooney, as the matriarch of the operation, received the longest sentence. She went down for sixteen years. Wig was sent away for ten for drug dealing and tax evasion. The children were not spared. Debbie and her police chief husband were convicted of twenty-eight felonies, including drug conspiracy and tax evasion. Debbie was sent to prison for ten years, David Ramey for fifteen. No one could fix the jury for Brenda this time, and she left her children with a sister while she served nearly four years.

After their arrests, the Preeces sold out people they once controlled, laying bare the reach of their power and money. Among the sixty-nine people subsequently convicted were Mingo County sheriff Charles Hilbert, who was jailed for paying a $100,000 bribe to get his job in 1983. Hilbert once held a press conference to show off a marijuana seizure as evidence his force was busting drug dealers. Then he sold the drugs to the Preeces.

Half of the money Hilbert paid to get his job went to county commissioners who made the appointment. The other half went to the outgoing sheriff, Johnie Owens, to recommend him for the post. Owens got fourteen years for that. He was chairman of the Mingo County Democrats and the Committee for Good Government, which gave him influence over votes he delivered up for the Preece family.

Owens was also jailed for taking a bribe to fix the murder trial of a man accused of shooting his own cousin. He could get the conviction reduced only to second- from first-degree murder. In retaliation, the accused's father, who paid the bribe, reported Owens for corruption.

Hamrick, the school board president, was also director of the county's Economic Opportunity Commission, which dispensed largesse to the poor and gave him authority over about twenty-five hundred jobs—one quarter of all the employment in Mingo County. Hamrick answered to Wig when it came to deciding who did and didn't get work or welfare. He was jailed for twelve years for stealing public funds. Savage described the commission as "the reverse of Robin Hood." "They were stealing from the poor and giving to the rich," he said.

The jury foreman who fixed Brenda Preece's trial was convicted of conspiracy. Federal investigators even bagged a magistrate and a prosecuting attorney.

The FBI said the Preeces were making $1 million a year from selling drugs. Debbie Preece scoffs at that, but the Feds seized houses, Mercedes and Cadillacs, boats, and $300,000 of diamond rings from the family.

Savage described the roundup of the Preece clan and the breaking of its grip on Mingo County as "the best thing that could happen to West Virginia." "We reclaimed part of America. The area will never be as bad again," he said.

The Preece family was to discover how wrong Savage was, but this time it was on the other end of the drug deal.

• • •

FOR DEBBIE PREECE, prison time was the hardest thing she'd ever done. She unhesitatingly admits she was guilty. The drugs, the money, the family conspiracy, she admits it all. But her chatty back-and-forth gives way to protective pauses when we touch on what Savage called "the mountain mafia." She loves her parents dearly, she said, and doesn't want to say anything that might look bad. There are the grandchildren to consider. They know, of course. Too many people went to prison to keep it a secret. But they are shielded from the details. "We're not the same people we were back then," Debbie ventures. "We're good people, making amends."

Debbie discovered God anew and was elected to the town council. One of her sons is principal of the local school.

Wig became a born-again Christian and went back to being fire chief for a total of fifty-nine years. When he died in 2014 at the age of eighty-six, the *Mingo Messenger*—"your source for all things Mingo"—proclaimed him a hero "who unfailingly placed everyone else's safety and well-being above his own." Its report on the funeral made no mention of arson or prison. It did say that representatives from fifty fire departments attended the burial and that Kermit's mayor called Wig a great asset to the town. Tomahawk, the son arrested for marijuana who set the family drug business in motion, was appointed the new fire chief.

Cooney died five years before Wig, at the age of eighty-one. She was remembered as a tough woman and the driving force behind the family operation.

By the time I met Debbie Preece for the first time, she had other battles to fight. She had separated from David Ramey, the former police chief, and lived with her second husband, David Dodd. A photo of an elderly Wig and Cooney postprison—both white haired, his arm around her shoulders as they stand in front of a red truck—rests in a glass frame on a table in the hall. It has the single word *Mom* inscribed to one side.

Dodd is from the state capital, Charleston. He got his first taste of Mingo County before he met Debbie when an uncle asked for a lift down to Williamson to get a prescription. "I said, 'My goodness, from Charleston? We got clinics, everything in Charleston. Why you want to go down there?' He said, 'You go down there, and you'll get some medicine.' So we came down. He got his prescription from Hoover and walked to Hurley Drug. When they called his name, he stood up and fell on the floor and died. Right there in the drugstore," said Dodd.

Debbie has stage-four brain cancer. She is uncertain if she will survive. If she's going to die, there's some unfinished decade-old business, a score she'd like to settle before she goes.

After his release from prison, her younger brother William, "Bull" to all who knew him, went back to mining, working underground on a coal face about forty miles away. There was a rock fall. He was sent up to Huntington for treatment and his first prescription of OxyContin. It took two years before the family realized Bull was addicted. "We were saying he was in denial. We could see the changes in his behavior. Seeing him high and just passing out. We knew, we knew. He passed out a lot. He would just be sitting here, and you look over and he'd be asleep. He'd say, 'I'm okay. I'm just tired.' Well, you're not just tired. He was high," acknowledges Debbie. "We'd try and talk to him. He agreed to go to rehab. I took him myself and checked him in. But the only rehab we had here would only keep you three days unless you could get a court order from the judge."

Bull lost his job. Debbie blames the addiction. The injury meant he got a payment from the West Virginia workers' compensation, was ruled disabled, and put on Social Security. "I think he could have gone back to work if he had not been addicted, and I think he would have.

"We took him to a methadone clinic in Williamson. We had to get up every morning and drive him there. We paid twenty-five dollars a day. He was on that for a while, and he did good. And then, as most of them do, he would just fall off the wagon. I know he went to a lot of people for help."

Bull bounced between addiction and recovery programs of various stripes, but always he returned to the pills. Debbie never gave up, but the struggle to haul her brother back to the man he was got tougher by the day. Bull and his wife, Donna, who was also using drugs, had a small grocery store. Instead of using the income from sales to buy new stock, they bought pills. The shop went bust.

Bull's Social Security wasn't enough to pay for prescriptions and keep up the mortgage payments on their house, so they lost it. Bull split with Donna and moved back in with his parents. "He lost everything he had," said Debbie.

Bull still had his life, and Debbie worked hard to keep him away from the pills. He had to travel from Kermit to get a prescription, even if only to Williamson, twenty miles away. Debbie tried to keep an eye on his whereabouts. But then James Wooley reared his head.

Wooley owned the Sav-Rite pharmacy, an ugly red squat building next to Kermit's post office. He looked on Williamson's drugstores with envy. Trade at his own pharmacy was so slow that Wooley also ran a used car lot.

"He's a fine fellah," said Charles Sparks, Kermit's mayor until 1990 and then twice again through the 2000s. "He was easy going, mild mannered, do anything in the world for you. Had a big garage. You'd go in and say you need a car. You'd pay a hundred down and a hundred a month to him. Of course, if you didn't pay him, they'd come after you and repossess your car. You couldn't beat him as a person. But he just got into that other business, and it starts snowballing and greed took over. You know how it is: if I can make a million, I can make two."

Wooley knew the Williamson doctors Shafer and Hoover well. Larry Barnett, who owned the Family Pharmacy, used to work for him at the Sav-Rite in the late 1980s. When he saw Barnett was raking in a small fortune dispensing opioids, Wooley saw no reason he couldn't do the same, but he needed a doctor to direct prescriptions his way. He knew just the person, and it wouldn't be long before he was out of prison.

Dr. Gregory Wells used to practice ten miles up the road the other side of the Kentucky border until he was arrested for illegally prescribing excessive amounts of opioids for a friend and former Kentucky police officer. That was before OxyContin swept in, but even then there was the demand. Wells was locked up for five years. A couple of months before his release, Wooley paid the doctor a visit at the Ashland federal prison in Kentucky and offered him a future.

The pharmacist persuaded his assistant at the drugstore, Debra Justice, to set up a medical clinic with Wells just outside Kermit. The doctor would prescribe, Justice would administer, and Wooley would dispense. They'd all make a fortune.

But when the state medical board refused to reinstate Wells's license because of his conviction, Wooley urgently needed another doctor. Wells recruited an acquaintance, Dr. John Tiano. He assured Tiano the job would not interfere with his work as a full-time resident at Marshall University's medical school, more than an hour away in Huntington, West Virginia. All he had to do was lend his name and DEA number to prescriptions and show his face for a few hours a week. The real work would be done by a half-dozen nurse practitioners, even though they did not have the authority to write long-term opioid prescriptions.

The Justice Medical Complex opened in the spring of 2005, a ten-minute drive from town, following the rail line north and turning down Stonecoal Road into the woods. Prescriptions were sent directly to the Sav-Rite. Word about the new clinic spread rapidly, and Kermit soon resembled Williamson, not least because some of the out-of-state cars clogging the streets and the people arriving by the van load came directly from its near neighbor, looking to double up their opioid supply.

Within a few months, Wooley was filling a prescription a minute. The year after the Justice clinic opened, drug wholesalers delivered more than 3 million doses of hydrocodone to Sav-Rite in a community not much bigger than a hamlet. The pharmacy bought more of the opioid than any drugstore in West Virginia, Kentucky,

Pennsylvania, Virginia, or Ohio that year. Sav-Rite ranked twenty-second in the nation among retail pharmacies for hydrocodone purchases. Gross sales surged above $6.5 million—the equivalent of $15,000 per head of Kermit's population.

Mayor Sparks watched the influx: "Oh, we were aware. We knew what was going on. The citizens would come and say, 'Why don't you do something about that up there?' The average person doesn't know or doesn't stop and think that you can't just go in. You have to do an investigation before you can stop something like that. People said nothing's being done."

The police made arrests, usually of people so out of their heads they weren't in any fit state to drive. Occasionally, they were found passed out at the wheel or driving down the wrong side of the road. Sometimes officers seized large quantities of pills, but if someone was waving a prescription the police didn't think there was much they could do.

Bull Preece was one of Tiano's early patients. He arrived at the Sav-Rite on September 16, 2005, to collect a prescription for ninety hydrocodone tablets. It had Tiano's name and DEA number on it. The prescription was supposed to last a month, but two weeks later Bull was back at the Sav-Rite to pick from another script, this time written by Dr. Kiser, just months after his arrest in Williamson, for ninety high-strength oxycodone and sixty lower dose opiates. Together they contained four times the narcotic of the earlier prescription. Bull paid nearly $500 in cash. That night he was dead.

Eleven years after Bull's death, Debbie Preece still struggled with it. "I get emotional about it because I can't get over it," she said, her voice breaking. "I've been to a psychiatrist, and they're like, 'You should have been over this by now.' Well, where are they from? You don't get over that. All of my sisters and brothers live within a block of each other. We're just a very tight-knit family."

Bull was not taking the drugs on his own the night he died. After he collapsed, the others robbed and abandoned him. They grabbed the rest of his pills and took his car. The next day, Debbie received a call from a man across town to say someone had crashed Bull's car into his house. "He told me he knew the car was stolen because it didn't have a key in it. It had a screwdriver."

The driver fled, but the house owner looked in the vehicle and found a bunch of prescription receipts written in Bull's name. "He kept his receipts inside a book. I looked at this and I was, 'No way.' It was an enormous amount of pills. Come on. This cannot be legal," said Debbie. "The new doctor comes along, and they're giving him drugs no questions asked. He's addicted, and they hand him this enormous amount of drugs. They don't ask any questions down at the Sav-Rite. They just go on giving him the pills. It didn't make sense. It couldn't be right."

Debbie wanted the police to investigate, and she went looking for a lawyer to see if she could sue over Bull's death. The first lawyer she approached, in Charleston, told her she needed to understand her brother was an addict and a court would not put much value on his life. A wave of realization and anger hit Debbie. "I said, 'Let me tell you something. Obviously, he didn't value his life very much because he was on the drugs. But it was priceless to me, and I won't be in need of your services.' And I hung up," she said.

Debbie was determined her brother would not be remembered just as a drug addict. "My brother is not going to go down like this. He's not going to be just another drug addict that's gone. I will not let that happen. I will fight and do whatever I can to make sure that he's not just buried and forgotten," she said. "Nobody really knows what it's like. And nobody wants to know. Nobody cares. You're just an addict."

Debbie tried another Charleston lawyer, Jim Cagle. He listened sympathetically and told her she needed evidence. Debbie started her own investigation. She watched the pharmacy and the Justice Medical Complex. She counted the cars outside the Sav-Rite and noted when someone overdosed in the parking lot. When the lines were long, the staff handed out popcorn and candy. Debbie made sure to collect her own prescriptions from the drugstore so she could get a good look at what was going on. "They had about ten girls working in there, and it's no bigger than this kitchen. They were throwing the pills over the counter. I was, Jesus Christ, every thug in the world is in here."

Jim Cagle could hardly believe what he was hearing, so he came to see for himself. "I've never seen anything like it in my damn life," he told Debbie, and he sent someone to quietly film the scene.

The Preece network still had some life in it. Word leaked back about a dinner at a steak restaurant outside Williamson owned by Don Blankenship, the coal magnate who was jailed a few years later over the deaths of twenty-nine miners in an explosion at the Upper Big Branch pit. Wooley and Justice were at the table along with the doctors Hoover, Shafer, and Ryckman. To Debbie, it looked like a gathering of conspirators, particularly when the group was over-heard discussing the opioid business. "They had a goal. They were going to make this amount of money," she said. "I said to myself, 'If these people think they're getting by with this, they're way, way wrong."

In 2007 the West Virginia medical board received an anonymous tip that Tiano was prescribing illegally at the Justice Medical Complex. The board investigated and the following year reprimanded Tiano. It ordered him to write a "book report" on *Responsible Opioid Prescribing: A Physician's Guide*—the document that had done so much to promote the use of painkillers among doctors. Marshall University told Tiano to stop his moonlighting at the Justice clinic. In the two years he lent his name to prescriptions there, Tiano made more than $250,000.

Debbie thought a book report was a ludicrous punishment. In any case, Tiano's departure did not mean the end of Wooley's scheme. As one last act, the doctor recruited his successor, Augusto Abad, a former emergency room physician working as a general practitioner and diabetes specialist. Abad started at the Justice clinic in January 2008. By then, Debra Justice's son, Cameron, a heavy equipment driver by trade, was running the center. He paid Abad's health insurance, leased him a new Mercedes, and gave him $10,000 to get started before the cash rolled in.

Abad rarely saw patients in person. His job was to "supervise" the nurse practitioners writing prescriptions under his name and DEA number. If he reviewed their cases at all, it was often from his house in Charleston by looking at photographs sent by the clinic. He usually went to Kermit for a couple of hours on a Thursday. Business was so good that in 2008, Wooley opened a second Sav-Rite next to the Justice Medical Complex.

By then, a second anonymous tip—this time to the Drug Enforcement Administration—drew the attention of the feds. The informant claimed that "Debra Justice and Wooley had hatched a get rich(er) quick scheme to open a pain clinic that would refer all of its prescriptions for controlled substances to Sav-Rite Kermit" and that they were "handing out drugs like candy.'"

The DEA, FBI, and state police began watching. Mary Ann Withrow, a federal agent, said investigators recorded that the Sav-Rite and the clinic were "excessively busy," with so many people there was nowhere left to park or sit. Many of the patients traveled long distances rather than use their local clinics and pharmacies. "Individuals openly discuss the fact that they come to do so because it is relatively easy to get controlled drugs," Withrow said in evidence for a search warrant. "One undercover agent was actually startled by the fact that prescriptions are filled at such a rate that Sav-Rite workers literally throw bags containing drugs over a divider and onto a counter in order to keep up the pace."

An agent observed that the cash drawer at the second Sav-Rite next to the clinic was so full, the clerk could not close it properly.

Investigators watched patients walk out of the pharmacy and divide up their drugs with people waiting in the parking lot.

Cagle filed a lawsuit against Wooley on behalf of Debbie, forcing him to give a deposition. He proved a remarkably unobservant pharmacist. He didn't remember articles in trade magazines warning about doctor shopping or the dangers of OxyContin addiction.

He had no idea Kiser had been arrested, even though it was on the front of a newspaper he sold in the drugstore. Nor had he heard a word about it from one of his own counter staff, Ladonna Smith, who just happened to be married to the policeman who arrested the doctor.

Debbie was as surprised as she had been in 1986 to discover the police had been watching Kermit. The feds and state police raided the clinic and the Sav-Rite pharmacies in March 2009. Ciccarelli, the FBI agent, was part of the raid on the Sav-Rite in town. Even with police at the door, people kept arriving to collect their opioids.

The drugstore made $10 million in three years just from Medicare and Medicaid payments for prescriptions. The Justice clinic had billed Medicare more than $500,000.

A YEAR AFTER our first meeting, I was back in Debbie's kitchen. She was in her pajamas, weak from cancer treatment. But she was optimistic: she had been given an experimental treatment that worked for former president Jimmy Carter, and at the very least it was buying her time.

Tomahawk arrived with his young son. He is still fire chief and now a member of the town council. He had just come from doing a lift, one of the routine jobs the volunteer fire department gets called out for. "We've got some older people so big they can't get in their house by themselves. We have to go load them up in their vehicles so they can go to the doctor, and then when they get back we got to go unload them and take them back in the house," he said. "We were helping this one guy who weighs 480 pounds. He can't get around. Whenever he falls, the family calls the fire department to come pick him up. It takes three or four of us when he falls on the floor to get him back up. They keep us busy with just that one man."

Tomahawk would rather be doing that than the other frequent calls. Kermit's fire department covers the northern part of Mingo and the lower end of neighboring Wayne County. "Our first-responder calls have more than tripled in the last two years. If somebody calls for an ambulance, if it's an overdose, they'll send us first because we get there before the ambulance does. In the past three months we've have four overdose calls, and three of them didn't make it. They all died. Pills," he said. "This last one was right down the road here, about two miles. She's thirty-two years old, and there stands her son, ten years old. And she's laying there OD'd on pills. That's a hard thing for a kid to handle. We're doing CPR. There weren't nothing we could do."

A few months earlier, an investigation by Eric Eyre in the *Charleston Gazette-Mail* revealed that drug distributors pumped 780 million doses of opioid painkillers to West Virginia over a six-year period. Enough for 433 pills for every person in the state. During that time, overdose deaths rose by two-thirds.

Most of the drugs went to the southern part of the state. Top of the list for hydrocodone deliveries was the Sav-Rite in Kermit. It bought 9 million doses of the opioid in the two years before the police raid. The Tug Valley and Hurley pharmacies in Williamson made up the rest of the top four, alongside a drugstore in neighboring Logan County.

Even in Kermit, where everyone had seen what was going on, they were shocked by the numbers. "Almost 9 million pills in this little town," said Sparks, the mayor. "It boggles my mind. I was blown away. I thought, 'My God, almost 9 million pills in two years went out of here, and Wooley said that he made $500,000 a month in a little town of 400 people.'"

Back then Wooley wasn't telling the town how much he was making. On that income he should have been paying about $175,000 in business taxes to the council every quarter. He was paying closer to $10,000.

Tiano and Abad were each jailed for a year and Cameron Justice for two and a half. Tiano lost his medical license. On his release, Abad was deported to his home country, the Philippines, where he continues to practice.

Wooley pleaded guilty to illegally selling prescription medication and conspiracy. Prosecutors reached a plea deal with a sentence of two years' probation for the pharmacist, but the judge balked and sent him to prison for six months. He also paid a $500,000 fine for Medicare and Medicaid fraud.

None of the newly convicted showed remorse other than for the difficulties they now found themselves in.

After Wooley's arrest, the insurers of his drugstore settled out of court with Debbie. She was at a difficult point in the battle with her cancer and didn't have the strength for a full trial. She regrets that now, wishing that Wooley had been forced to explain himself to an open court and in the process establish that Bull was a victim.

Tomahawk flatly refuses to talk about family history. Debbie tiptoes around it. She doesn't do comparisons with the past and prefers to stick to what she regards as the industrial-scale delivery of death at the hands of something much bigger than the locals. Like many in the area, she thinks Mingo was targeted because it is marginalized. "I don't know if we were unnoticed because it's a poverty-stricken area and they think, 'Who cares? It's a small town. Everybody there's on drugs. We're making lots of money. Who cares? Nobody's going to pay attention to those people,'" she said. "It's a sad situation that once people are hooked, no one cares about them. They become problematic for families, and some families would rather they just not come around. We were different. Lot of love. Lot of family support."

Sparks was elected mayor again in 2016 after stints on the council and as town clerk. The council looked at the numbers and then at who was responsible, and its eye settled on the wholesalers delivering massive amounts of opioid pills. The three largest US drug distributors—McKesson, AmerisourceBergen, and Cardinal Health—shipped more than 400 million doses of narcotics to West Virginia, with a population of fewer than 2 million people, in the five years to 2012.

Twelve million of those drugs were delivered to tiny Kermit. "I'm not going to say that we're totally clean. We're not. Not in this area," said Sparks. "You have a lot of coal miners. You have a lot of people that work. They get hurt. They get put on these opioids. A lot of these people don't abuse them. A lot of these people need them. But there was a lot of people that were coming in here that didn't need them. That were just selling them to make the money. The drug distributors should have been aware of what was going on. I mean, stop and think, 9 million pills in two years. That's ludicrous. That's crazy."

CHAPTER 15

A Free Pass

AMERICAN LAW IS straightforward on the legal obligations of drug distributors if they suspect prescription drugs are falling into the wrong hands. The Controlled Substances Act obliges them to report "suspicious orders"—most likely sudden increases in demand by a pharmacy—and to halt deliveries while the DEA investigates.

Joe Rannazzisi saw this as an uncomplicated if largely ignored regulation. In 2005 he was finally in a position to do something about it.

Rannazzisi is a pharmacist and lawyer by training, but, conservative and by the book, his natural habitat is law enforcement. He joined the DEA in 1986, working a series of jobs investigating illegal drug labs, narcotics dealing, and homicide. Abrasive and direct, he can quickly get on the wrong side of people.

After a stint in Detroit, Rannazzisi was posted to Washington, DC, in 2004 as deputy director of the Office of Diversion Control, the law enforcement end of the agency, and promoted to head the division a year later.

The black market in prescription opioids was no secret by then, and the DEA was struggling to rein in a surge of hydrocodone sales by online pharmacies. Sellers on the Internet were hard to track, and so the agency cast its eye back up the supply chain to the wholesalers.

Diversion control launched the "Distributor Initiative" to remind wholesalers, including some of the country's largest firms such McKesson and Cardinal Health, of their legal obligations. Perhaps they didn't know. Perhaps they had forgotten. Rannazzisi reminded them.

As he saw it, what was asked of distributors was neither difficult nor onerous. Wholesalers kept comprehensive records of which pharmacy was buying what drugs. Changing patterns in orders were easy to spot. If they saw something odd, they needed to get the sales reps on the ground to ask questions of the pharmacy buying the drugs. Why the sudden demand? If answers didn't ring true, the wholesaler should tell the DEA and suspend deliveries.

To Rannazzisi, distributing highly addictive and potentially lethal drugs wasn't the same as delivering chocolate bars. He regarded the lucrative licenses the wholesalers held—McKesson is the fifth-biggest company on the Fortune 500 index with around $200 billion in revenue—as carrying particular responsibilities: "These companies have one task, and that is the safe and secure distribution of drugs, particularly prescription drugs. Otherwise, FedEx or UPS could do this role. This isn't a compliance challenge, like gender discrimination at a tech company, which is horrific, but it's not fundamental to their operation. This is the equivalent of a tech company failing on cybersecurity. If these companies were doing their job right, you shouldn't be seeing black-market prescription painkillers."

The DEA diversion chief thought pressure on the companies to live up to those responsibilities would be more effective if they were confronted individually and denied the opportunity to form a united front. "They said, 'Oh, yeah, this is great. Thank you for telling us. We're going to look at this closely. Yes, we understand.' But in reality, nothing. They weren't doing anything. . . . It was like a joke. It was almost like, 'DEA's just checking a box, so we're just going to continue doing what we're doing because quite frankly we're making a lot of money.' "

Internet pharmacies were eventually curbed by legislation, but the business moved to regular drugstores and demand for prescription opioids kept rising.

The DEA wrote a series of letters to the distributors, again reminding them of the legal requirement to report suspicious orders and instructing the wholesalers that they needed to "know their customers" by asking questions about where prescription pills were going. The distributors thought investigations were the job of law enforcement. As they saw it, all they were doing was acting as the middle man between the manufacturer and the pharmacist filling prescriptions written by a doctor. Determining whether a patient should be getting pills meant wading into medical decisions. They were the delivery boy, not the doctor.

Rannazzisi's irritation rose as the DEA gathered evidence of distributors ignoring warnings from their sales reps about pharmacies handing out opioids on a grand scale.

The Office of Diversion Control decided the only way to get the wholesalers to take the regulations seriously was to haul the big names into court. The DEA had never taken action against a Fortune 500 company before, and Rannazzisi reckons the firms never saw it coming.

First on the list was AmerisourceBergen. Rannazzisi remembers shocked company executives protesting that they had no idea they had been doing anything wrong. "They gave us all that nonsense after all the meetings, all the reminders. But it's hard to come up with a denial when you look at the numbers and you look at the ordering patterns. We had them over a barrel," he said.

"I wanted to hammer these people. They had had more than enough chance. But it was their first time through the ringer, so the attorneys wanted to go easy. We could have slammed them for a lot more than we got them for."

In 2008 the big three agreed to pay comparatively paltry civil fines and change their ways. Cardinal Health was hit with a $34 million penalty without admitting illegality. McKesson paid $13 million. AmerisourceBergen didn't pay any fine but promised to obey the law.

Rannazzisi thought they'd been let off too lightly. The fines were a pittance compared to their profits, but at least the message had gotten through and the DEA would finally get some cooperation. "These people were just walking away smiling because they really got hit with very little, but they all signed memorandums of understandings to comply with the act with specific requirements of what they were supposed to do."

Then there was the kind of publicity any corporation can do without. "McKesson Corporation fueled the explosive prescription drug abuse problem we have in this country," the acting head of the DEA, Michele Leonhart, proclaimed after the fines were imposed.

Rannazzisi saw an uptick in suspicious order reports for a year or so but noticed them fade again just as DEA agents on the ground were reporting a surge in the number of pill mills, particularly in Florida. "It was the same thing over again. Instead of the corporate office saying, 'There's no reason why a small pharmacy in this little town in Florida should be ordering 2 million tablets of oxycodone, shut 'em off, they don't have a legitimate explanation, they're not near a hospital, they're not near any kind of clinic,' instead of that they just kept shipping them," he said. "Two million tablets for a small pharmacy in one year, of one drug, is pretty amazing. That's a lot of money, a lot of income for not only the pharmacy but the distributor."

Rannazzisi said some smaller distributors tried the trick of filing a suspicious-order report for every delivery in the hope of giving themselves legal cover, but that didn't work because they didn't follow through on the second part of then halting delivery.

The diversion division decided it was time to get the distributors back in and warn them that they would face more serious action if they didn't shape up.

Putting aside the fact of their legal obligations, a good corporate citizen has moral obligations to ensure the safety of the people they are even supplying. But to heck with the moral obligations, I could stand on the legal obligations. Corporations have no conscience. They're not individuals. They're not living, breathing entities. They're just these things with no conscience, and all they're driven by is making money. The fact is, they were making a lot of money, so why the heck are they going to change their way of doing business when they're bringing all this money in? They didn't want to change the way they were doing anything.

IN 2009, A year after the distributors paid their fines and said they had changed their ways, a pharmacist in West Virginia called the DEA with his suspicions about a doctor in the state's eastern panhandle. The doctor was Rajan Masih, the target of Purdue's sales pitch soon after he had arrived from Texas. Dr. Masih was now prescribing very large numbers of opioids to some patients, including members of his own family. In fact, the scripts were forgeries: the doctor was taking the pills himself.

Dr. Masih had developed a passion for racing Indy light cars. In 2004 he lost control of his car in the rain, hit a guardrail, and demolished the vehicle. He walked away, but his back was injured. The next day Masih was on duty as director of the hospital emergency department, and he was still in pain. "Back then we had a sample closet that was just full of everything you could imagine, mostly for indigent patients. I took the samples of hydrocodone. Norco. It was unbelievable. Not only did it take away my pain, but I immediately felt, wow, this is amazing. I like my job. I like talking to people. I'm not irritated and angry with patients all the time."

Masih kept taking the pills, convincing himself they were to stave off some pain or other until he knew they weren't. "I know full well as a board-certified physician that people become addicted to this. I prescribed narcotics in ER every single day for all kinds of things. So I knew that potential, but I enjoyed it and I liked what this did to me," he said.

Within months, the doctor crossed the line between taking hydrocodone because it made him feel good and needing it to stave off withdrawal. He switched up doses and frequency. The pills gave him energy, but the supply from the sample closet dried up. Masih started writing prescriptions for his own use but using his mother's name. "That was the first act right there. I wrote it in various family members' names. I did not want anyone to know. I would try to quit, but I found it was just not possible. This withdrawal is so severe."

Withdrawal meant diarrhea, nausea, pain. Masih's wife found the pills and flushed them down the toilet, but the doctor wrote himself another prescription: "I was in the unique position that I'm never running out of pills. Never. Which is different from the average person in West Virginia."

Masih's preferred drug was hydrocodone, but the acetaminophen or Paracetamol in the pills is toxic to livers if taken in quantity. "I'd do ultrasounds on my liver to see if something's going on. I'd get liver-function tests done. There's a medicine that we use for Tylenol overdose that's present in ER. I'd be chugging some of that just to make sure that I'm not going into liver failure," he said.

Masih used five or six drugstores so as not to raise suspicions, but an alert pharmacist reported him. He reckons that his arrest by armed DEA officers at his clinic saved his life. "I could not and I would not stop, and I couldn't see any path out of this. It was just like a downward spiral."

The doctor saw himself as a victim driven off the rails by addiction. The DEA saw a predator physician prescribing to anyone who asked. Dr. Masih and his brother had opened a clinic in Moorefield, a twenty-minute drive from Petersburg. To the DEA it looked like another pill mill. The agency identified at least three of Dr. Masih's patients who had died of drug overdoses in the two years before his arrest. He prescribed one of them hundreds of opioid pills, far above recommended dosages, immediately before the man's death. He also prescribed the fentanyl patches that killed a woman. The DEA was not reassured when it found a pile of unlicensed guns in the trunk of Dr. Masih's car, including a Kalashnikov and an AR-15 assault rifle.

The physician faced more than one hundred charges but reached a plea deal, admitting a single count of illegally supplying opioids to a patient he knew to be injecting them. He was jailed for four years and lost his license to practice medicine.

Many in Petersburg speak highly of Dr. Masih. Hundreds of people signed an online petition praising him as a doctor and calling for his release. Others are more skeptical, including the county sheriff, who regarded the doctor as guilty of more than he was convicted of. Dr. Masih said he prescribed "recklessly" but not intentionally. "*Recklessly* to me means my barometer is off because I just took six hydrocodone, and obviously this is not a sane decision-making process," he said.

Recklessly also means he excuses himself of responsibility for the deaths. "I realize that many people became addicted to drugs or dependent on drugs as a result of me. I believe that people may have overdosed on medications that I prescribed. But these were people who already had been on narcotics for years through other doctors. I basically continued to do what their physicians had prescribed for them," he said.

Investigators were not persuaded by Dr. Masih's insistence that it was all a terrible lapse of judgment caused by his own addiction. A stamp on his desk used to mark every prescription "Fill at Judy's" reinforced suspicions of a conspiracy.

Judy's Drug Store was one of several pharmacies in Petersburg, but almost all of Masih's prescriptions were dispensed there. The family-owned business did so well out of the doctor that it opened a second branch close to Masih's clinic in Moorefield.

That was enough for prosecutors to conclude the pair were working together. The DEA had a criminal prosecution lined up, but the owner of the drugstore died, so Judy's Drug Store paid a $2 million civil penalty to settle the case in 2014, a huge amount for a small business, reflecting the scale of the profits it was making from opioids.

By then the US Attorney's Office had traced further up the supply chain and landed at the McKesson distribution center in neighboring Maryland. McKesson had not filed a single suspicious-order report about Judy's, even though under the 2008 settlement it had established a Controlled Substance Monitoring Program to put a hold on unusually large orders by small pharmacies.

When McKesson learned it was under investigation, the Maryland distribution center suddenly filed hundreds of the reports. The company said the failure to send them in earlier was because its monitoring program was flawed, but it would put that right. Rannazzisi thought McKesson had never made an effort, got found out, and was trying to game the system.

The company's position was not helped by a separate investigation of its distribution center in Colorado. Over the previous three years, it had only filed suspicious-order reports about a single pharmacy, even though opioid deliveries and deaths escalated in that time. The DEA concluded that most of McKesson's thirty distribution centers across the United States were failing to report unquestionably suspicious deliveries. That included the Sav-Rite in Kermit and the Tug Valley pharmacy in Williamson. No suspicious orders reports were filed about either drugstore by McKesson or its competitors. Neither did the big three see anything of concern in the delivery of 423 million pills to West Virginia in the six years to 2012 to warrant any action.

The DEA wasn't convinced by the company's pleas and launched a new investigation. McKesson insisted it had done nothing wrong, but kept buying its way out of a public airing of its practices in open court. In 2012 the company paid $190 million to settle a legal action by twenty-nine states alleged that it had inflated drug prices, causing public health programs to overpay.

IF RANNAZZISI WANTED to prosecute, he had to put together the evidence, take it to the Justice Department, and persuade a US attorney there was a case. But he did have one power at his disposal he was free to use without outside approval. The DEA can impose an "immediate suspension order" on a distributor, pharmacy, or doctor to shut down the supply by them of a prescription drug.

In 2011 Cardinal Health learned the DEA was about to impose an immediate suspension order against its Florida distribution center over deliveries to two CVS pharmacies filling prescriptions of pills that were rapidly turning up on the black market.

Rannazzisi thought the case watertight, so he was surprised in early 2012 to get a summons from the deputy attorney general James Cole, demanding he explain himself. The attorney general may head the Justice Department, but the DAG oversees the daily operation of the department.

The message came down: the DEA was not to take any action until Cole had been briefed. Rannazzisi smelled outside pressure. "I got in there, and I basically said, 'I'm just curious. We've done hundreds of actions over these last few years and no one's ever even asked me to come over and brief them, and this is a major corporation and now everybody wants to know what we're doing. I'm just curious, is there something special about this case I don't know about? Why would you want to know about this case?'" said Rannazzisi.

Cole's chief of staff, Stuart Goldberg, jumped in to say that they were just trying to make the legal case better. Years later, Rannazzisi learned the background to that meeting. Cardinal Health had hired a former deputy attorney general, Jamie Gorelick. The average lawyer rarely gets a look in with senior Justice Department officials, but someone who held Cole's post before him was virtually assured of a hearing.

Gorelick sent a seven-page letter in late 2011 questioning the legality of Rannazzisi's planned action and offering a long defense of the company. She claimed that shutting the distribution center would deprive hospitals of essential drugs, said the DEA's action was "both unlawful and inconsistent with the public interest," and lamented the agency's failure to respond "to our attempts to begin a dialogue."

Early the following year, fearing the DEA was about to impose the suspension order, Gorelick emailed Cole's office. The next day the DAG summoned Rannazzisi for the meeting to explain why he was planning to shut Cardinal's warehouse. Rannazzisi was exasperated to be asked by Cole whether he had tried to negotiate with the distributor: "He said I should foster better relations with an industry that refused to comply with the law. The DAG's office wanted to have a meeting with industry, and I refused to do it. They wanted to bring all the industry reps in, and I said it's inappropriate. Some of these people are under investigation."

Rannazzisi told Cole he was listening to the wrong people. "Why don't we bring some people in who lost kids or family members? Give them an audience. How about that?" he snapped.

The DEA filed the suspension orders against Cardinal and CVS to stop deliveries of prescription drugs. The distributors asked a district court in Washington, DC, to block the move. Judge Reggie Walton put a temporary stay on the DEA's action but, after reviewing the evidence, sided with the agency and put the suspension orders back in place.

Three months later, Cardinal agreed to stop deliveries of prescription drugs from its Florida warehouse for two years. Finally, the suspicious-order reports from the company started rolling in.

DEA INVESTIGATORS SAW Cardinal's climb down as an acknowledgment the company was in the wrong. That shook the big-three distributors. It was one thing for the feds to cut off a few doctors and pharmacies. It was another for the DEA to have the power to unilaterally shut down deliveries by some of the country's biggest corporations to entire states and regions. If the agency couldn't be reined in by pulling strings inside the Justice Department, then the distributors would have to work on Congress.

Their trade group, the Healthcare Distribution Management Association (HDMA), set about persuading individual members of Congress that wholesalers were doing all they responsibly could to prevent opioids ending up in the wrong hands but that it was hardly their job to behave as policemen. It called the DEA's suspension orders "draconian," complaining that there was not even a court process before they were imposed. The trade group painted the DEA as an unreasonable agency misusing its powers to go after drug distributors for making minor mistakes in their paperwork when all the industry wanted to do was help.

A month after the suspension orders, Representative Mary Bono chaired a subcommittee hearing on the DEA's moves against distributors. Even before the questioning got going, the apologists for the distributors leaped in. G. K. Butterfield, a North Carolina Republican, piled on the praise. "It seems to me that the security and safeguards these entities employ is very impressive and goes beyond what might be expected. They use layers upon layers of security," he said. "Understandably, though, the further down the supply chain a particular drug travels the greater are the opportunities for diversion." Butterfield said that regulators had gotten it all wrong.

David McKinley, a congressman from West Virginia, lobbed softball questions. He asked whether the industry was being "compensated for doing this police work for the DEA?"

No, the industry rep said. Enforcement was generously paid for out of the distributor's own pocket.

Marsha Blackburn, a Tennessee Republican, wanted to know why there wasn't more "give-and-take or dialogue" between wholesalers and the DEA. "Is there a more proportional approach to take rather than just going to an immediate suspension?" she said.

John Gray, president of the HDMA, played an old favorite. It was essential, he said, that nothing was done to interrupt the supply of opioids to the seriously ill patients who needed them. Then he pleaded innocence. What were the distributors to do? They were neither the manufacturer nor the physician. They don't dispense medicines. How are they to know who is buying these drugs?

Bono wrapped up the session with a lament about inaction in tackling the epidemic. "If thirty thousand Americans died every year from food poisoning, Congress would take action. If thirty thousand Americans died from pesticide exposure, Congress would take action. For that matter, if thirty thousand dolphins died and washed up on our beaches every year, Congress would take action. So why are the victims of prescription drug abuse treated any differently?" she asked.

After years of rejecting one piece of legislation after another proposed by Rogers, Bono, and other representatives to combat the epidemic, the US Congress was finally ready to act—but on behalf of the industry. The HDMA championed a bill, the Ensuring Patient Access and Effective Drug Enforcement Act, requiring the DEA to warn pharmacies and distributors if they were in breach of regulations and to give them a chance to comply before licenses were withdrawn. One of the architects, Representative Peter Welch, a Democrat from Vermont, said it was intended to save the DEA from having to "waste their time on protocol issues with distribution centers."

The same companies paying tens of millions of dollars in fines to avoid criminal prosecutions, a move reasonable people might regard as an implicit admission of guilt, were now being allowed to rewrite the law that held them accountable.

Rannazzisi ridiculed the legislation as a "free pass" for companies he regarded as institutional drug traffickers: "This doesn't ensure patient access, and it doesn't help drug enforcement at all. What this bill does has nothing to do with the medical process. What this bill does is take away DEA's ability to go after a pharmacist, a wholesaler, manufacturer, or distributor," he said. "This was a gift. A gift to the industry."

In meetings with congressional staff, Rannazzisi was hearing the same message he got from Cole. The DEA needed to work with the industry and be less confrontational.

Rannazzisi regarded the staffers as a block between him and members of Congress. It offended him that lobbyists could swan in the door and get a meeting with the people's representatives, while he, a senior official in a federal agency, was fobbed off with staff for whom he had little respect. The lack of respect only sharpened his abruptness. "Quite frankly, no offense, but some twenty-seven-year-old who's never done anything in his life other than go to school and maybe work for a congressman or senator, who has no idea what real life is, is telling us what to do? I was the guy who was overseeing and supervising street-enforcement operations in Detroit, was out there buying dope, was out there doing regulatory policy and enforcement policy for many, many years," he said.

Rannazzisi later denied it, but Representative Tom Marino of Pennsylvania, a sponsor of the bill and leading recipient of drug company donations, accused him at a hearing of telling congressional staffers that their bosses were "supporting criminals" with the legislation. Marino used an appearance by the DEA administrator, Michele Leonhart, to say that her subordinate's alleged comment "offends me immensely." Blackburn, the Tennessee Republican, demanded the Justice Department investigate Rannazzisi for trying to "intimidate the United States Congress."

The Justice Department obliged. It was the beginning of the end for Rannazzisi's pursuit of the distributors. A year later, a new DEA administrator took office. Chuck Rosenberg said he was there to work with industry. Rannazzisi regarded it as a capitulation by the DEA and a disturbing victory for the drug distributors.

Crucially, Rosenberg withdrew the DEA's objections to the Ensuring Patient Access and Effective Drug Enforcement Act. Members of Congress shrugged and said that if the agency no longer had objections, then they would not stand in its way. The law passed in 2016. Of all the legislation the 114th Congress could have passed to address the opioid crisis, the first piece the people's representatives chose to vote into law was written to protect business interests.

The HDMA president, John Gray, called it a victory.

CHAPTER 16
The End of Days

MIKE SMITH, THE West Virginia police sergeant, spent years investigating Williamson's pill mills and was increasingly unimpressed by what he regarded as the lack of enthusiasm on the part of federal prosecutors to go after rogue doctors. Smith had some success in the early days with those doctors who clearly—by swapping drugs for sex—committed fraud. But by the late 2000s, the doctors writing the largest number of prescriptions in the city, Katherine Hoover and Diane Shafer, were still going strong. The lines at the clinics were as long as ever. Smith was frustrated that no matter what evidence he took to prosecutors, they shied away from charging doctors for illegally writing prescriptions. He thought the US attorney in Charleston, Booth Goodwin, was afraid to prosecute cases he might lose and that his office was too soft on physicians who were no different from heroin dealers. "I know that's his perspective, and he's expressed it to me forcefully and to my face," said Goodwin. "Mike was one of the most vociferous: 'Dammit, Goodwin, why can't we do this?' He's entitled to his opinion, and I like Mike and I appreciate that's his viewpoint. But he also did not go through all of the challenges that we would face if we were to try to prosecute those doctors on drug-dealing charges."

Goodwin thought that without indisputable evidence a doctor was prescribing pills in the knowledge they would be used to get high, he would never get a jury to convict. The physician would claim the patient said they were in pain and needed pills and that the doctor had no reason not to believe it. The defense would drag in other doctors to say how difficult it is to judge pain, and reasonable doubt would be established. "You're then in a position as a prosecutor, if you're going to prosecute them for drug dealing, you'd better overcome that hurdle of medical necessity," said Goodwin.

Smith began investigating the opioid trade years earlier knowing nothing about medical law, but now he was steeped in every detail of the legal obligations and procedures for doctors writing prescriptions for narcotics. He knew the law required physicians writing prescriptions under a DEA number to see the patient and diagnose a condition requiring treatment. That often also required some kind of evidence, such as an X-ray. Doctors were also obliged to complete a prescription in full at one sitting, including signing and dating.

Smith sent an undercover officer into the Williamson Wellness Center to see Dr. Katherine Hoover. The officer claimed to be suffering from back pain. After waiting for several hours, he saw Hoover fleetingly and walked out with a prescription for opioids. The clinic refused to send the prescription to the Walmart pharmacy and gave him the list of the five approved drugstores from which to choose. The undercover officer returned to the clinic a month later for his refill. The receptionist told him that next time he would have to come back with an X-ray or MRI to document his supposed injury. Smith was convinced that the clinic was not interested in properly diagnosing the man so much as providing cover if the place was raided. His suspicions were confirmed when he sent the officer back four weeks later without the X-ray. Camille Helsel, the nurse practitioner, gave him a lecture. "Camille Helsel comes in and says: 'Let me tell you something. If the feds come in right now, I want to have some kind of documentation to justify giving you narcotics. So work with me here. You need to help us out here.' He ends up getting his pills," said Smith.

The police arranged an X-ray. "We get the idea to X-ray a German shepherd, a dog, and see if they're even paying attention," said Smith.

His bosses weren't amused by the dog ploy. So Smith sent his undercover officer back with a generic X-ray of a featureless spine— not his own and showing no special characteristics. It was essentially just a random skeleton but it was more than good enough for the office assistant. According to Smith, "Nobody even looked at it other than the fact to see that his name was on it. There was no diagnosis or anything."

Smith upped the game. The officer returned each month, spinning tales about killing a big deer and dragging it for two miles when he was supposed to be suffering from crippling back pain. Smith thought that if the medical staff were making even a pretense at looking out for addiction and abuse, they should have had questions. "It was things people should have caught up on. Narcotics should be for chronic pain, acute injuries. And he's telling them that is dragging deer around," he said.

Smith collected testimony from people convicted of drug-related crimes at the Williamson courthouse. "Everybody basically said the same thing. That the Wellness Center is like pushing cattle through to get the pills. Cash only."

He saw the same kinds of lines and patterns of prescribing at Shafer's clinic and the pharmacies. He also saw that Vinson had a hand in both. "To me it was pretty obvious that these were not competitors," said Smith.

Although Vinson no longer lived in Williamson, he had inherited the building with the clinic after mother died in 2006 and was regularly seen about town.

• • •

IN 2009 THE state police homed in on a member of Shafer's staff, Lisa Baisden, after a number of people said she was supplying prescriptions in the doctor's name in exchange for cash or some of the drugs. Baisden was responsible for maintaining the clinic's register of which patients got what narcotics. Under questioning, she said that Shafer routinely signed prescriptions without dating them so they could be picked up without seeing a patient or if she was out of town. Baisden also told the police that Shafer disregarded warnings from her staff that some patients were coming in to renew prescriptions before their existing supplies should have been used up.

Baisden handed the police the register for the previous thirteen days. It showed Shafer took in a total of $89,000, or $6,800 day, in cash payments alone. Prosecutors calculated that the doctor made about $1.36 million in 2009 and that she had pulled in $7 million in cash payments since 2002.

Baisden's information was useful, but Smith needed evidence in his hand to get a warrant to raid Shafer's practice. The break came when someone in the doctor's office slipped up and issued a prescription without specifying it needed to go to one of the five drugstores in on the racket. The patient took it to an outside pharmacist who spotted that the script was dated with a different-colored ink and handwriting from the rest of the prescription. He reported it.

Baisden told the police Shafer suspected she was being watched and that the doctor was thinking of setting fire to her center and its records to cover up the crime and collect on the insurance. When he learned that, Smith got a search warrant.

Neither the state police nor the FBI trusted officials in Williamson's magistrate's office not to tip off Shafer. The local magistrate, Eugene Crum, was a friend of hers who was under observation by the FBI on suspicion of corruption and drug dealing. So Smith had someone sit in Crum's office, watching that he did not make any phone calls, until the raid on Shafer's practice was underway.

The West Virginia police sergeant arrived at the clinic to find thirty people lined up outside waiting for prescriptions. "I've never been in an office like that. It was more messy than just about any crack house or drug house I'd ever been in. There was trash stacked in rooms to the ceiling. The exam table had a xylophone and a bunch of trash on top of it. The bathrooms weren't working. Somebody had defecated in the sink," he said.

When investigators opened the clinic's files, they found dozens of presigned prescriptions. They discovered records showing Shafer had consultations with more than one hundred patients the previous day even though she wasn't in Williamson. Then the police headed for the bank to get at the doctor's safe-deposit box. It was stuffed with a half-million dollars in cash.

Shafer was out of town, traveling to Ohio to study to become a mortician, the same profession as her old friend Henry Vinson. Smith couldn't work it out. "People could not understand why you would want to walk away from a cash cow and venture into the funeral-home business when you've got so much money," he said.

The answer came in a visit from a local official who said Shafer had been telling people around Williamson she was planning to get into the body-parts business. Shafer was saying that corpses were money.

A few months later, the police raided the Wellness Center, now renamed Mountain Medical, where Hoover had her practice. Smith also got a warrant to go into Shafer's house, where Hoover stayed when she was in town. "There was purses and stuff laying everywhere, full of cash. Then you'd look around, you'd move clothing on the floor, and there'd been $100 bills, $20 bills that had been ground into the carpet. It wasn't like it was even trying to be hid. Under the bed there was wads of money. Just laying with trash and everything else." The police found $95,000 in bills.

Joe Ciccarelli, the FBI agent, led the raid on the home of Myra Miller, Vinson's administrator at the clinics. She was married to a retired state police sergeant, J. J. Miller.

"We opened a safe in the basement that had $400,000 in cash which J. J. tried to begin to explain to me: 'Well, when I was in the state police I booked a lot of overtime.' I said, 'Stop, just stop. Nobody's going to believe that. Just stop,'" said Ciccarelli.

"We took four or five hundred guns. J. J. had a standalone garage with an apartment over the top of it that was filled with guns. If he had one kind of collectible gun, he had three of the same kind. We were there all night loading a U-Haul truck and inventorying the guns he had. Because what are you going to do when you have all that cash? You're gonna buy something with it."

THE FEDERAL AUTHORITIES calculated that Hoover was the single largest prescriber of controlled substances in all of West Virginia between December 2002 and the end of 2009. Smith laid out her record on a spreadsheet, a total of 355,132 prescriptions—about 200 for every working day. Hoover, in a town of a few thousand, was prescribing more than all of West Virginia University's hospital. "There was some days she prescribed to 400 people. In a day. That's just not possible," Smith said. "I interviewed her at length. No remorse. In her mind she was convinced that what she was doing was right. She was very evasive when I showed her the amount of patients she was seeing. She said, 'I don't count the patients. I worked very hard, I'm very busy, I put in long hours.'"

Another of the doctors at the clinic, William Ryckman, was equally unapologetic. Smith learned that the physician was big in his church back in Pennsylvania but the congregation had little idea what he was up to in West Virginia. "I don't think a lot of people who knew Ryckman knew what he was involved in."

Smith reserved his greatest contempt for Diane Shafer. She wrote 118,445 prescriptions between 2002 and the raid on her clinic, or at least that was the number issued in her name. In 2009 her patients filled 17,065 prescriptions. The police calculated that she "saw" 113 patients a day on average, which meant consultations far too short to properly assess a person's medical needs. The truth is she didn't see most of them at all.

Smith saw no remorse in Shafer: "It was pretty much, 'I'm a doctor, I went to medical school, I'm allowed to do this.' She was very arrogant."

Ciccarelli ran up against the same self-righteousness when he spoke to Shafer. "All she could talk about was all the things she'd done for the community. How she donated flowers," he said. "I don't think they get it. They're simply in it for the money. They're the bottom feeders of their profession."

Diane Shafer and Will Ryckman went to prison for six months apiece and were barred from practicing medicine. Katherine Hoover went on the run. "She sent a bunch of letters to the judge and prosecutor's office accusing them of crazy stuff. Saying that they were attempting to prosecute her for no reason," recalled Smith.

Hoover reemerged in the Bahamas and refused to give the court an address or email to contact her. She left behind a large rotting house in Lost Creek.

The feds went after the profits of addiction. Investigators calculated that in 2009, Williamson Wellness/Mountain Medical took in $4.6 million in cash alone. Technical ownership of the clinic had changed hands a couple of times after Vinson went to prison, but in reality he continued to own the building and Ryckman the business. Between April and July 2009, more than $1 million was deposited in one of several bank accounts in Ryckman's name. The doctor claimed to know nothing about it, and the money was confiscated.

The government seized nearly $600,000 from Shafer, divided between cash stuffed in two safe-deposit boxes, money in four bank accounts, and bills strewn around her house and office.

Federal authorities seized Hoover's assets, and she was stripped of her medical license. She is expected to face charges if she returns to the United States.

Miller lost the $465,000 found in her home and a few thousand more in her bank account.

Vinson avoided a third bout in prison by agreeing to give the government the building that once housed Williamson Wellness Center in return for an assurance he would not be prosecuted. The building was officially valued at $1 million, but it stood empty seven years later, with the federal seizure order still taped to the window.

Shafer tried to get her medical license back in early 2017. She told the West Virginia medical board she was an upstanding member of the community who taught CPR and first aid, was a lifeguard at a local pool, and choir director at her church. Sergeant Mike Smith painted a less flattering picture of her for the hearing.

The medical board refused to reinstate Shafer's license. It said she lied repeatedly, still did not accept she had done wrong, and suggested she was fortunate not to have faced more serious charges.

In the end, Smith felt the doctors got away with it: "If they'd been dealing in crack, they'd have been hammered."

SHAFER REGARDS HERSELF as a victim of this tragedy. She repeatedly avoids questions about her prescribing practices and claims the raids on her office were illegal because the warrant did not have her name on it. It was made out in the name of the clinic. "They stole money, jewelry, cell phone, and a brand-new Mac Notebook. They spent the day stealing and looting without a search warrant," she said. "They tore down doors, broke door facings, and acted like barbarians in my opinion. They violated my rights by not having a search warrant for my office with my name on it. Not using proper legal channels must be the way they crush people." She called the search "barbarian." "Do not be fooled by the misrepresentations of the government."

Shafer said many of those seeking treatment were "coal miners hurt from coal mining injuries." "The opioid crisis is not as easy as federal agents make it sound. Incarcerating physicians is not the solution," she insisted.

She accused the federal government of trying to "destroy doctors." "Incarcerating patients and doctors has not reduced drug usage. It has been an ineffective strategy. My guess is that federal agents love to steal from doctors, so doctors are at risk. The publicity makes them famous and ruins the doctors."

To this day, Vinson does not accept responsibility for what transpired in the properties he owned and managed as millions of pills went out of the door. "The medical clinic was rented on a daily basis, including staff and all the equipment necessary," he said.

Vinson deflects questions about the criminal actions of the doctors who paid him by making out that the investigation of Williamson Wellness was part of a "nationwide trend." "That criminal activity did not involve me. If there's a patient-care issue, I would think that's between the physician and a patient," he said. "Certainly, I've made lots of mistakes in my life, and I've paid dearly for the mistakes I have made in my life, but I have moved on and I'm trying to do the best I can. I've gone back to school. I've got a master's degree in integrated marketing. I've been attending law school. So Williamson is a different time and place."

IT IS IMPOSSIBLE to calculate the human cost of the conspiracy between the doctors and pharmacists of Mingo County and what might at best be regarded as the negligence of the drug distributors and regulators. The tens of millions of pills that passed through one small corner of West Virginia were distributed far and wide. Their toll was exacted in death or lives reduced to scavenging for the next hit or subsumed to heroin. It was measured in children orphaned, taken into care, and born dependent. Further down the bill were jobs lost, marriages wrecked, families impoverished. It was a price exacted every mile the pills traveled beyond Mingo.

In 2009 Willis Duncan's son Brian overdosed and died. He was thirty-four years old. "Went to sleep, never woke up," said Willis. "It was a month before he was getting married."

Even Brian's death could not shake his parents from their dependency. Each month, Debbie Duncan was collecting a prescription
with Hoover's name on it for 120 Lorcets and 120 Xanax. She would
often swap them for Opanas because they were so much stronger.
After Hoover's arrest, Debbie was forced to travel farther to get
prescriptions.

Debbie Duncan overdosed and died on September 3, 2011. She
was fifty-one years old and had been hooked for fourteen years. The
autopsy report said she was killed by a combination of Opanas and
other opioids.

Willis's voice breaks as he talks about Debbie's death. He pushes
forward a picture taken a week before she died. "She looks healthier
than me and you," he said. It's true.

Willis lost a son and a wife and even then he kept getting high.
"There was maybe two years out of twenty when none of us were
addicted."

Finally, the money pushed him over the edge. He was spending
hundreds of dollars a week, sometimes more than a thousand. He
couldn't afford it any longer. In 2014 he asked a doctor for help. He
has stayed off opioids since. "I've just screwed up so damned much
of my life, and it's all been over medicine. Stupid stuff. You get on it,
into it, and before you really realize it, it's got a hold of you," he said.
"I'm still trying to clear my mind as to why the heck I done what I
done and why it got hold of me like that because I've always been a
much stronger person than that."

As Willis sees it, he was sucked in by a conspiracy of people more
interested in money than human life.

These people messed a lot of people up. Me being a dumbass
hillbilly, I didn't understand what was going on. I didn't
think that they would hurt you and make you keep wanting and wanting. They all worked together. The doctors. The
pharmacies. They didn't give a rat's fuck. If you paid cash,
you get your stuff. There was never no doctor who said we

want to cut you on this one, cut you on that. More, more, more, more, more, more, more. Just kept increasing.

I had to go through this the hard way. I lost a son, a wife, a multitude of friends at a really, really early age. They're still dying off over it.

It's like end of days. We done witnessed it.

ACT III
WITHDRAWAL

CHAPTER 17

The Public Health

IN 2009 THE Food and Drug Administration admitted an out-sider to its inner circle. Dr. Peter Lurie previously headed Public Citizen, a watchdog in Washington, DC, and an often strident critic of the FDA and its relationship with big pharma.

Lurie was appointed associate commissioner for public health strategy and analysis. His new boss, Joshua Sharfstein, asked him if he had ideas about the opioid crisis. "I pulled up some graphs of over-dose deaths, and I was amazed at what I saw," said Lurie. "I'd seen graphs that sort of showed the numbers going up, but I don't think I honestly had adequately appreciated the magnitude of it. It's easy to look at trends, but what struck me more was the numbers and the numbers were already massive, greater than many other things that we were worried about at the agency."

Prescription opioid deaths in 2009 rose past 15,500—three times the number of a decade earlier. Total overdose deaths, including other drugs such as cocaine and heroin, were more than double that. For the first time, overdoses outnumbered fatalities in car accidents, claiming a life every fifteen minutes. The toll in large parts of the country reached levels once restricted to a handful of states. Close to a half-million people were being delivered to hospital emergency rooms because of drugs, twice as many as five years earlier.

OxyContin sales were up to $3 billion a year, one-third of total revenues from opioids. Hydrocodone prescriptions had surged to 130 million, bringing in about $650 million for the drug makers. Pain was very profitable.

Lurie was feeling his way at the FDA. Working in the commissioner's office put him at the center of power in the agency and he quickly came to appreciate that by far the most influential division was the Center for Drug Evaluation and Research which approved new medicines. Part of its strength lay in the hundreds of millions of dollars it brought in through user fees but it also had a reputation in other parts of the agency for a set of uncompromising officials who did not welcome outside interference.

The FDA's standard for approving a drug is whether it is safe and effective when used as prescribed. Lurie began to wonder aloud in conversations with colleagues and at meetings whether there needed to also be a public health consideration in the drug approval process that took on board not only how a medicine was supposed to be used but how it was actually used. What if numbers about how similar products already on the market were factored in to the approval process?

Lurie didn't push his idea hard, dropping it in at opportune moments. He knew how strong the pushback would be, particularly from the division that dealt with opioids, Anesthesia, Analgesia, and Addiction Products, now headed by Dr. Bob Rappaport. The division had a reputation for being locked into the view that the real epidemic was of untreated pain and for feeling increasingly under siege from the criticism that only hardened its stance.

Some FDA officials viewed Rappaport's fiefdom with frustration. They saw it as wedded to a narrow and legalistic view they felt all too conveniently marginalized the addiction crisis as not really the agency's problem.

Lurie wasn't the only new face at the FDA. Shortly after moving into the White House, Obama appointed Dr. Margaret Hamburg, the former health commissioner for New York City, to head the agency. She put down an early marker in an article in the *New England Journal of Medicine*, saying that under her, the FDA would consider the broader potential harms of a medicine, not simply the narrow findings in clinical trials, in determining whether it met the test of benefits outweighing risk. "A public health approach recognizes that the potential good of a new medical product or policy must be balanced against the potential harm. Some benefits are not worth the risk; some risks are worth taking," she wrote.

IN 2010, PURDUE Pharma launched a new version of OxyContin with an "abuse deterrent formula" that made it much harder to crush and turn into an instant high. By then, the shape of the epidemic was evolving. The CDC's statistics were getting attention, and some doctors began to prescribe more cautiously, although the numbers of opioids dispensed remained, and remains, much higher than in any other country.

More than 200 million prescriptions a year were being written for narcotic painkillers. Most were for the lower-strength instant-release opioids that provided the fertile soil in which OxyContin burrowed deep. Now Purdue hoped the changes to OxyContin would take some of the focus, and the blame, off of its drug, although it didn't withdraw the old version until the new one was ready.

But the FDA soon dashed any hope that the remaking of OxyContin might mark a shift in the agency's stance on high-strength opioids. In 2012, the year after the director of the CDC, Tom Frieden, called the epidemic by its name, the FDA announced a hearing to consider approval of the most powerful hydrocodone pill to date.

Zohydro ER has up to ten times the level of narcotic of the best-selling prescription opioid in the country, Vicodin. The manufacturer billed it as a slow-release pill, dribbling the drug into the system over twelve hours, just like OxyContin. But it frankly admitted there was

nothing to stop Zohydro from being crushed and snorted or injected
to give an instant, massive, and dangerous hit similar to OxyContin
and Opana.

The FDA convened an advisory committee of doctors and specialists to consider approval of the drug. The death toll from opioids
had ratcheted up to nearly seventeen thousand people the previous
year. Congressman Hal Rogers was alarmed the FDA should even
consider allowing another high-strength opioid on to the market, let
alone one that could so easily be turned into a fix in a needle. He
saw it as evidence of the agency's tone deafness toward the epidemic.
Others regarded the hearing as a provocation.

The meeting was overseen by Bob Rappaport, who framed the
process in familiar terms. He conceded that Zohydro might worsen
"the already critical public health problem of prescription opioid
abuse and misuse" but urged the committee not to forget "the other
major health problem we're facing—the widespread, inadequate
treatment of pain."

The manufacturer, Zogenix, told the committee its drug filled a
"clearly unmet medical need" for patients who build up a tolerance
to lower level doses of opioid and as an alternative to drugs such as
Vicodin and Percocet containing acetaminophen, a toxin that can
cause liver failure if taken in quantity or over long periods.

But Zogenix's president and cofounder, Dr. Stephen Farr, was
savvy to what was really on the committee's collective mind. He
swiftly moved on to the company's plans to take "immediate and
meaningful action" if Zohydro fell into the hands of the addicted. It
would even cut off deliveries if necessary.

Farr also put store in the Risk Evaluation and Mitigation Strategy program the industry had persuaded the FDA to make voluntary.
But by the time of the Zohydro meeting, confidence in REMS was
waning no matter how much the drug companies tried to talk it up.

Farr said he was committed to ensuring Zohydro did not become
the next OxyContin. Patients would be monitored and overdoses
reported, with the process overseen by a board of experts. Zogenix
even took a pop at Purdue's criminal marketing campaign. "We are

committed to commercializing Zohydro ER in a responsible manner," said Farr.

Following a presentation by a series of the company's paid hires, Zogenix might have thought it was home free. It had ticked the boxes about combating abuse and painted itself as on a mission to help the pain afflicted. But what had been a run-of-the-mill hearing full of data, charts, and technical issues veered off into uncomfortable territory.

An anesthesiologist on the advisory committee, Dr. Vesna Jevtovic-Todorovic, wondered if the relatively small number of people who would benefit from Zohydro was worth the "huge risk" of unleashing another powerful opioid. Jane Maxwell, a scientist at the University of Texas addiction research unit, questioned how the company was going to carry through on its plan to monitor for "signals" of abuse in its patients. She was not impressed when told Zogenix would do it by keeping a watch on drug treatment centers. "I'm very concerned because I've spent a lot of time listening to other similar alleged systems that need a lot of work. Now, then, you've answered enough for me to indicate what you don't know," she said.

Maxwell was also scornful of Zogenix's plans for an oversight board, saying that she had seen them before and "it ends up being self-serving."

When the hearing was thrown open to public comment, the first to speak was Avi Israel. The retired electrician from Buffalo, New York, struggled to contain his contempt as he eyed the FDA representatives. Avi regarded the agency as so corrupted by drug company money he doubted what he had to say would make a difference. But he thought it important to speak in any case, and so told the story of what led up to the day in June 2011 that he relives without end. Of his son Michael's operation for Crohn's disease. Of his repeated opioid prescriptions and the rise of the addiction tearing at his body. By the end, Michael was crushing painkillers and snorting them to keep the torture at bay. When it all became too much, the young man shot himself. Michael was eighteen years old. "My son took his last breath while in my arms. Half his face was plastered all over the wall, and he was struggling to breathe," Israel told the doctors and scientists around the horseshoe-shaped table. "My son Michael had a medically sanctioned addiction. He wasn't out on the street looking for drugs. He got his prescriptions from a doctor, and then he filled them at our local pharmacy."

Avi, angry but composed, said he wasn't trying to take opioids away from people who really needed them, the dying and cancer ridden. But these were not who most of the drugs were prescribed to.

A long time ago, a committee just like you decided to approve hydrocodone for moderate pain and long-term use. They did it without knowing or thinking of the consequences, that that decision gave a license to pharmaceutical companies and their mouthpiece, the pain management people. They brainwashed our medical society into prescribing the magical pill for everything, including for an eighteen-year-old that weighed eighty-seven pounds and suffered from Crohn's disease. So here you are today and you could be making the same mistake. But you need to ask yourself a question: Is this medication really going to help somebody? Do we really need another pill in this country? Do we really need another narcotic pill to help anybody with pain? We can't handle what we have.

Other parents followed. Cheryl Placek spoke about her twenty-eight-year-old son, Daniel, a navy veteran, who hanged himself at the Veterans Administration's hospital in Buffalo within hours of being admitted for treatment for addiction to prescribed hydrocodone. Pete Jackson, whose daughter Emily died after swallowing a single Oxy-Contin pill in 2006, urged the panel to address the addiction crisis before adding a new drug: "There are already multiple available treatments for pain. Let's address the ongoing epidemic before considering additional products that will offer more of the same risks without any demonstrable benefits over currently available opioid formulations."

Dr. Daniel Busch, a psychiatrist at Northwestern University's Feinberg School of Medicine, who lost a son to opioids, said he was "disturbed that the FDA is even hearing the new drug application for Zohydro ER."

Rappaport, perhaps sensing what was to come, attempted to mark out what was acceptable territory for discussion. He warned the committee that its recommendations should be within "the regulatory framework within which those of us at FDA must function." He said that so long as Zohydro was no more likely to cause harm or addiction than the similar opioids already on the market, OxyContin and Opana, then it must be approved.

Some members of the committee were incredulous at being asked to judge Zohydro by the standards of OxyContin, a drug that was approved before the epidemic it drove took off and before the dangers were evident. Even worse, Zohydro was to be compared to the old version of OxyContin before it was reformulated to make it harder to crush and snort or inject. To some of the doctors, that flew in the face of common sense.

Rappaport countered that since the FDA had never required the manufacturers of OxyContin or Opana to reformulate their drugs, and the companies had done it of their own accord, then it could not make it a requirement of Zohydro. He suggested the skepticism from the committee was "punishing this company and this drug because of the sins of the previous developers and their products." More than once he reminded the committee that the FDA was obliged to provide "a level playing field for industry."

Dr. Judith Kramer, a professor of medicine at Duke University, was astonished the committee was being asked to ignore the experience of the past two decades. "I realize there has to be a level playing field in terms of business practice, but the primary thing has to be the public health," she said. It seemed perverse to some doctors to be using a drug that had been pulled from the market as the benchmark for approving a similar narcotic.

Avi Israel grew so agitated by what he regarded as Rappaport's fixation with the drug companies' rights to make money at the expense of people's lives that he stood up holding a twenty-dollar bill over a picture of his dead son and shouted, "The FDA, they don't see people, they see money." Then Israel threw the cash in Rappaport's direction and told him to stop trying to influence the committee's decision.

In the end, the panel voted by eleven to two against approving Zohydro. In two other votes, the committee split on whether it was an effective long-term treatment and overwhelmingly, by nine votes to five, said that Zohydro was not safe even for those it was intended to be prescribed to.

The votes amounted to a wholesale rubbishing of the manufacturer's claims for Zohydro and the need for it. Avi Israel walked out of the room relieved that common sense had finally prevailed. "It was really a good feeling to know we were able to do that," he said.

A few months later, in October 2013, Israel received a call from Dr. Doug Throckmorton, the deputy head of the FDA's drug approval division. He said that after years of pressure by Congressman Hal Rogers and activists, the agency had decided to move hydrocodone to a more restrictive prescribing schedule—the same one as oxycodone. The agency had resisted the move for a long time, but Margaret Hamburg was in favor.

Israel wondered if finally the tide was turning, so he was a little surprised to receive another call from Throckmorton the next day around lunchtime. Throckmorton said the FDA had decided to override its advisory committee and approve Zohydro.

The drug approval division was determined not to be driven by what it regarded as a growing lynch mob against opioids. The committee was merely advisory, and the agency was within its rights to overrule the vote, so it did.

Some saw the timing of the announcement rescheduling hydrocodone as a cynical move to dampen criticism of Zohydro's approval. If so, it failed. The backlash was furious.

Congressman Hal Rogers introduced legislation to ban the drug. Senator Joe Manchin called the FDA's decision "indefensible" and accused it of compromising patient safety on the altar of drug company profits. He proposed legislation to force the FDA to explain before Congress any future decisions to override its own review committees' recommendations.

Manchin raised questions about whether what he called the "pay to play" IMMPACT meetings had been used to create a "scientifically questionable methodology for drug approval." "If true, we have an alarming explanation for the indefensible decision of the FDA to approve Zohydro," he said.

Mary Bono, who by then had left Congress, said it demonstrated how out of touch the FDA was with what was going on outside of its offices: "I think that was the most offensive moment to all us advocates. You had to wonder what rock they were living under."

Attorneys general of twenty-eight states wrote jointly to Margaret Hamburg, pleading with the FDA commissioner to withdraw approval of the drug: "Those on the front lines of the battle against the worsening opioid drug addiction epidemic recognize that the FDA's reckless decision to approve Zohydro represents a remarkable failure to act in the best interests of protecting public health."

Rogers told me he thought the decision to approve Zohydro was "incredible." He described his reaction as "shock, surprise, consternation" and confronted Hamburg about her decision to override the advisory committee. The FDA chief told him the drug was necessary for a small subset of patients with liver issues who had trouble with the acetaminophen in the hydrocodone combination pills.

The Zohydro reaction shocked the FDA. Some officials dismissed it as driven by bereaved parents unreasoned by grief and opportunistic politicians looking for simplistic solutions to a complex problem. But Hamburg acknowledges that the reaction reflected a broad anger at the failure of Washington's institutions, the medical establishment, and political leaders to take the epidemic seriously. The FDA in particular was seen as arrogant and detached from the sense of crisis.

It really was an indication of how heated the concerns were. Tensions over certain issues had been simmering for some time before I even got to FDA, and I think there had been an underappreciation of just how serious a problem this was. It was too bad because I did feel that it became a wedge when we needed more collaboration and communication. At times we felt embattled. Whether or not Zohydro was approved was not going to change the course of the epidemic. But it got in the way of much more important discussions because it became a lightning-rod issue. I would have been saved endless headaches and difficulties if there had been no Zohydro, but at the end of the day I did feel that there was a medical indication for it.

Margaret Hamburg was right. There was no great surge of overdoses because of Zohydro, but it did change the course of the epidemic to the extent that the political and public backlash was a turning point for the agency.

Hal Rogers had helped establish an annual drug abuse summit that evolved into a leading forum for debate about the epidemic, attracting scientists, activists, and politicians. The meetings also became a focus for pressuring federal agencies to take the opioid crisis seriously.

Rogers was impressed that Hamburg agreed to address the summit several years in a row, knowing that she would not receive a warm welcome. In 2014, after Zohydro's approval, the FDA commissioner was booed by some in the audience. "I like Peggy Hamburg, but she was not aggressive enough. At our summits we would really put the pressure on her and FDA to change these various policies. She would meet the victims, and I think that got to her. I think she realized then that FDA was more than just regulating medicine; it was dealing with a national epidemic that her policies were a big part of. So I think she became much more attuned to the magnitude of the problem and the depths that it was taking people," he said.

But Rogers still did not see the changes he hoped for, and he put that down to the influence of the drug companies. "I certainly think that the pharmaceuticals had a lot of sway with FDA and the policies they put forward," he said.

Pete Jackson, whose daughter was killed by a single OxyContin pill, met Hamburg just after Zohydro was approved. "We felt like we were starting to get in some doors in the Congress in the later years, speaking with some of the decision makers, but FDA seemed like a tough nut to crack. I sat down with Dr. Hamburg. I put my daughter's framed picture in front of her and told her Emily's story. I looked in her eyes, and I just pleaded with her. I was pleading with her, and I don't think she was listening," he said.

Mary Bono also struggled with the FDA: "There seemed to be a disbelief at the FDA that it was occurring at the numbers that it was. We were in a meeting with just Peggy Hamburg and six or eight of us, Republicans and Democrats, hammering her on this, and they were just not listening. It almost seemed she was prepared to take a congressional smackdown and walk away and let it roll off her back."

Did Hamburg justify the FDA's position? "No. No. No. Nor did she say, 'We recognize the problem and we're going to address it,'" said Bono.

Some of the congressional staff dealing directly with the FDA described the agency as "extremely defensive" and "digging its heels in" when it was asked to explain its policies. They saw a contradiction in the position of its officials who claimed there was insufficient data to pin the epidemic on prescribing but appeared unconcerned by a similar lack of evidence for the benefits of long term use of opioids.

Andrew Kolodny, the activist doctor who founded Physicians for Responsible Opioid Prescribing, attended meetings with Margaret Hamburg. He sensed that while she was moved by the personal tragedies, she did not connect them to FDA policies. "I think she was pretty useless. I don't think she got it at all. At that time, unlike today where everybody's talking about it, it wasn't yet on the national radar. President Obama wasn't paying any attention to the issue. I just don't think she really got it. She would nod and say 'I hear you,' but I don't think she could care less about what we were saying," he said.

Dr. Kolodny is not alone in thinking Hamburg was unwilling to confront her own staff in the drug approval division. "She was not somebody who was going to tell Janet Woodcock or Doug Throckmorton or Bob Rappaport that there were concerns about the way they were handling things. She completely deferred," he said.

Fed Up! wrote to the Health and Human Services secretary, asking the Obama administration to remove Margaret Hamburg as FDA commissioner.

Hamburg is saddened and to some degree mystified by the criticism. She acknowledges that the FDA blundered in approving OxyContin without closer scrutiny, although that was not on her watch. "I wish that the FDA had really looked more aggressively at the claims being made when OxyContin first came into the marketplace. The company downplayed its addictive qualities, and the evidence to support the product's marketing claims did not appear to be adequately supported by evidence," she said.

The former FDA chief said that during her tenure the agency pushed hard to address the epidemic by encouraging treatments for drug addiction and pressing manufacturers to develop nonopioid pain medicines and formulas to prevent pills from being misused. Hamburg also considers education programs and REMS a success. "I think FDA got a lot of criticism for not being proactive enough, but FDA was very concerned and committed," she said.

Hamburg said she wanted to see obligatory opioid training for doctors but said that would have required the cooperation of the DEA by making it a condition of the license to prescribe narcotics. The DEA did not cooperate.

She agreed that drug approvals "should be assessed not just in terms of 'Is it effective against pain if used properly?' but also the risk of improper use." But that did not happen while she was in charge, in good part because the drug approval division remained an obstacle to moves to reduce access to opioids.

Kolodny, as president of PROP, filed a petition in 2012 seeking to have the FDA place limits on the dosage and time an opioid can be prescribed for noncancer pain. He also wanted a change to labels to say the drugs were to be prescribed only for severe pain. The agency was under a legal obligation to respond, and a political one, too, given the surging death toll.

FDA officials don't like Kolodny. They characterize him as unreasonable and difficult. One described him as a "complex character."

But outside of the drug evaluation center, there was a recognition that at least some of Kolodny's views about the epidemic had merit. Still, his name on the petition was enough to harden the response.

The FDA latched onto Kolodny's request for specific limits on time and dosage. The agency said the numbers were arbitrary because it was impossible to define a specific point at which the risk of addiction or overdose rises sharply. It depends on the individual. The petition was refused.

Lurie thinks that was a mistake. He said the FDA should have agreed to a general warning that higher doses of opioids are more dangerous and cautioning in favor of low doses for as short a time as possible. "What often happens at FDA is they answer only what's asked for, and then the answer is no. And that's just a total missed opportunity," he said.

Kolodny did win one victory. In 2013 the FDA agreed that the labels of long-acting opioids would no longer say they were approved for "moderate to severe pain." The new wording was more cautious, saying the drugs were for the "management of pain severe enough to require daily, around the clock, long-term opioid treatment and for which alternative treatment options are inadequate." The new label also added further warnings about the risk of addiction.

Hamburg acknowledged that there had been "heated debates for years" about the labeling and that those pressing for stronger warnings were right.

The same year, the FDA also effectively admitted that the original version of OxyContin was unsafe when it refused to let a generic version of the drug onto the market on the grounds that Purdue's pill had been withdrawn "for safety reasons." That did not explain why the agency had permitted the company to keep selling the old drug while it developed a supposedly safer version, but it had been a win-win for Purdue. It had gone on making money from an unsafe drug until it developed an alternative, and now its competitors were barred from marketing the same drug.

Dr. Lurie said that getting the drug approval division "to show creativity was a real struggle all the way through." Dr. Hamburg agreed. She said "there was concern about rigidity on the part of review teams and the legal assessment" in trying to move opioid approval beyond the narrow focus on the needs of individual patients in order to consider broader public health considerations. "We began discussions about how to bring this broader frame to the analysis. And that was why we also really began to push hard on trying to encourage companies to do research and develop new products to treat different types of pain with nonopioid products," she said.

Margaret Hamburg nonetheless repeated the FDA's original case in favor of opioids, insisting that the agency's lawyers were firm on its obligation to approve painkillers that met the legal standard of being safe and effective when used as prescribed.

Those arguments no longer washed with doctors such as Nathaniel Katz, the former chair of the FDA's analgesic advisory committee. He was among those who pressed for wider prescribing of opioids but had grown increasingly exasperated with the agency's failure to face up to the addiction crisis. "The FDA missed enormous opportunities. Missed them and has continued to miss them for the best part of twenty years," he said. "The people in charge of the FDA don't really care about this problem. They are like a sailboat buffeted in the wind where the captain is more concerned about keeping the ship upright. The FDA's constantly under siege by Congress and by the American Medical Association, by pharmaceutical companies, by all sorts of entities. Their concern is maintaining their own equilibrium so they don't capsize as opposed to defining the problem and coming up with solutions. And that's why they never had a strategy and have never implemented any tactics to achieve any strategy."

DR. HAMBURG LEFT the FDA in 2015. Early the following year, her soon-to-be replacement as commissioner, Robert Califf, used the *New England Journal of Medicine* to signal a change in direction. He said the agency would reexamine the balance between the risk and benefits of opioids to take into consideration the "wider public health effects." Califf, until then the deputy commissioner for Medical

Products and Tobacco, acknowledged that opioids sometimes did more harm than good and said there should be a focus on alternative ways of treating pain. The FDA would finally look at ways to take proper account of the risks of narcotic painkillers to wider society and not only those for whom they were prescribed.

Califf said "things are getting worse, not better," and that the FDA could not go on as before.

It was what Lurie had been waiting to hear. "We were thrilled about it," he said of the article. "But it was quite unclear where it went and what it meant."

Califf needed to create momentum, so he turned to the National Academy of Sciences, Engineering, and Medicine (NAS) to consider how to turn ideas into action. Some FDA officials were skeptical that Califf could get those kind of changes past the drug approval division.

The NAS invited Lurie to speak about what policy changes he wanted to see. The doctor saw an opportunity to explain to some of his FDA colleagues that they weren't as constrained by regulations as they claimed. He made a robust case for consideration of broader public health issues by pointing to the requirements put in place for some nonopioid drugs. Labels on antibiotics consider their impact not just on the health of the user but on the population as a whole by warning that pills should be taken only as prescribed to prevent their overuse and the development of drug-resistant bacteria.

Lurie told his audience that immunization strategies have a similarly broad outlook in vaccinating large numbers of people against viruses they may not be at any great risk of falling ill to. "Herd immunity" limits the opportunity for a virus to spread and infect someone who may be harmed. Males are immunized against the human papillomavirus virus to protect females, for instance.

Other agencies also take on broader public health considerations. The process of approving pesticides considers not only their effectiveness in killing insects without damaging crops but also their impact on the environment.

Lurie's trump card was the most awkward of the FDA's responsibilities, regulating tobacco. Wider public health considerations are at the core of the process for approving tobacco products, such as the impact of secondhand smoke or whether electronic cigarettes will encourage more young people to smoke.

The FDA official built his case with one example after another. The law gives the agency considerable latitude in deciding what kind of data, and how much, it requires to assess whether a drug is safe and effective, he said. Drug makers are also obliged to include an "environmental impact," although that is not a factor in the approval criterion.

To Lurie, these represented a lot of levers at the FDA's disposal if it wanted to maneuver toward enforcing a wider public health consideration in drug approval.

The strongest pushback came, not surprisingly, from within the drug approval division. Lurie said that the idea of incorporating a public health dimension to drug approvals "does not come naturally to them." The division had the backing of the agency's lawyers, who continued to argue that it was legally obliged to consider nothing but the clinical studies and that it could be sued by any manufacturer whose drugs were kept off the market. "It's really not true. Around the edges, under duress, you sometimes have found a way to do it right," said Lurie.

In late 2014, Bob Rappaport was replaced by his deputy, Dr. Sharon Hertz. Within other parts of the FDA she was regarded as what one official called "a terribly rigid person, unimaginative, a real bureaucrat." But momentum was building. Lurie could not see how the FDA could just go on as it had.

As it turned out, the fears that Zohydro would help drive the rise in prescription opioid addiction and death proved to be largely misplaced. It was not because Zohydro was benign; instead, its illicit market had already been stolen—by heroin, and worse.

CHAPTER 18

Russian Roulette

JOE RAYMOND IS unflinchingly upfront about how he landed where he did. He liked drugs. He had none of the family trauma he heard about from other junkies. His parents loved him. He suffered no injury that led him to prescription drugs. It was simpler than that for Joe: "It's drugs, man. I like getting high. As a kid, I grew up in the Boston punk and hardcore scene. The chaos of that always drew me to it. My dad managed a venue in Jamaica Plain. I was there all the time when I was a kid, seeing bands. I started getting stoned on pot when I was twelve years old. Probably got good and truly drunk the first time when I was thirteen. I would try anything when I was a kid."

Fatherhood brought narcotics to his doorstep. Raymond was eighteen when his first child was born. The mother came home from the hospital with painkillers.

After that Raymond took whatever he could find. His father was a roofer and started using Percocet following surgery on his rotator cuffs. "It was never a big deal for my dad to throw me a couple of

Percs if I asked for them. I don't think my dad was, 'I don't give a fuck if my son gets hooked on drugs.' It was just we didn't realize how big of a deal it was. I would do anything because they were fun until it wasn't fun."

Heroin was only just working its way into Boston in the mid-2000s, as the Mexican cartels recognized that since opioids were back, they had a product to sell. The drug still carried the stigma of the 1970s, not least the idea it was the choice of the black inner cities, and Raymond looked down on people who stuck a needle in their arm. For him, there was a clear distinction. Heroin was "dope." Prescription pills were entertainment. One represented addiction. The other was a lifestyle choice.

But Raymond, like so many others who thought an opioid tablet was no more risky than the beer he washed it down with, eventually stared into an abyss where heroin was all that was on offer. The seeds planted by Vicodin and Percocet, and nourished so vigorously by OxyContin, flowered in the revival of a drug no one had given much thought to for nearly four decades. The new wave of users was different from the 1970s, though. Back then, people went straight to heroin as the drug of choice. By the late 2000s, three-quarters of heroin users were driven to it via prescription opioids.

Looking back, that made sense to Raymond, even if he didn't see it at the time. After all, what are painkillers if not heroin in a pill? The drug cartels in Mexico understood the same thing.

IN THE MID-2000S, Raymond worked at a large Toyota dealership just outside Boston, selling car parts. Like members of a secret society, the workers there who popped pills all knew each other. One of them was a delivery driver and biker. She came to Raymond saying she could get her hands on a load of OxyContin they could sell. The drugs moved so fast that the consignments became regular and grew larger. Before long, Raymond was taking delivery of a thousand OxyContin every two weeks. He was making a lot of cash, but he was also using increasing amounts of his own wares. Then the day came when the delivery didn't. Aggravated people called wanting their drugs. Raymond wanted them, too. "I'm not thinking I probably have a physical addiction to these things I've been doing every day for months. I'm sitting there, damn, I'm really sluggish today. I can't get up and go. My nose is running, and it's ninety degrees out. What the fuck? I think I have the flu. One of my buddies says, 'You're dope sick.'" That didn't compute for Raymond. Dope sick was what you got from heroin withdrawal, not from a few pills.

On the other side of Boston, Chris Landry was another Oxy-Contin dealer who messed around with drugs since his early teens. First it was ecstasy and weed. Then Vicodin and Percocets. Addiction was never in the cards. "I thought it was just kids' stuff. OxyContin started to make its way around. 'Hey, try this. It's like Percocet times ten.' I crushed and sniffed, and the feeling was great. It was like doing Percocets, just more intense. Never had a problem with Vicodins, Percocets, so why would I have a problem with OxyContin?"

The only problem with OxyContin was the cost: the more he took, the more he needed. The answer was staring Landry in the face: stop buying and start selling. Demand was surging, and so were prices. It was easy money.

Landry was twenty when he began his runs to Broward County in Florida, which had rapidly gained a reputation as the Disney of drug dispensing. "I was going down there and getting thousands upon thousands of them and bringing them back by plane, by car, every week. I stopped working. It was a whole different lifestyle than I was used to."

But, like Raymond, he was consuming large quantities of the drug, too. "My habit got up to fifteen, twenty a day. I'd just crush 'em and sniff 'em. That's what I'd do all day long."

Landry made money "hand over fist" for a couple of years. The Florida police seemed indifferent, but the federal authorities eventually paid attention and dealers started disappearing to prison. Landry faced a quandary: if he kept dealing, he knew he'd eventually get caught. But if he stopped the delivery runs, then he had no money to feed his ever-growing habit. "So I tried to stop them. Stop the pills and get back to the gym. I was violently sick as soon as I came off them."

Landry didn't make the connection until a friend told him he was dope sick. "I told him I'm not a junkie. I hadn't a clue."

Landry had been doing a dozen or more OxyContin a day. His friend urged him to do a couple of pills, and he'd see that everything would be all right again. "Sure enough, I crushed up three of them, sniffed it, and within ten, fifteen minutes washed away that sickness. I realized I was fucked. There were people having unbelievable hard times coming off two, three, four of them, and I was running a twenty-a-day habit for close to two years," he said.

Joe Raymond wasn't even trying to give up when he went around to his dealer to buy pills, only to be told that all he had was heroin. The dealer laid out a couple of lines for Raymond to sniff and told him it was no different from the ten OxyContin pills he was taking each day. Raymond hesitated. Crossing to heroin was a big leap. It amounted to an admission to himself that he was addicted. That he was no different from the junkies on the street he looked down on. But he was seriously dope sick and in need of a fix. "I snorted those two lines. Immediately felt better. After that it was, why am I spending forty dollars a pill, eighty dollars a pill, when I can buy this bag of heroin for forty dollars, and that'll last me the whole day and still have some for the morning? Everything changed for me the day I did heroin."

Raymond had been spending increasing amounts of money just to maintain an opiate equilibrium, but no matter how many Oxys he popped, the highs never seemed as intense as the early days. "I was just maintaining a normal feeling in my life. 'Staying off empty,' as we call it. When I did that first line of heroin, not only was I off empty, but I thought, 'I remember this. I know this feeling.' And then I was off and running." The old OxyContin rush was back.

Heroin had been hard to find and expensive during the early years of the epidemic, but by 2008 it was readily available in Boston and the price was plummeting. Within two years, it cost around half the price of OxyContin for the same hit. But just as with the pills,

Raymond needed ever-larger doses. In 2009 he was caught embezzling money from work and fired. But he still needed his drug. "I came from a good family. I never thought I would be robbing a runner with a syringe filled with my own blood as a weapon: 'Give up what you have, or I'll give you HIV.' I don't have HIV, but he doesn't know that. I'd like to tell you I only did that once, but that wouldn't strictly speaking be true. No one thinks they're going to get to that point."

Chris Landry was struggling with withdrawal. He'd always been against heroin, against needles, but the pain was overwhelming, and when a friend offered to shoot him up for the first time he went with it. "All that washed away. I felt like a million bucks. Like I just hit the lottery. The second chapter is you become addicted to the needle. I wouldn't sniff it. Too slow. Anything through a needle because it's instantaneous. That feeling you're looking for is going to be there in one second."

Landry needed work and got a job as a trash collector, earning around $300 a day in cash, sometimes almost double that, but it still wasn't enough to pay for his habit and the everyday costs of living. The drugs came first.

> I got wads of cash on me all the time from this job. All that money you go to hell with. For a couple of months I was living in a car. Then I was living in an alley for well over a month. I'd wash up at Dunkin' Donuts. Charge my phone. Call my doper. Max out. Go sleep in an alley. Wake up and go do trash all day wearing the same clothes. Not showered for well over a month. And the $300 a day wasn't enough to support my habit. Come the weekend, I'd do other stuff to make money. Illegal shit. Drop somebody. Hold something up. For all the money I was making, I couldn't make it through the weekend with the cash I had.

Landry shot up in gas station bathrooms and passed out on the floor until the staff broke in and threw him out. He stank from collecting trash and not washing. To the world he looked like a hobo, although he couldn't see it himself. "You can be deprived of everything, living in a filthy toilet bathroom, and be perfectly happy so long as you had dope."

BY 2010 MAJOR pill mills had been put out of business from West Virginia to Florida, and the growing awareness of an epidemic was making some doctors more cautious about prescribing. Opioids were still being dispensed in huge numbers, but as they got that little bit harder to obtain, the laws of supply and demand pushed up the price. On top of that, the changes to OxyContin in 2010 to make it hard to break down to an instant high made it far less attractive on the black market. Mexican cartels filled the gap by shipping much more heroin, which got cheaper by the day and easier to find. Dealers appeared at the end of a text message, modeling their service on modern American businesses practices: quick and reliable. Competitive pricing soon meant a hit of heroin cost less than the pills required for the same effect. In 2014 heroin overdose deaths overtook those from prescription opioids, even though they were still rising, too. About 15,400 people were killed by heroin, 1,000 people more than painkillers. The opioid epidemic had a new drug of choice.

As demand grew, the cartels struggled to keep up. Heroin was hugely profitable, but growing and harvesting poppies, and turning them into heroin, is labor intensive and time-consuming. Then the drugs have to be smuggled into the United States. So by 2013, another drug started turning up in coroners' reports in alarming numbers: fentanyl, a synthetic opioid.

Fentanyl is so much more powerful than heroin that only small quantities are needed to reach the same high. That meant easy profits for the cartels. The DEA calculates that a kilo of heroin earns a return of around $50,000. The same weight in fentanyl brings in $1 million. Small but valuable quantities of the drug were much easier to carry across the border into the United States, or just put in the mail.

The drug mostly came from China, usually via Mexico. Cartels already had long-standing relationships with legitimate Chinese firms supplying chemicals to make meth amphetamine, so it wasn't difficult to switch to deliveries of fentanyl powder made in Chinese factories. Deliveries moved between multiple freight handlers. Larger shipments were hidden in shipping containers. Six Chinese customs officials fell ill, and one into a coma, after seizing more than seventy kilograms of fentanyl from a container headed to Mexico in 2015.

The cartels stretched supplies of heroin by mixing it with everything from baking soda to powdered milk and then added fentanyl to make up for the loss of strength. But getting the mix wrong could be fatal, and the drug suddenly started turning up in overdose deaths.

As the death toll from tainted heroin rose, some users became more wary, and prescription opioids started to command a premium on the black market because their strength was a known quantity. So cartels moved into pressing counterfeit tablets. But, as with mixing fentanyl into heroin, making pills from the ultrapowerful synthetic required the kind of precision not usually associated with drug traffickers. A few grams too much is enough to kill. The DEA likens buying black-market opioids to playing Russian roulette.

Jerome Butler didn't even know he was putting the gun to his head. The final picture of the twenty-eight-year-old African American man shows him propped immobile in a hospital bed, eyes closed, sustained only by a clutch of tubes and wires. It was the spring of 2016, and these were his last hours of life. His mother, Natasha, made the near-impossible decision to let him die even as she was still trying to understand what had snatched her son away. Natasha Butler had never even heard of fentanyl until a doctor told her a single pill had pushed Jerome to the brink of death. "The doctor said fentanyl's a hundred times more potent than morphine and fifty times more potent than heroin. I know morphine is really, really powerful. I'm trying to understand. All that in one pill? How did Jerome get that pill?" she wondered.

The pill that killed Jerome was stamped M367, a marking used on a brand of hydrocodone prescriptions pills, Norco. Investigators determined that it was one of a batch of fake tablets responsible for fifty-three overdoses in Sacramento over a few days in the spring of 2016. Twelve people died.

It was a matter of luck. When investigators sent seized counterfeit pills after the Sacramento poisonings for testing, they found a wide disparity in the amount of fentanyl in each one. Some had as little as 0.6 mg. Others were stuffed with an almost certainly fatal dose of 6.9 mg of the drug. The DEA reckoned that the difference was probably the result of failing to mix the ingredients properly with other powders, which led to uneven distribution of the fentanyl.

The police did not have to look far for the source of the drug that killed Jerome. He was staying with his girlfriend at the house of her aunt, Mildred Dossman. Jerome and Dossman's son were smoking cannabis and drinking beer. Then they both popped fake Norco pills supplied by Dossman. The next morning, Dossman found her son unable to speak or move. He survived thanks to an antidote. Jerome was foaming at the mouth and had gone into cardiac arrest.

Dossman was charged with distributing fentanyl and black-market opioid painkillers. Investigators said she was a local dealer.

Weeks after Jerome died, DEA agents raided a San Francisco apartment where a married couple were churning out fake prescription pills made of fentanyl.

Candelaria Vazquez and Kia Zolfaghari sold the drugs across the country via the Darknet, using Bitcoin for payment, and shipped them through the local post office. The couple operated the pill press in their kitchen. A dealer told the DEA that Zolfaghari manufactured large numbers of tablets: "He could press 100 out fast as fuck."

The pair made so much money that agents searching their apartment found luxury watches worth $70,000, more than $44,000 in cash, and hundreds of "customer order slips" that included names, amounts, and tracking numbers. On one occasion Zolfaghari converted $230,000 worth of Bitcoins into dollars. The apartment was also stuffed with designer goods. The seizure warrant described Vazquez's shoe collection as "stacked virtually from floor to ceiling." Some still had the $1,000 price tags on them.

Zolfaghari was arrested carrying a 9mm semiautomatic gun and envelopes with about five hundred pills he was preparing to take to the post office. The couple was convicted of distributing fentanyl, but in early 2018 they were fugitives after fleeing on bail.

HEROIN INEVITABLY WORKED its way into West Virginia. Joe Ciccarelli, the FBI agent who helped bring down the Mingo County doctors, left the bureau in 2014 and returned to Huntington as police chief. The city is the worst hit by heroin in West Virginia, and it is not lost on Ciccarelli that the success of his earlier work helped fuel the second wave of the epidemic. "The cases that were directed toward the providers—the physicians, the pharmacies—drove the price of the pills sky high because the supply was gone, and that drove people to heroin. The entrepreneurs in Detroit very quickly saw this is the market, and now we're awash in it. You can see the numbers after 2010 just skyrocket in terms of heroin. We still see the pills. They are what led us to this point. But now it's heroin, heroin, heroin."

If the path to the new wave of heroin addiction is different, Ciccarelli said so are the workings of the cartels delivering it.

The Mexicans have shut away some of the violence that puts the spotlight on them and become more like the traditional organized crime families in the United States, keeping a low profile and doing business and making money. The typical way heroin is dealt now is the dealers don't want any of these addicts coming around where they've got their dope stashed. It's done by cell phone. Meet me in a convenience store lot. The Burger King parking lot out here on Route 60, it's every day. It's heroin central. Even if they don't overdose, they're driving away high on heroin. We just had a woman up on the interstate near Milton. High as a kite, three kids in the car, crosses the median, hits a tractor trailer head-on. She survives. The seven-year-old survives with a broken leg. The two tiny ones both killed.

One afternoon in August 2016, one call after another hit the 911 lines in Huntington—people overdosing in gas station bathrooms, passing out in the bath, collapsing outside the Burger King. Twenty-eight people overdosed over a period of four hours. All but two were saved by an antidote to the heroin contaminated with fentanyl. Ciccarelli said the city should expect to see a lot more of that.

Overdoses in Huntington escalated to more than twelve hundred in 2016, nearly double the previous year. Paramedics reported going into homes to save a life and finding almost everything has been sold to pay for drugs or children sitting in the middle of the living room floor while their parents are passed out in the bedroom. One in ten babies born in Huntington is dependent on opioids.

There was nothing unique about the city. It had become Everytown in the heroin epidemic. You could find a Huntington from New England to Tennessee and California. None of them could cope.

"I don't know the answer. A year ago I might have said we're going to work our way out of this. But look at the numbers now. I think it's going to be one of those things that only history is going to be able to tell us ten or fifteen years down the road if we're doing the right thing," said Ciccarelli.

In Petersburg, on the eastern side of the state, the same rush of heroin was being blamed on the legacy of Dr. Rajan Masih. The DEA calculated the rogue doctor wrote thirty thousand prescriptions in the five years before his arrest, and that did a lot to drive the demand for opioids in the city.

The heroin came in from Baltimore, Detroit, and Columbus, Ohio. The cartels preferred to find local dealers to sell it who wouldn't catch the eye of the police on the lookout for strangers hanging around the streets. Breanne McUlty fell into the role after meeting a man on a bike. She goes by Bre and was on the path to addiction and dealing before she knew it. Her father used cocaine and methamphetamine and drank excessively when she was a child. Then he branched into prescription opioids. "He couldn't get out of bed without them," she said.

Bre's mother left home, taking her younger sister. Her father was spending so much money on drugs, he couldn't keep up the mortgage payments, and they were forced to sell the house. He dragged Bre from one place to another. Other addicts were ever present. Drugs were so much part of the daily routine that when the parent of one of Bre's friends asked her to sell some morphine, it seemed like a perfectly natural request. She was fifteen years old.

At sixteen Bre was about to have a baby, homeless, and on probation for stealing a pair of shoes. "Some anonymous call said I was pregnant and I was walking the streets. Sometimes I was barefoot and looked helpless, I guess. My dad was driving by one day and saw me and said, 'You've got a court order,' and gave me the papers," she said.

The court told Bre to move into a shelter for teenage mothers, but she soon fled to Maryland, where her daughter was born. She returned to Petersburg and slipped back into dealing whatever she could get her hands on to make money. At that time it was mostly pills. Alcohol was her drug of choice, but it was backed up with crystal meth. "It gives you a lot of energy, but after a while your mental health starts floating away. You get really, really thin. It eats away at your teeth. It messes with your brain. You start imagining things. Hallucinating. You hate it but can't stop."

Bre was doing a run to Ohio to pick up pills with her boyfriend when a dealer on a bicycle pulled up and offered her heroin to sell back home. It was gone in a flash, and Bre understood the opportunity: "I would buy an eight ball for about $600, and I could make thousands out of that because I'd get the ball and cut it off into little chunks so small, and I would go to 7-Eleven, get colored straws, and cut them into different prices for different colors. This one's a little bigger, this one's a little more. And you could sell so much," she said. "There is just so much money to be made in West Virginia, it's kind of hard to walk away once you get the hang of it."

Bre found herself in the unusual position of selling heroin to the Mexicans in Petersburg she had been getting her meth from. She was smart and careful and avoided arrest. When she did finally get busted, it was while taking a ride with a friend to a birthday party. The police stopped the car and found a meth lab. A few months later, sitting in jail, Bre learned that another woman in the car was cooperating with the police. Bre wrote her threatening letters, warning that she would get killed or her house burned down. "I guess if I'd had the chance, as mad as I was, I probably would have done something. But I don't know if I would have burnt their house down."

Bre was never charged for the meth lab or drugs, which weren't hers, but she was sentenced to four years for intimidating a witness. "Federal prison saved me. This was my way out. I grew up in prison."

Rajan Masih felt the same way about his prison sentence. It also gave the former physician an education from other inmates on the web of deception used to get opioid prescriptions and "doctor shop." He learned they changed one letter of a surname to bypass prescription monitoring programs. Married women used maiden names to double up on prescriptions. Men carried artificial urine pumped through false penises to pass drug tests. But it was the dealers who were most organized. They shuttled groups of hard-up elderly people to the doctor for opioid prescriptions, paying them a few hundred dollars for half of the pills. And they brought buyers in from out of state by the busload. "The medical community has no idea how organized this is as you sit in your office. It was just unbelievable to me."

Bre McUlty and Rajan Masih emerged from prison within a few months of each other, both determined to apply the lessons they had learned. Bre was twenty-five. "I came home from prison thinking I was going to make a difference. I'm going to help all these people. It was a slap in the face when everybody was: 'Screw you. You think you're better than us now.' A lot of people I've talked to, they started doing drugs because of their situation. Products of their environment or something bad happened to them, and they're just trying to get over the depression. Sometimes they just look for entertainment. That's what being American is about. I think people just live to party and don't think about the things that really matter."

Bre is not optimistic about Petersburg. She ticks off some of the people using or dealing in drugs, including a couple of prominent names. "You can't trust anybody in this town. It's a wreck. If you want to stay clean, you've got to stay alone."

Two years after her release from prison, Bre decided she had to get out and moved to Atlanta. "When I was a teenager, you're not somebody unless you've got drugs in your pocket. I don't want my kids to grow up in the same situation. I know it's everywhere, but here it's everybody."

Masih struggled to find work as a convicted felon stripped of his medical license but landed a post running an addiction recovery center in Petersburg. "What we are seeing is that there are those older people who started with narcotic pain pills, transitioned to heroin because it's dirt cheap. Then there are those eighteen- or twenty-year-olds who went straight to heroin. They started smoking it. Very rapidly it evolves to injection."

For those who survive the epidemic, and worked to shake off addiction, a long struggle awaited.

In Boston, Joey Raymond and Chris Landry both went into rehab. Repeatedly. They rotated between treatment centers, half way houses, sober homes and turning back to the needle. "I've been through sixty to eighty detoxes," said Raymond.

He stayed off heroin for a couple of years, but then his seventeen-year-old son, Mason, was murdered. "I went off the spinner for six months or so. I got arrested in the middle of this tear."

Raymond was confined to a locked recovery facility, a place he described as little different from a prison except everyone is an addict. "It helped me because I kind of pulled it together while I was in there. I realized I've got two other kids that lost their brother. It wasn't just me that took this loss. It comes to a point where, as clichéd and as stupid as it sounds, you have to get to your breaking point. You have to get to the point where this just isn't going to work for you anymore."

Raymond went from halfway house to a sober home for people recovering from addiction, which he now manages. "This past halfway house was the first one I ever completed because for years I thought completion of a halfway house is the end game. It's not the end game. It's the fucking beginning. I'll never be cured."

Chris Landry has cycled through detox and sober homes too. When we spoke, he had been clean for four months and intended to stay that way. He sees things clearer now that he's out of the forest. "Pretty much 95 percent of it is because of OxyContin coming around. That's the start of all this. The epidemic, the heroin. There wouldn't have been any of it without OxyContin."

IN 2016 FENTANYL deaths surged past heroin and prescription opioids, taking more than twenty thousand lives. Just three years earlier, fentanyl had been a bit player in the epidemic, claiming around three thousand lives. As the drug worked its way into the cities, it drove a sharp rise in deaths of African Americans in urban areas as rates started to catch up with those for whites in cities. In Washington, DC, the rate of drug overdoses doubled in a year. At the same time, fentanyl continued to keep West Virginia far in front for overdose deaths.

Some officials began to talk in terms of two epidemics. There were at least steps the government could take to rein in the supply of prescription pills. But they struggled to combat heroin, fentanyl, and similar illicit opioids seeping into every part of the United States.

Dr. Peter Lurie, the former FDA official, reckoned there was a time when the epidemic could have been reined in by curbing prescribing. But now, he said, the government faced the "scary possibility" that reducing access to opioids was feeding the demand for heroin, and it had no way of dealing with that.

A 2014 study found that 94 percent of heroin users said they came to the drug "because prescription opioids were far more expensive and harder to obtain." Nearly half of the people in the study said they preferred prescription opioids if they could get them because they were safer and there was less risk of arrest.

"What's going on now is a maturing of the epidemic," said Lurie. "This epidemic's probably got fifteen years to run. People are addicted, and that means they're going to keep needing it. It's going to be years that they stay on it until they finally get over it. If they don't get killed. So it has a very very long tail on this epidemic, even worse than people appreciate."

CHAPTER 19

Dodging Torpedoes

B Y 2015 DR. Tom Frieden, the director of the CDC, thought the time had come to state the obvious.

The years of cooking up complicated REMS programs, debating medical education, and developing abuse-deterrent formulas had not slowed the price exacted by false claims for opioids and less than discriminating prescribing. Deaths from legal narcotics continued to climb even as heroin and fentanyl began their sprint.

The crackdown on the pill mills and greater awareness on the part of doctors led to a small drop in the number of opioid painkillers dispensed after 2010, but Americans were still prescribing narcotics at five times the rate of the United Kingdom or France. Doctors and dentists continued to send patients home with a month's supply of narcotics after simple procedures when a few days would have been sufficient.

By calling the epidemic by its name, the CDC director played an important part in drawing national attention to the crisis that should have happened years earlier, particularly on Capitol Hill. But Frieden

feared that without further curbs on prescribing, deaths would continue to rise and a new wave of Americans would be sucked into
addiction. He decided to take the unusual step for the CDC of telling doctors to rein in their prescribing.

Frieden's mind was made up by the realization that none of the
other major agencies were going to step up to the plate. There were
hints of change from the FDA, but whatever it was planning to do
wasn't happening fast enough. In any case, its credibility had just
been mauled over Zohydro. Other federal agencies had in effect
relinquished responsibility beyond putting together studies and plans
that never seemed to change much on the ground. The states were
supposed to oversee medical practice, but many, although not all,
had failed to have an impact. Medical education for doctors continued to be funded by the pharmaceutical industry.

Frieden concluded the CDC needed to take the initiative. "If not
us, who? It became rapidly clear to us that most of the people working in this space were heavily conflicted. The industry influence was
all over the place. It was funding a lot of medical groups. It was funding medical boards in the states. It was funding massive education."

The CDC director was also skeptical about several of the measures embraced by the FDA, such as abuse-deterrent formulas that
were supposed to make it harder to get high from prescription drugs.
He thought they muddied the waters.

> It only gradually became apparent, to me anyway, that when
> pharma comes and says, "We've got this great new drug that
> is much harder to melt and inject," what's not to like, right?
> But then you realize that abuse-deterrent formulations are
> very similar to what tobacco did with "lite cigarettes." It's
> something that really doesn't cause less harm but confuses
> people about whether it causes less harm. The data is clear.
> Lots of people believe abuse deterrent means nonaddictive. I
> don't think that's a mistake on the part of the drug compa-
> nies. This was a way of them extending their profit margin.
> Sure, something that's harder to melt is good, but it doesn't

make a big difference. It's still a lethal drug if you swallow too many pills, and it's not that much harder to melt down either.

The CDC put together a "Core Expert Group" of seventeen specialists to draw up guidelines on best practices for doctors. Frieden knew it would be politically controversial. The drug industry would push back hard against recommendations that challenged opioids as the default stop for pain. He also knew that despite the growing body of research showing narcotics were neither effective nor safe for long-term treatment of chronic pain, there was no definitive evidence either way. "We wanted to be very careful. We wanted to be cleaner than Caesar's wife if you're going to be doing something that's controversial. We knew that the evidence base wasn't as strong as we would like it, because who has an economic interest in proving that these drugs are dangerous? Nobody." But as Frieden saw it, if the CDC waited for definitive evidence it would take years, and that would mean more lives lost and more people becoming addicted.

The agency approached Dr. Roger Chou to lead the Core Expert Group. The Oregon pain specialist had worked for other federal agencies on long-term opiate therapy and addiction, and he was prepared for the hostility coming down the road. He had previously sat on a panel that dared to question whether OxyContin should be prescribed in ever-increasing doses. "We basically said there's really very little evidence showing that high doses are effective for chronic pain, and there may be some serious risks. People got really angry with that. Doctors. They are yelling at us at meetings. They were very offended that we would tell them how to prescribe opioids."

The CDC's move immediately attracted the suspicion of pharma. It wanted its people on the panel and public hearings it could flood with patients demanding no restrictions on access to opioids. Instead, the CDC chose a set of experts who weren't taking the industry's shilling.

When a copy of the draft guidelines leaked in late 2015, the manufacturers and advocacy groups were appalled. In pressing for a significant scaling back of prescribing, the CDC made the case that opioids were not only addictive but didn't work very well other than in the treatment of short-term acute pain. It said they should be prescribed far more cautiously and in more limited quantities. The drug industry could live with doctors being told to be careful, but it had spent years combating anything that questioned the basic effectiveness and value of opioids.

The Pain Care Forum went to work on Capitol Hill. The industry cast the CDC as having gone rogue. The Washington Legal Foundation, which two decades earlier led a fight on behalf of the tobacco industry against further regulation of smoking, threatened a lawsuit against the CDC for "blatant violation of federal law" for supposedly failing to adhere to transparency regulations. The Academy of Integrative Pain Management, a member of the Pain Care Forum, pressed Congress to investigate whether the CDC was influenced by special interests. Other forum members joined the pushback in trying to rally political pressure on the agency.

Congressman Jason Chaffetz obliged. The chair of the House Committee on Oversight and Government Reform, who was among the recipients of the largest drug company political donations in Congress, wrote to Frieden, saying his committee was investigating whether the CDC had broken the law by appointing a biased advisory panel because its expert group included Jane Ballantyne.

Then the congressman fell back on the old favorite. "We expect CDC's guideline drafting process to seek an appropriate balance between the risk of addiction and the need to address chronic pain," wrote Chaffetz.

Other members of Congress suggested that it was not the job of the CDC to advise doctors on prescriptions. But the mood on Capitol Hill had shifted. Congress was not so willing to dance to the industry's tune now that public attention was focused on the epidemic. Senator Joe Manchin of West Virginia, long a vocal critic of the opioid makers, described resistance to the CDC guidelines as being pushed by interests "concerned we're going to take away their candy."

In the end, Chaffetz turned up no evidence of wrongdoing.

The proposed guidelines also came in for stinging criticism from within the FDA. Dr. Sharon Hertz, who succeeded Rappaport as head of the analgesia division, told a meeting of federal agencies that the evidence for the CDC guidelines "is low to very low and that's a problem." "I think we need to recognize that CDC wants to substantially limit opioid prescribing. Period," she told the panel.

The FDA had found a sudden enthusiasm for hard evidence in making opioid policy after years of allowing it to be directed by scant and misrepresented data.

At the same meeting, Dr. Wanda Jones, Obama's deputy assistant secretary for health, said the CDC's guidelines "fly in the face of science." "Damn the torpedoes, full speed ahead," she scoffed. Jones said that focusing on the opioid epidemic was a distraction from dealing with pain.

Tom Frieden called her remarks, and similar views expressed by members of the National Institutes for Health staff, "sleazy." "NIH was really conflicted on this. They had lots of industry money, and they had bought into this pain perspective, that we're vastly undertreating pain and we need to do a much better job treating pain, and that's why we need opiates."

Frieden regarded the demands for indisputable evidence before acting as unreasonable. The CDC would not require a comprehensive study to recommend people not jump out of an airplane without a parachute. "The strength of the evidence doesn't necessarily relate to the strength of recommendation," he said.

Even as it worked on the guidelines, the CDC continued to pile up evidence about the shape of the epidemic. It released a study showing that for many people who became addicted, it took just a few days of pills to get hooked. The likelihood of addiction increased sharply with prescriptions for more than five days.

When the guidelines were finally published in March 2016, they were substantially the same as the draft in spite of the pressure. "The campaign didn't have any effect. None," said Frieden. "We were determined to go forward."

The guidelines recommended that doctors should try other therapies before prescribing opioids for the first time, and where they were prescribed it should be the lowest effective dosage for as short a time as possible. High-dosage extended-release drugs such as OxyContin were mostly to be avoided. The CDC said that after surgery, three days of pills would normally be sufficient, and more than seven should be rare.

The agency went on to recommend that doctors set specific goals for treatment so that the effectiveness and risks of opioids could be judged as they are used. It also said that doctors should avoid prescribing opioid pain medication and benzodiazepines, such as Xanax, together because they greatly increase the danger of death.

The CDC also considered the contentious question of setting a recommended maximum dose, which Andrew Kolodny had asked the FDA to do and been refused. The claim that patients could be given ever-increasing doses of opioids to match their pain and would not become addicted was by now widely discredited. The CDC set the recommended daily limit at no more than 90 mg of morphine and warned doctors to be cautious above 50 mg. "The problem with the dose thing is that it's like speed limits. There's no magic threshold. The lower you go, the fewer overdose deaths you'll have," said Chou, the chair of the CDC committee that drew up the guidelines. "The 90 mg is based on data that shows a lot of the overdose deaths occur at 90 mg. We have 50 mg because you get about a doubling of the risk once you hit 50 mg or so in most studies. So there's some reasoning behind both of those numbers, but there's nothing magic about them."

Chou got pushback from some doctors who objected to being told what to do by the government or who claimed it would cause them to withhold opioids from legitimate patients. But he is weary of members of his profession failing to act. "This idea that physicians can manage it on their own, that we don't want more government regulations telling us what to do, if that was the case, we wouldn't have gotten into the situation."

Tom Frieden made his case for the new guidelines in a paper in the *New England Journal of Medicine*. He laid out the undeniable link between increased prescribing and overdoses. The paper, cowritten with Dr. Debra Houry, director of the CDC's injury prevention center who was instrumental in getting the guidelines through, said the push for wider opioid use in the 1990s "failed to adequately take into account opioids' addictiveness, low therapeutic ratio, and lack of documented effectiveness in the treatment of chronic pain." "It has become increasingly clear that opioids carry substantial risks and uncertain benefits, especially as compared with other treatments for chronic pain," wrote Frieden and Houry

The CDC had now repudiated the entire thesis of the opioid evangelists. The agency's guidelines were, the two officials said, intended to "chart a safer, more effective course."

The two doctors noted the lack of data to back up claims for the long-term effectiveness of opioids and said that what studies there were showed the opposite. "The few randomized trials to evaluate opioid efficacy for longer than six weeks had consistently poor results. In fact, several studies have showed that use of opioids for chronic pain may actually worsen pain and functioning, possibly by potentiating pain perception," they wrote.

While opioids were of questionable use for long-term pain, there was little doubt about the risks of addiction and overdose. The two doctors said that nearly all opioid painkillers on the market "are no less addictive than heroin" and that dependence among people taking them for chronic noncancer pain was as high as one in four patients. "We know of no other medication routinely used for a nonfatal condition that kills patients so frequently," they concluded.

CHAPTER 20

The National Nightmare

OTHER COUNTRIES LOOKED on in alarm as they grappled to understand if the US experience marked the beginning of a global wave of opioid addiction that would eventually engulf them.

Part of the answer lay in a question too few in the United States seemed to be asking. If the country was in the grip of an epidemic of untreated chronic pain, why were other developed nations not reporting the same crisis? Surely, they do not suffer less pain.

As it happens, reported levels of pain are not hugely different on either side of the Atlantic. The distinction lies in how the numbers are interpreted and how pain is treated. On paper, doctors in the United States and Europe follow similar guidelines on the use of opioids. Practice diverges under myriad influences from the "pill for every ill" culture to the expectation of living pain free and the financial workings of the US health care system.

No other country prescribes narcotic painkillers at the level of the United States. Per capita daily opioid consumption by the British and French is less than one fifth that of Americans. Life expectancy in both countries is higher than in the United States.

American doctors are also more likely to prescribe a dangerous mix of drugs, notably benzodiazepines, such as Xanax and Valium, alongside narcotics. Both suppress breathing, and the two types of drug are found together in about one-third of overdose deaths in the United States. Benzodiazepines are dispensed more sparingly in most other developed countries and far less frequently in combination with opiates.

Foreign doctors look askance at America's profit-driven health system as more of an industry than a service. "Medicine is business oriented in the US. It's very production line," said Dr. Jane Ballantyne.

Yet doctors in Europe see signs that opioid prescribing is on the rise there too as the influence of the painkiller culture spreads.

THE US GOVERNMENT made its own efforts to understand what went wrong. A commission appointed by President Trump called the opioid crisis "the most devastating drug epidemic in our nation's history." It identified a dozen factors as catalyzing the crisis. They ran from the misrepresentations of the Porter and Jick letter on addiction and the use of "low quality" research claiming opioid narcotics were safe for the routine treatment of chronic pain to the "educational campaigns" run by drug makers. The commission also singled out the movement to treat pain as a fifth vital sign, the financial interests of insurance companies, and the "insufficient response of federal regulators." "A nation awash with prescription opioids became fertile ground for diversion by acquisition from medicine cabinets, through rogue pharmacies, rogue physicians, and for opportunistic sellers of illicit heroin, fentanyl, and other deadly opioids."

The commission assigned blame to an array of institutions, but some of the sharpest criticism focused on the FDA, not least because of the agency's acceptance of Purdue's claims that opioid addiction was "very rare" and that the delayed absorption of OxyContin reduced misuse of the drug. "The FDA provided inadequate regulatory oversight. Even when overdose deaths mounted and when evidence for safe use in chronic care was substantially lacking, prior to 2001, the FDA accepted claims that newly formulated opioids were not addictive, did not impose clinical trials of sufficient duration to detect addiction, or rigorous post-approval surveillance of adverse events, such as addiction."

The commission said the FDA failed to consider whether the risks from misuse of opioids outweighed the benefits provided by their intended use.

The report's conclusions were a stinging rebuke to the FDA, but it said there had been a failure of leadership across the board, including within the White House drug czar's office and other federal institutions, such as the National Institute on Drug Abuse. "I think the fundamental problem is the absence of leadership in that there is really nobody in charge of this problem," said Dr. Nathanial Katz.

Former FDA chief Margaret Hamburg agreed. "Was there the political will and commitment to actually make sure that things got done? I think more should have been done, and I think the same holds true today as we're speaking."

Katz continues to believe that used the right way, prescription opioids can help large numbers of people deal with pain. But he said doctors remain "blinded by lack of adequate data" and thinks medical policy has been hijacked by the industry. "What we said was selectively quoted, amplified a millionfold by forces that were much more powerful than any of us were, and that created this gap between the theory and the practice or even between the recommended practice and the actual practice," he said. "It was not subtle, and it was not unintentional. That was done deliberately."

Katz said the industry overstated the extent of chronic pain in America and then framed the response as a choice between using opioids or denying treatment. Doctors who didn't prescribe were characterized as lacking in compassion. The drug makers' grip on opioid policy has killed what Katz once believed could be a reasoned approach to the use of narcotics. "I used to think that if I put enough energy into it, I could actually contribute to shaping of intelligent policy in this area. I no longer think that. I don't really see any prospect for intelligent policy in this arena in the United States."

THE DRUG INDUSTRY eventually exacted its revenge on Darrell McGraw, the West Virginia attorney general who sued Purdue Pharma. It backed his Republican challenger in the 2012 election, Patrick Morrisey, a former lobbyist for the pharmaceutical industry's trade group and for the drug distributor Cardinal Health.

Cardinal contributed to Morrisey's campaign and paid for his inauguration party when he won by a slim margin. McGraw is philosophical. "Sooner or later they'll get you. You can't stand up in the political process; you can't win in the long run; no individual can win at the state and local level against endless amounts of money. The pharmacy people in the opioid business assembled with others, which is their right, to dispose of their tormentor."

Morrisey inherited a clutch of lawsuits filed by McGraw against opioid makers and distributors. Among them was Cardinal Health, which at the same time hired Morrisey's wife as a lobbyist and paid her firm nearly $1.5 million. Morrisey recused himself but was later revealed to have met with company representatives several times.

Eventually, all of the lawsuits against the drug companies were settled out of court.

McGraw reckoned that the corporate backing of his political opponent was intended as a warning to other state attorneys general. If so, it came too late.

By the time McGraw was out, state governments, counties, and even little Kermit were filing a wave of lawsuits against those they accused of profiteering from addiction. The manufacturers and distributors who so enthusiastically latched on to the simplistic narrative of an epidemic of untreated pain suddenly embraced a claim of "it's complicated."

Purdue Pharma declined to answer detailed questions about its practices or its criminal conviction. These days it tries to keep the focus firmly on the history of OxyContin since it was reformulated in 2010 to make it harder to break down into an instant high.

The drug maker placed ads in the *New York Times* and other newspapers protesting that it is doing all it can to combat the epidemic. "We manufacture prescription opioids. How could we not help fight the prescription and illicit opioid abuse crisis?" it pleaded.

In its response to questions, Purdue described itself as "an industry leader in the development of opioids with abuse-deterrent properties, funding and advocating for the use of prescription drug monitoring programs and partnering with law enforcement to help provide access to naloxone."

But even as it proclaimed itself committed to doing the right thing, Purdue was not above further misrepresentation. It failed to say the changes to OxyContin's formula were made under pressure because the original claim that the drug was less addictive and safer was patently false. And while the company did indeed develop a deterrent formula, it kept selling ever-increasing amounts of the old pill with its large hit of easily accessible narcotic for years until the new version was ready. Purdue said it did not want to interrupt supplies to patients who need the drug. As it happens, the flow of billions of dollars in profits was not interrupted either.

Then the company went on to the defensive. "Suggesting activities that ceased before 2002 related to OxyContin is responsible for today's complex and multi-faceted opioid crisis is deeply flawed. The vast bulk of opioids prescribed are not OxyContin, which represents less than 2% of current opioid prescriptions. Today's crisis is being driven by the illegal trafficking and abuse of heroin and illicit fentanyl," the company said in a careful piece of dissembling.

OxyContin's share of the opioid market has never been more than 10 percent of total opioid prescriptions, but that does not reflect its impact on the epidemic or the part played by Purdue in pushing mass prescribing of narcotic painkillers. Less powerful instant-release opioids, such as Vicodin and Percocet, were more popular and more widely misused. But if they were the gateway for many people, OxyContin supercharged opioid addiction. It was far more powerful than other readily available narcotics. OxyContin tipped some users over the edge, spilling them into addiction. And for all of Purdue's attempts to characterize its drug as a bit player in the epidemic, when more than 200 million prescriptions a year are being written, its share still ran into the millions. The trail to the Florida pill mills was known as the Oxy Express for a reason.

For all its attempts to place the weight of the responsibility for the epidemic on the doctors it pressed to prescribe its drug and the "abusers" who became addicted, in 2018 the company announced it would no longer market OxyContin to physicians and dismissed its entire sales staff.

As attention on the actions of Purdue and its fellow manufacturers intensified, they did their best to disperse responsibility for the epidemic so far and wide that in the end, everyone was to blame, so no one was to blame. Except "the addicts."

Endo, the maker of the high-strength narcotic Opana and Percocet, defended itself from a raft of lawsuits by describing the epidemic as "a complex problem with root causes that are difficult to disentangle." The company described accusations by Ohio's attorney general Mike DeWine that pharmaceutical companies caused the addiction crisis as a "stunning oversimplification" and dismissed as "offensive" his claim that they "laid waste to Ohio as only the worst plague could."

Endo was not alone in assuring anyone who would listen that it had spent years trying to combat the epidemic and bemoaning the fact that "litigation and vilification" would not bring about an end to the crisis.

Congress dragged in the heads of the major drug distributors in May 2018 to put it to them that they have a responsibility for the opioid epidemic. The chiefs of the big three—McKesson, Amerisource Bergen, and Cardinal Health—outright denied it. Only the CEO of a small distributor, Miami-Luken, conceded that his firm did indeed play a role.

The executives stuck to the industry strategy of trying to disperse responsibility as wide as possible in order to diminish their own role while claiming that "playing the blame game" will not help end the epidemic.

It was an approach that infuriated Representative David McKinley, a Republican from West Virginia, who accused the distributors of "deflecting responsibility." "The fury inside me is bubbling over. . . . For several of you to say you had no role in this whatsoever, I find particularly offensive."

Much of the hearing focused on wholesalers swamping McKinley's state with pills. The questions homed in on McKesson's supply of 5.6 million opioids to the Sav-Rite in Kermit over just two years and Cardinal Health's large deliveries to drugstores in Williamson.

McKesson's CEO, John Hammergren, was asked how, when his company's own monitoring system required that orders larger than 8,000 opioid pills a month should be scrutinized, the firm was delivering the equivalent of 9,650 pills a day to the Sav-Rite. Hammergren admitted that deliveries "should have been terminated sooner" but put the failure to do so down to error. The system had broken down, he said. By an apparent remarkable coincidence, the other distributors suffered from the same kind of breakdown that allowed them to go on delivering millions of pills for years on end.

Hammergren remained defiant throughout the hearing. George Barrett of Cardinal Health took a more conciliatory line in expressing "personal regret" at his company's failure to cut off deliveries to Hurley Drug in Williamson. "With the benefit of hindsight, I wish we had moved faster and asked a different set of questions. I am deeply sorry we did not," he said.

Representative Diana DeGette confronted the executives over internal memos in which some staff at the distributors flagged concerns about the scale of deliveries to the Mingo County pharmacies but were ignored. The deliveries continued. She said the wholesalers had to have known. It was all over the news. The DEA was telling them. Yet they kept shipping the pills. "I mean, come on," DeGette said.

The CEOs gave a collective shrug.

McKinley asked why, if doctors and pharmacists have gone to prison, drug distributor executives should not be jailed too. "I just want you to feel shame about your roles, respectively, in all of this," he said. "What's the punishment that fits the crime when 900 people in West Virginia lose their life? Just a slap on the wrist? A financial penalty? Or should there be time spent?"

For all its protestations of innocence, McKesson paid a record $150 million fine in 2017 for violating the law requiring the reporting of suspicious orders, its second penalty for the same offense. The settlement required the firm to suspend deliveries for several years from some of its distribution centers, including those in Florida and Ohio. McKesson said it paid the penalty "rather than engage in time consuming, contentious and expensive litigation."

The agreement was a vindication for Joe Rannazzisi's claim that the distributors paid their fines as the cost of doing business and continued delivering opioids without much concern for who was using them. The former DEA agent thought the company got off too lightly, given the size of its revenues at nearly $200 billion a year.

Rannazzisi resigned in 2015, but that was not the end of his influence. President Trump tapped Tom Marino, the former member of Congress who introduced the legislation curbing the DEA's ability to shut off opioid deliveries, as his new drug czar. It was Marino who told Rannazzisi he was "immensely offended" at the suggestion the new law protected criminals and who backed a Justice Department investigation of the DEA official. In late 2017, Rannazzisi appeared on CBS's *60 Minutes* recounting Marino's actions, forcing the former congressman to withdraw from consideration as drug czar.

Following the publication of his opioid commission's report, President Trump ordered the declaration of a public health emergency in response to what he called the "national shame and human tragedy" of the "worst drug crisis in American history." The president spoke powerfully about the human toll of the epidemic, including the large numbers of babies suffering opioid withdrawal. "Beyond the shocking death toll, the terrible measure of the opioid crisis includes the families ripped apart and, for many communities, a generation of lost potential and opportunity," he said. "Nobody has seen anything like what's going on now. As Americans we cannot allow this to continue. It's time to liberate our communities from this scourge of drug addiction."

What that means in practice remained unclear nearly two years into the Trump administration. It announced plans to bring down the number of opioid prescriptions and to pursue its own lawsuits against the pharmaceutical industry to recover the cost to the government of the epidemic. But little changed on the ground for states desperate for treatment facilities and help with the social costs of the tragedy.

The White House estimates the crisis has cost the United States $1 trillion because of the demands on health care, policing, the courts, and lost jobs and productivity and is likely to cost half that amount again over the next few years. The epidemic costs West Virginia alone more than $8 billion a year, about the same as the drug industry makes from opioids.

A study by Princeton economist Alan Krueger calculated that the opioid crisis accounted for about 20 percent of the fall in men in the labor force, with nearly half those of working age who were without jobs taking pain medication daily.

The president offered a throwback to the days of crack and mass incarceration of African Americans as part of the War on Drugs by proposing the death penalty for traffickers. But few these days suggest that prisons and punishment are the path out of the epidemic, and Trump's comments only went to highlight how very different official attitudes are today and why. "I don't think you can understate the importance of, to be very blunt, this is happening to whites not blacks," said Tom Frieden, the former CDC director. "It's so hypocritical. I'm glad that people are saying now that addiction is a disease, but these same people, a lot of them were saying, 'Lock those addicts up.' It's a disease when it's white people, and it's a moral failing when it's black people? I think there's a lot of racism in how we dealt with epidemics over time. I think the more enlightened approach now is a reflection of the more diverse population affected."

The unrelenting efforts of some of those who responded to personal tragedy by working to ensure it did not happen to others delivered some victories. Bob Pack, who lost his two children to a driver high on opioids in 2003, finally saw his campaign to require doctors in California to consult a monitoring system before prescribing opioids come to fruition after fifteen years. The state was expected to implement the system in late 2018 after California's medical association backed off its delaying tactics in the face of increased public scrutiny.

In Florida, Janet Colbert, the nurse who first saw the wave of opioid addiction as she treated babies born with withdrawal symptoms, could finally claim success in her campaign to limit painkiller prescriptions to three days and to make prescription monitoring mandatory for doctors after the state legislature passed new laws in 2018. By then ninety-two thousand children had been taken into care in Florida as a result of drug addiction. Their successes were replicated by campaigners in other states.

Jane Ballantyne, who described the swing to mass prescribing of opioids for chronic pain as a "leap of faith," faced another backlash when she argued in the *New England Journal of Medicine* that doctors should stop focusing on bringing down pain levels as a measure of health. She said that it resulted in ever-higher doses of opioids that not only defeated themselves but worsened quality of life and led some into addiction and death. It also distracted from tackling the causes of the pain, frequently rooted in psychological or social factors.

Advocacy groups denounced the paper as a call to stop treating pain. One doctor denounced it as an "atrocity" and demanded Ballantyne be fired. She described the reaction to the article as "vitriolic." "The backlash comes from patients who are already dependent on opiates because they cannot conceive of living without the opiates. I sometimes worry that I'm going to be shot walking down the street," Ballantyne said with strangled laugh.

The response was a reminder that changing the medical profession is one thing, shifting the patient culture of opioids as a right is another.

To me that's the cultural change that's needed—for people to believe that they don't need opiates. They just don't
need them. It's very bad pain management. It's medical malpractice, especially now with the knowledge we have. We
shouldn't be doing it because it's not safe, it doesn't work,
and we need to change the culture. There's no doubt chronic
pain is a problem, and it does affect people's lives adversely.
But that doesn't mean you throw opiates at them if you know
it's going to make those lives worse. It means you help them
in all these other ways you can help them. Spend more time
with them. You fix their social situations.

In March 2018, the *Journal of the American Medical Association*
published a study that contributed to the growing body of support
for Ballantyne's warning fifteen years earlier that opioid painkillers are not effective for many of the types of chronic pain for which
they are most commonly prescribed as a long-term treatment. The
tests showed that patients generally had slightly worse pain and more
adverse side effects. As Ballantyne said. All in all, prescription opioids were no better than over-the-counter drugs for large numbers of
patients.

But that is a difficult message to accept for chronic pain patients
convinced they are going to be left to writhe in agony. Some rejected
out of hand any possibility that the drugs themselves might be con
tributing not only to their pain but to their deteriorating health.

Advocacy groups pressed the CDC to change its opioid prescribing guidelines on the grounds that scaling back opioid levels is not
right for every patient.

Dr. Lynn Webster, the pain specialist who was an early advocate
of opioid prescribing, thinks the CDC guidelines are killing people. He accuses the agency of "intimidating" doctors into reducing
prescribing levels and said the guidelines were not based on science.
"It was highly politicized. Because the CDC guidelines have been
adopted by a number of states and organizations, doctors are afraid if

they don't follow them that it exposes them to some risk of sanctions. And so patients end up being forced down but their pain is not well controlled. I know there are a huge number of suicides because of it."

Dr. Sean Mackey, the chief of pain medicine at Stanford University School of Medicine who was instrumental in drawing up the controversial report claiming 100 million Americans are living with chronic pain, has described the attempts to rein in opioid prescribing as a kind of McCarthyism.

Dr. Roger Chou, one of the authors of the CDC guidelines, is not persuaded. "People even now will say we're swinging to the other side of the pendulum and we're underprescribing opioids. My response is, 'No, we're not.' We swung one way based on no data. Now we actually know what some of the benefits and harms are."

THE CHALLENGE NOW is twofold: to prevent new addictions and to provide relief to the estimated 2 million Americans hooked on opioids. Part of the solution is to scale back prescribing. It has fallen but only by enough to make a small dent in the total number of opioids dispensed each year.

President Trump appointed a new FDA commissioner, Scott Gottlieb, a doctor with a background in the agency but who was also a millionaire libertarian instinctively hostile to government intervention. By his own admission, Gottlieb spent years "lamenting the growing federal intrusion into the practice of medicine." But he changed his mind when it came to opioids and frankly admitted the FDA had failed to rise to the challenge. "We didn't get ahead of it. Nobody got ahead of it," he told the National Academy of Medicine. "The type of action we need to take to finally [address] this crisis is going to be far more dramatic than we would have had to do had we made certain decisions years ago."

Gottlieb endorsed a report drawn up by the academy recommending that approval of opioids take into account the public health effects of addiction—the move for which Dr. Lurie had long pressed.

A few months earlier, an FDA panel finally did what Walden and other bereaved parents had demanded for years and took account of how Opana was really being used. The panel voted to pull the drug from the market, saying the risks outweighed the benefits. This time the FDA listened to its own advisory committee and made a formal request to Endo to withdraw Opana from sale. The agency cited the increase in people injecting the drug and the resulting HIV and hepatitis C outbreaks as a cause. Endo bowed to the pressure.

Dr. Gottlieb took a number of other steps that suggested the FDA had abandoned the "balanced approach" denounced by Nathaniel Katz. The FDA chief called a public hearing on whether to introduce compulsory training of doctors to prescribe opioids nearly two decades after the first calls for mandatory education had been made. He strengthened oversight of the more popular opioids, like Vicodin and Percocet, and began to put in place mechanisms to tighten the approval process for new narcotic medicines. Trump's opioid commission noted that at the time of its report, the FDA was considering applications to approve fifty-two more opioid painkillers, more than double the number already on the market.

The shift in the agency's stance, and the earlier CDC moves, was widely welcomed by Congressman Hal Rogers, the parents of Fed Up!, and others who spent years pressing for action. But it also felt a little like bolting the stable door after the horse passed out in the paddock.

Gottlieb admitted that the epidemic is "five steps ahead of us." With heroin and fentanyl deaths surging, the crisis moved far beyond prescribing alone.

No one really knows how many have died from an overdose either caused by opioids or in combination with other drugs: the official count is 350,000 between 1999 and 2016. By 2018 deaths from drug overdoses had risen to more than 200 people a day, and were the single largest cause of mortality for people under the age of fifty. Some studies predicted that the toll could double or worse over the next decade, killing a half-million more Americans if the spread of heroin and fentanyl cannot be contained.

Not many of those on the front line are optimistic that those numbers will start falling any time soon. Former CDC chief Tom Frieden expects fentanyl and similar artificial opioids to percolate through the country for years. Ballantyne predicts the epidemic will take a decade or more to reverse.

Former member of Congress Mary Bono, who continues to campaign over opioids, does not see a lot of hope. "It's bleak. Very bleak. I hate to say that because I'm an eternal optimist. I don't believe we've turned the corner yet. We have a long way to go. If we don't prevent people from starting in the first place, shame on us. From preventing folks from using and abusing these pills, shame on us," she said.

Bono was in the Atlanta airport talking to Nora Volkow, the head of the National Institute on Drug Abuse, when a man sitting near them slumped over from an overdose.

In April 2018, the US surgeon general, Jerome Adams, said the situation was so dire that people should carry the overdose medicine naloxone as a matter of routine.

Fifteen years after Purdue Pharma launched its video promoting OxyContin as safe and effective, the *Milwaukee-Wisconsin Journal-Sentinel* tracked down the seven patients who appeared in it praising the drug. Two became addicted and died using opioids. Another person who became hooked lost her job and her home before finally overcoming her addiction to OxyContin. Three patients said the drug had worked for them. The seventh declined to answer the newspaper's questions.

In 2017 the *New England Journal of Medicine* posted a rare warning note over the online version of the Porter and Jick letter whose misrepresentation had been a foundation of the campaign by the opioid ideologues: "For reasons of public health, readers should be aware that this letter has been 'heavily and uncritically cited' as evidence that addiction is rare with opioid therapy."

AS THE EPIDEMIC gripped some of the poorest parts of the country, it became difficult to separate cause from effect. The drugs took hold because of the vulnerability of communities hit by poverty, the retreat of well-paid jobs, struggling schools, and, as so many describe it, despair. At some point opioids became a driver of those conditions. The narcotics robbed people who failed drug tests of jobs, hit education, wrecked families, compounded poverty.

West Virginia ran a contest for school students in 2017 to raise awareness of painkiller addiction. More than two thousand children entered the Kids Kick Opioids competition with drawings, poems, and stories. The winner was an elementary school student in Martinsburg, Jacey Rose Chalmers. She pasted a photograph onto a sheet of paper and beside it wrote: "This is a picture of me and my daddy and my little brother. I love my daddy so much. Then the next week daddy died from taking drugs. I cried and cried. I miss my daddy. I want to hug and kiss him every day. It is very sad when kids don't have their daddy to play with now. I still cry when I think about my daddy."

By then, West Virginia had placed more than six thousand children in foster care because of opioids and moved others out of the state because of lack of resources to look after them. Its Bureau for Children and Families expects the number to increase for years to come, with all the consequences that has for the next generation. Social workers see children grappling with the trauma, anger, and disbelief at losing a parent, sometimes two.

The West Virginia pharmacy board dismissed its director, David Potters, in 2017 following an emergency meeting after the *Charleston Gazette Mail* reported the board had failed to enforce its own regulations regarding suspicious orders of opioids, even as millions of pills poured into the state. Year after year, the board's inspectors gave a clean bill of health to the pharmacies in Williamson, Kermit, and other towns dispensing painkillers with abandon. Neither had the board found any reason to be concerned about the fact that wholesalers submitted just two suspicious-order reports over more than a decade.

Through most of the epidemic, West Virginia had the highest drug overdose rate in the country. It is still rising and likely to go on doing so for years, with "deaths of despair" estimated to increase by one-third by 2025.

The closure of the clinics and the rounding up of the doctors was
not the end of the story in Mingo County. Several of those regarded
by the FBI agent Joe Ciccarelli as complicit in protecting the pill
mills were brought down.

Judge Michael Thornsbury, the man described by Ciccarelli as
the "Boss Hogg" of the county, was undone in 2014 by his involvement in a bizarre conspiracy in which Dr. Diane Shafer had a walk-on
role not long after her release from prison. Thornsbury headed a slate
of political candidates calling itself Team Mingo. It included Eugene
Crum, the former magistrate who was suspected of tipping off the
targets of search warrants. Crum was running for sheriff as an anti-
drug crusader with the financial backing of Shafer. He won election
but months later learned that an FBI informant had fingered him for
using and selling opioids. The new sheriff framed the informant, and
Thornsbury sent the man to prison for up to fifteen years. Several
others were drawn into the conspiracy, including Mingo's prosecutor,
the chief magistrate, and a county commissioner.

A few weeks later, Crum was shot dead while eating lunch in his
police car in downtown Williamson by a man who alleged the sheriff
raped him as a teenager. Ciccarelli said the FBI was investigating
Crum for a series of crimes involving drug dealing, including unlawful possession of opioids and money laundering, and that he almost
certainly would have been prosecuted.

The FBI kept up its surveillance of Thornsbury and others members of Team Mingo who were jailed over the framing of the informant. The judge was also charged with trying to entrap his secretary's
husband, in part by planting drugs on him, in an attempt to have the
secretary resume an affair she had broken off.

Federal prosecutors described Thornsbury as at the heart of the
corruption of Mingo County. The judge who sentenced him to four
years in prison likened Thornsbury's behavior to that of a "Third
World dictator."

Kermit hired a lawyer, Truman Chafin, the former state senator who had raised no objection to the activities of the Wellness
Center just down the street from his office in Williamson. Chafin

said Kermit had been ravaged by drugs so multinational corporations could make money. "Now, there is nothing wrong with having money. However, as the Bible says, the *love* of money, which is
the calling card of these huge drug distributors, is the evil that has
caused over 3 million deadly opioid pills to be sent to this little town
with only four hundred residents," he said.

In 2017 Williamson's principal hotel, the Sycamore Inn, closed
for lack of business. It was converted to a drug rehabilitation center.

CHAPTER 21

Guilt

A VI ISRAEL MOURNS in public. He posts his pain at Michael's loss on Facebook. "I miss my little boy."

There's a picture of Michael's room for the world to see, preserved as if waiting for him to return. "We miss you Mikey."

Avi pours his energy into helping others newly arrived at the moment of hell he endured those years ago, their lives pulled apart by the agony of a daughter or son snatched from them by an epidemic they never saw coming.

The bereaved, mostly parents but also siblings and grandparents, gather at the offices of the support group Avi runs in central Buffalo, Save the Michaels of the World. There are a dozen or so people one chilly evening in early December. This is the worst time of year with the holidays on top of each other. Halloween, Thanksgiving, Hanukkah, Christmas. The memories come tearing back and with them regrets and self-recrimination. Holidays are a trauma.

Avi is Jewish, but, as he was out walking his dog, he bought a Christmas tree on impulse to give the group something to decorate and so perhaps ease the pain of the meeting. Some of the families no longer put up trees or decorations because they are so closely associated with a childhood of dreams now dashed. "I don't want to be sad," Avi tells the group. "I got tired of being sad every day."

But there's no escape. The grieving carry photographs and mementos but more than anything, they bear guilt. The parents tell each other what they wish they'd known and done. How could they have allowed their child to be prescribed those pills? Why did they not better understand what it means to fall into the grip of opioids?

Avi says they shouldn't torture themselves. "You can't go with 'what-ifs.' "

But they do. They can't stop themselves. The what-if they'd done something different that day, that week, that hour. Worst of all is the what-if of the last encounters.

Susan Durlack is wracked with guilt over some of her final words to her son Jimmy. "On Tuesday I told him I was sorry he was ever born. I told him if I'd known what he was going to be like, I would have had an abortion. On Thursday he was dead."

Susan, a psychiatric nurse practitioner, blamed her child when he was alive and herself now he is dead. Jimmy was thirty-two when he overdosed. She knew he was using prescription pills but did not know about the heroin. Susan's snipe about the abortion spilled out because she was exhausted by the demands of her son's addiction on her life. She slept with her debit card in her bra to prevent him from stealing it. "I'd had a bad day, and I said to him I can't take it anymore. He stole a check from my checkbook, so I went berserk on him. I didn't understand that he was suffering. I didn't understand it, and I'm so sorry that I didn't. I never threw him on the street, but I did blame him and I was nasty. I said, 'Get your act together. What's wrong with you? You're lazy. I can't trust you.' I said to him once, 'My girlfriends have sons, and I have you.' Because they say, 'Tell him to get his act together. You're letting him walk all over you. He's using you.' That stigma. Even when he died, one of my oldest friends said to me, 'Well, Susan, he did it to himself.' "

Marilyn Gentile carries the guilt of calling the police on her son Bobby because she couldn't see any other way to stop him from dying from heroin. At the support group she attended back then, they told her "tough love" was the way. "When you're at your wit's end and you don't know what to do and you're fearful that when they walk out the door it's the last time you're going to see them, your last resort is have them arrested."

When Bobby came home, Marilyn told him he needed to straighten out and grow up. She found him at dawn sitting at his computer, dead. "The horrible things you say," she lamented. "It's always with me. Never leaves you. There's reminders everywhere. Words that are said. It's in your brain forever."

THOSE WHO BEAR real responsibility for America's national nightmare show no such sense of guilt or torment. Even today, they shift responsibility for the epidemic onto those who fell victim to it.

In 1889 the British Parliament debated the morality of its empire forcing opium on China through war and invasion. One MP, Samuel Smith, denounced "the gigantic evil of this opium trade," calling it "England's greatest national sin" in an era when Britain had more than a few sins on the go. "I am quite aware that within the last few years a feeble and a futile effort has been made to persuade the British public that the use of opium is not noxious, that opium is a comparatively healthy drug, and that it may be used by the great mass of the Chinese without any greater harm than results from the use of beer by our population, or even with any greater harm than from tobacco smoking," he told the House of Commons. "I have never come across a single disinterested witness who did not regard the common use of opium as one of the most terrible curses that could befall humanity."

Yet the suffering of the Chinese was invisible to most Britons, and they looked away as the powerful multinationals of the age continued to profit from the cursed trade well into the twentieth century, unswayed by appeals to morality or anything but the bottom line.

Modern pharmaceutical companies are, at best, amoral. Many of their drugs save and improve lives, but their decisions are driven by profit, including which lives are of value. Senator Joe Manchin described the flooding of his state with opioids as a business strategy: "It's an epidemic because we have a business model for it. Follow the money." Darrell McGraw, West Virginia's attorney general, likened the opioid makers to the tobacco companies concealing the dangers of cigarettes. John Brownlee, the former federal prosecutor in Virginia, regarded Purdue Pharma as a criminal enterprise.

It would be a mistake to conclude that responsibility for the opioid epidemic lies only with the greed of the drug companies or that it is shared solely with corrupt doctors and pharmacists who profited from mass prescribing. They were facilitated by politicians, regulators, and a broader medical industry with an agenda or that chose not to see. The opioid makers were helped in that because, for many years, the primary victims were those it was easy to look away from— the "dumbass hillbillies," as Willis Duncan put it.

Purdue may have targeted some of the poorest parts of Appalachia because that's where the data said opioids were already being prescribed. But it proved a convenience that these regions were among the most marginalized in the country and the easiest to stigmatize as the drug makers pursued the disreputable tactic of blaming the victims for their addiction.

Like the nineteenth-century opium dealers, the painkiller manufacturers used the power of the huge profits of addiction to keep the faucets of mass prescribing open. The quarter of a billion dollars a year the drug industry spends on lobbying bought the complicity of Congress and organizations such as the American Medical Association through silence and distraction. The din of money drowned out the warnings sounded by Dr. Art Van Zee about the devastation already wrought to his Virginia community in the late 1990s and the research by doctors such as Jane Ballantyne that should have prompted critical questioning of the claims made for opioids. Congress and the FDA were told loudly and clearly that a national disaster was unfolding more than a decade before the CDC's Tom Frieden called it an epidemic.

Drawing on the tobacco companies' playbook, opioid manufacturers obscured the evidence of the dangers of their products even when it was staring the industry in the face. Instead, the drug makers and their front organizations sought to discredit those who advocated caution.

Some US states tried to sound the alarm as the morgues overflowed, their social services struggled to cope with children orphaned or taken into care, and communities disintegrated. They looked to Washington for leadership but did not get much from President Obama or Congress.

The pharmaceutical industry and parts of the medical profession took the view that an acceptable level of addiction was a price worth paying for the benefits of opioids. But they worked hard to avoid examining whether the benefits really did outweigh the risks. They did not want to know if their drugs were addictive any more than they wanted to know whether opioids were effective in combating pain in most of those to whom they were prescribed. Purdue Pharma made up claims for OxyContin instead.

Russell Portenoy has at least had the courage to express regret for what can only be regarded as a reckless distorting of statistics and academic papers in his evangelism for the possibilities of opioids. It's not quite an admission of guilt, but it is further than most others who bear responsibility have gone.

The Food and Drug Administration has struggled to admit its role. In the absence of a frank acknowledgment of its mistakes, the agency's belated reversal of earlier opioid policies can be taken as an implicit admission of its failings through this epidemic. The FDA says it has learned the lessons of the past but declines to discuss its mistakes or what those lessons are. It remains secretive about its decision-making process.

Still, even the FDA now acknowledges that the method of its approval of OxyContin was a stark error. The agency's complicity in allowing Purdue's false claims during the first five crucial years when the drug spread like wildfire was only a beginning.

That mistake could have been overcome if the voices pleading caution in the early 2000s had been heeded. Had at least been taken seriously enough to pause the headlong rush into mass prescribing. But they were drowned out as the American medical system was hijacked by a mix of bad science and corporate money.

The result was a lost decade—the years between the unequivocal warnings from those grappling with the early impact of mass prescribing of opioids and the CDC stepping up to the plate—in which the epidemic could have been contained and hundreds of thousands of lives saved.

There are no shortage of lessons to be learned. One is about what happens when commercial interests wield influence over medical policy. But the epidemic should also cause the country's leaders to reflect on who fell victim and why.

In large parts of the United States, opioids were popular because they were a fix. A fix for emotional pain. A fix for failing bodies. A fix for struggling to make it in a society that promises so much, and judges by what is achieved, but turns its back on so many of those who fail to live up to that promise.

THERE WAS SILENCE over the years from another quarter too. Even as the plague unleashed by their company swept the country, the Sackler brothers were not to be heard from. Mortimer died in 2010 and Raymond seven years later. Both lived to see the destruction, but neither had a word to say in public about the misery inflicted by OxyContin or the criminal activities of Purdue. There was never an explanation, let alone an apology. But the Sacklers were far from invisible.

The vast profits of addiction made the family among the richest in America. It was estimated to be worth an extraordinary $14 billion by 2015, equivalent to about one-third of all the profits from

OxyContin. The Sacklers mainlined a slice of the bonanza into buttressing their reputations as exceptionally generous benefactors of humanity. The family name is branded onto galleries, research institutes, and museum wings from California to Tel Aviv, New York to Cambridge. There's the Sackler Wing at the Met in New York and the Serpentine Sackler Gallery in London. The brothers didn't forget the opportunities offered by Glasgow when they were unwelcome at medical school in their hometown. A bridge at Kew Gardens and galleries at the Smithsonian carry the Sackler brand.

But while Mortimer and Raymond, and the trusts they created to handle their incredible wealth, vigorously promoted the family name, they were rather more reticent about its ties to Purdue Pharma. The source of the money was rarely publicized. Nowhere in the announcements of their latest act of generosity did it mention that it was funded by the profits from Purdue and the wrecked people of Mingo County.

Like so many others, the Sacklers looked away.

Timeline

The Making of a Tragedy

1980

☤ Two doctors at Boston University Medical Center, Jane Porter and Hershel Jick, write a brief letter to the *New England Journal of Medicine* noting a low incidence of addiction in a set of patients treated with opioids. The conclusions are highly qualified.

1986

☤ Pain specialists Russell Portenoy and Katherine Foley publish a paper challenging the medical community's long-standing aversion to morphine because of the risk of addiction and claiming opioid painkillers are a safe treatment. The paper is based on the cases of just thirty-eight cancer patients. A growing number of pain specialists join the movement.

1995

☤ Henry Vinson begins recruiting doctors to run what will become one of the most prolific opioid pill mills in the heart of a region worst hit by the emerging epidemic.

1996

☤ Purdue Pharma releases a new and powerful opioid pill, Oxy-Contin, and unleashes an unprecedented marketing campaign that claims the drug is less addictive and more effective than other narcotic painkillers.

Dr. James Campbell, president of the American Pain Society, introduces the concept of "Pain as the 5th Vital Sign" alongside other measures of health such as blood pressure and pulse.

1999

☤ The first flickers of the epidemic to come are seen in sharp rise in drug overdoses in southwestern West Virginia.

The Veterans Health Administration adopts "Pain as the 5th Vital Sign."

2000

☤ OxyContin sales rise to $1 billion a year.

2001

☤ Dr. Art Van Zee warns Purdue Pharma and the Food and Drug Administration that OxyContin is devastating communities in parts of Virginia, Kentucky, and West Virginia.

The Joint Commission for Accreditation of Healthcare Organizations requires the nation's hospitals to prioritize pain treatment and pairs with OxyContin's manufacturer, Purdue Pharma, to publish a guide claiming the risk of addiction is low.

The West Virginia state police launch an investigation into escalating opioid prescribing as coroners report a surge in drug overdoses.

2002

Katherine Hoover becomes the most prolific opioid prescriber in West Virginia.

A patchwork of counties in southwestern West Virginia, eastern Kentucky, and Virginia emerges as the epicenter of the growing epidemic.

2003

The FDA warns Purdue that it is illegally promoting OxyContin in ads that downplay the dangers of the drug.

A Government Accounting Office report details Purdue Pharma's marketing practices in selling OxyContin and its influence over federal regulators.

West Virginia attorney general Darrell McGraw wins an out-of-court settlement with Purdue over pushing its drug to doctors.

The *New England Journal of Medicine* publishes an article by one of the United States' leading pain specialists, Dr. Jane Ballantyne of Harvard Medical School, warning that opioid painkillers do not work as long-term treatment and may even make a patient's condition worse. Her warnings are dismissed as "extreme."

2004

OxyContin sales pass $2 billion a year.

2005

☤ Amid growing questions about the dangers of mass prescribing of opioids, pharmaceutical companies establish the Pain Care Forum to shift the focus from addiction to what it claims is an epidemic of untreated pain.

2006

☤ A Centers for Disease Control official, Dr. Len Paulozzi, compiles data showing a direct link between rising prescribing and opioid deaths. He describes the crisis as an epidemic.

The Pain Care Forum attempts to shift the focus by organizing a briefing before members of Congress, "The Epidemic of Pain in America," claiming that the real issue is not addiction but people living with pain.

The high-strength opioid Opana is approved by the Food and Drug Administration three years after its initial rejection.

2007

☤ Dr. Charles Lucas, professor of surgery in Detroit, publishes a paper warning that the focus on pain treatment is killing some patients.

Purdue pleads guilty to federal criminal charges over its false claims for the safety and effectiveness of OxyContin. Three of its executives are also convicted.

The country's three largest drug distributors—McKesson, Cardinal Health, and AmerisourceBergen—flood West Virginia with opioids. They will deliver 780 million doses over the next five years.

2009

☤ Drug overdose deaths outnumber lives claimed by traffic accidents in the United States for the first time.

2010

Deaths from prescription opioids rise to 16,651 this year. The formula for OxyContin is finally changed to make it harder to crush and extract the narcotic, and some doctors are more cautious about prescribing. But people already hooked on the drugs still need a fix, and demand for heroin begins to surge.

2011

The head of the Centers for Disease Control, Tom Frieden, says there is an epidemic of opioid addiction.

The Institute of Medicine issues a highly controversial report claiming 100 million Americans are living in chronic pain.

2012

Doctors write more than 250 million prescriptions for opioids, enough to provide a bottle to every adult in America. The United States consumes more than 80 percent of the world's prescription narcotics.

2013

Coroners start to record the first deaths from fentanyl, an artificial opioid fifty times more powerful than heroin.

2014

Heroin deaths overtake prescription opioids for the first time. Total drug overdose deaths rise to 47,055. Sales of prescription opioids are now four times higher than in 1999.

An FDA committee overwhelmingly votes against the approval of a new and powerful opioid drug, Zohydro. The FDA ignores the decision, approves the drug, and creates a political uproar.

2016

☤ Fentanyl deaths surge past heroin and prescription opioids, taking more than 20,000 lives. Total drug overdose deaths rise above 64,000—more than all the American soldiers to die in the Vietnam War.

West Virginia has the highest drug overdose death rate in the United States at 52 per 100,000, nearly double the rate in 2010.

The CDC issues guidelines discouraging doctors from prescribing opioids.

2017

☤ A presidential commission calls the epidemic a "national nightmare" and blames it in part on misselling of opioids and the failure of the FDA and other federal institutions.

McKesson pays a record $150 million fine for violating the law requiring the reporting of suspicious orders.

Endo announces it will stop selling Opana ER under FDA pressure.

2018

☤ The CDC estimates that drug overdose deaths rose above 200 a day in 2017, a 13 percent increase over the year before. It calculated that opioids have killed at least 350,000 Americans since 1999.

Notes

Among the books that informed my research and writing are several that have made an important contribution to understanding the present epidemic.

Barry Meier's excellent early account of the impact of OxyContin, *Pain Killer: A "Wonder" Drug's Trail of Addiction and Death* (Emmaus, PA: Rodale, 2003), should have been enough on its own to have brought about a rethink of the headlong rush to mass prescribing.

In *Dreamland: The True Tale of America's Opiate Epidemic* (New York: Bloomsbury, 2016), Sam Quinones writes a groundbreaking exposé of the rise of the heroin cartels alongside the mismarketing of prescription opioids.

Dr. Anna Lembke gives a good account of how the crisis unfolded from a doctor's perspective in *Drug Dealer, MD: How Doctors Were Duped, Patients Got Hooked, and Why It's So Hard to Stop* (Baltimore: Johns Hopkins University Press, 2016).

David Courtwright traces the path of opiate use from the middle class to the urban back streets over more than a century in *Dark Paradise: A History of Opiate Addiction in America* (Cambridge, MA: Harvard University Press, 2001).

Fran Hawthorne gives valuable insights into the workings of the Food and Drug Administration in *Inside the FDA: The Business and Politics Behind the Drugs We Take and the Food We Eat* (Hoboken, NJ: J. Wiley, 2005).

Ben Goldacre's *Bad Pharma: How Drug Companies Mislead Doctors and Harm
Patients* (New York: Farrar, Straus and Giroux, 2013) exposes how pharmaceutical companies manipulate doctors and the drug approval system.

CHAPTER 1

The account of Henry Vinson's history is drawn from my interview with him,
the police, and residents of Williamson along with Vinson's book, *Confes-
sions of a D.C. Madam: The Politics of Sex, Lies, and Blackmail* (Walterville,
OR: Trine Day, [2014]). The account of Vinson's arrest and prosecution in
Washington, DC, was also drawn from "From Small-Town Roots, a Big-
City Scandal," *Washington Post*, July 24, 1989.

The accounts of the histories and actions of doctors Diane Shafer, Katherine
Hoover, and William Ryckman are drawn from interviews, court records,
and depositions.

CHAPTER 2

The history of the Sackler brothers was drawn from interviews and several
sources, including Barry Meier, *Pain Killer: A "Wonder" Drug's Trail of Addiction and Death*; and Sam Quinones, *Dreamland: The True Tale of America's
Opiate Epidemic*. Both books also gave accounts of the Porter and Jick letter
and its misuse. Quinones revealed the extent to which that letter came to
influence academic papers with hundreds of citations.

David Courtwright's explanation of the history of morphine addiction in the
nineteenth and early twentieth centuries was drawn from his book *Dark Paradise: A History of Opiate Addiction in America*.

The account of Dr. Russell Portenoy's part in the liberalization of opioids is
drawn in part from a 2016 interview with Marcia Meldrum, a historian at
the University of California–Los Angeles specializing in the history of med-
icine and biology. Meldrum conducted the most extensive interview with
Portenoy to date in 2003. Some of Portenoy's quotes are from that interview:
"Oral History Interview with Russell K. Portenoy," April 17–18, 2003 (Ms.
Coll. no. 127.67), John C. Liebeskind History of Pain Collection, History
& Special Collections for the Sciences, UCLA Library Special Collections,
Louise M. Darling Biomedical Library, University of California, Los Angeles.

Portenoy's admission that he exaggerated claims for the safety of opioids was
made in a 2011 interview with Physicians for Responsible Opioid Prescribing: https://www.youtube.com/watch?v=DgyuBWN9D4w.

The Robert Kaiko memo was uncovered by a *Los Angeles Times* investigation by
Harriet Ryan, Lisa Girion, and Scott Glover, "'You Want a Description of
Hell?' OxyContin's 12-Hour Problem," May 5, 2016.

CHAPTER 3

Willis Duncan and Wilbert Hatcher were interviewed in Mingo County in 2016.

CHAPTER 4

Dr. Rajan Masih was interviewed in Petersburg, West Virginia, in 2017.

The Purdue marketing memo was obtained by the American Public Media program Marketplace, www.marketplace.org/2017/12/12/health-care /uncertain-hour/opioid.

Purdue's marketing tactics were exposed in a Government Accounting Office report in 2003: "Prescription Drugs: OxyContin Abuse and Diversion and Efforts to Address the Problem." They are also described in Meier, *Pain Killer*.

Sean Thatcher's account of his time as a Purdue sales rep was given in an affidavit as part of a lawsuit by the state of Montana against the company.

Purdue's predicted sales of OxyContin were reported in "Painkiller's Sales Far Exceeded Levels Anticipated by Maker," *Wall Street Journal*, May 16, 2002.

CHAPTER 5

Dr. Art Van Zee was interviewed in St. Charles, Virginia, in 2017.

The role of Dr. David Haddox was drawn from Art Van Zee's interview, Barry Meier's *Pain Killer*, and public records.

Dr. Nathaniel Katz was interviewed in 2017.

CHAPTER 6

Mike Smith and Joe Ciccarelli were interviewed in West Virginia in 2017.

The accounts of the actions of doctors and pharmacists are drawn from interviews with patients, witnesses and investigators, court documents, and depositions.

The numbers of opioid pills delivered to Mingo County was exposed by Eric Eyre in "Drug Firms Fueled 'Pill Mills' in Rural WV," *Charleston (WV) Gazette-Mail*, May 23, 2016. Eyre won the Pulitzer Prize for his reporting.

CHAPTER 7

This chapter is based in part on interviews with Dr. Charles Lucas in Detroit, Dr. Jennifer Plumb in Salt Lake City, and Dr. Jane Ballantyne and Dr. Roger Chou in Portland, Oregon.

CHAPTER 8

Congressman Hal Rogers was interviewed on Capitol Hill in 2017.

The series of stories on opioids in eastern Kentucky was published in the *Lexington Herald-Leader* in December 2003 and January 2004.

Interviews with Dee Davis and Steve Mays were conducted in Beattyville in 2016 and Davis again in 2018.

The Anne Case and Angus Deaton study appeared in their article "Rising Morbidity and Mortality in Midlife Among White Non-Hispanic Americans in the 21st Century," *Proceedings of the National Academy of Sciences* 112, no. 49 (2015): 15078–15083.

CHAPTER 9

The account of Frances Oldham Kelsey and thalidomide appeared in " 'Heroine' of FDA Keeps Bad Drug Off Market," *Washington Post*, July 15, 1962.

The history of the FDA was in part drawn from Fran Hawthorne, *Inside the FDA: The Business and Politics Behind the Drugs We Take and the Food We Eat*.

Emily Walden was interviewed in 2017.

Ten years of IMMPACT emails between Turk and Dworkin were obtained from the University of Washington with the assistance of Craig Mayton. Extracts of the emails previously appeared in "FDA and Pharma: Emails Raise Pay-for-Play Concerns," *Milwaukee Journal Sentinel/MedPage Today*, October 7, 2013; and "Pharmaceutical Firms Paid to Attend Meetings of Panel That Advises FDA, E-mails Show," *Washington Post*, October 6, 2013.

CHAPTER 10

This chapter is based on interviews with Darrell McGraw in Charleston, West Virginia, and John Brownlee in Virginia as well as court documents.

CHAPTER 11

All of those quoted in the chapter were interviewed in 2016 and 2017.

Janet Colbert published an account of her campaign to close Florida pill mills and change laws: *STOPPNow: (Stop the Organized Pill Pushers) Now* (Pittsburgh: RoseDog Books, 2017).

CHAPTER 12

This chapter is largely drawn from interviews, including with former member of Congress Mary Bono, Congressman Hal Rogers, Dr. Nathaniel Katz, and Dr. Jane Ballantyne.

The role of the Pain Care Forum was first exposed in detail by a joint investigation by the Associated Press and the Center for Public Integrity, "Pro-Painkiller

Echo Chamber Shaped Policy amid Drug Epidemic," September 19, 2016, www.publicintegrity.org/2016/09/19/20201/pro-painkiller-echo -chamber-shaped-policy-amid-drug-epidemic.

The Institute of Medicine report was called *Relieving Pain in America: A Blueprint for Transforming Prevention, Care, Education, and Research* (June 2011).

Figures for pharmaceutical company spending on political lobbying were obtained from the Center for Responsive Politics.

Bill Brewster's denial that he pressured congresswoman Mary Bono was made to the Associated Press and the Center for Public Integrity in "Pro-Painkiller Echo Chamber."

CHAPTER 13

Dr. Len Paulozzi and Dr. Tom Frieden were interviewed in 2017.

CHAPTER 14

This chapter is in part based on interviews with Debbie Preece, who spoke to me several times, along with Jim Cagle, David Dodd, Charles Sparks, and residents of Kermit who did not wish to be named.

The history of the Preece family's involvement in drug dealing in Kermit was drawn from several newspaper accounts: Barry Bearak, "Sweep of Hollows: Unraveling Corruption's Traditions," *Los Angeles Times*, April 21, 1988; "Almost Heaven? This Corrupt Corner of West Virginia Was More Like the Other Place," *People*, November 14, 1988; and "Mountain Town Shaking Reign of Drugs, Corruption," *Orlando Sentinel*, May 1, 1988.

The accounts of the role of doctors and pharmacists in Kermit and Williamson were drawn from interviews with state police, the FBI, Mingo County residents (some of whom chose to remain anonymous), and court documents.

Detail on the scale of drug deliveries came from Eric Eyre, "Drug Firms Poured 780M Painkillers into WV amid Rise of Overdoses," *Charleston Gazette-Mail*, December 17, 2016.

CHAPTER 15

Joe Rannazzisi was interviewed three times between 2016 and 2018. Dr. Rajan Masih was interviewed in 2017.

CHAPTER 16

Mike Smith and Joe Ciccarelli were interviewed in 2017.

The account of the actions of doctors and pharmacists was drawn from interviews and court documents.

CHAPTER 17

This chapter is in large part drawn from interviews with Dr. Peter Lurie in 2017 and Dr. Margaret Hamburg in 2018, as well as Hal Rogers, Mary Bono, Avi Israel, Andrew Kolodny, and Nathaniel Katz.

The FDA declined to make officials still on its staff available for interview. Dr. Rappaport did not respond to several requests for an interview.

CHAPTER 18

Joe Raymond and Chris Landry were interviewed in Boston and Natasha Butler in Sacramento.

The 2014 study on heroin users moving from prescription opioids appeared in "The Changing Face of Heroin Use in the United States: A Retrospective Analysis of the Past 50 Years," *Journal of the American Medical Association* (July 2014).

Joe Ciccarelli was interviewed in Huntington, West Virginia, in 2017.

CHAPTER 19

This chapter draws on interviews with Dr. Tom Frieden, Dr. Len Paulozzi, and Dr. Roger Chou in 2017.

The fall in opioid prescribing after 2010 was documented by the CDC: "Vital Signs: Changes in Opioid Prescribing in the United States, 2006–2015."

The Washington Legal Foundation letter threatening the CDC can be found here: www.wlf.org/upload/litigation/misc/CDCComments-Opioids.pdf.

The CDC guidelines can be found here: www.cdc.gov/mmwr/volumes/65/rr /rr6501e1.htm.

Frieden and Houry's paper defending the guidelines was "Reducing the Risks of Relief: The CDC Opioid-Prescribing Guideline," *New England Journal of Medicine* (April 21, 2016).

CHAPTER 20

Interviews with Jane Ballantyne, Lynn Webster, Roger Chou, and Joseph Rannazzisi were conducted in 2017.

The forecast of a higher death toll was made in Max Blau, "Opioids Could Kill Nearly 500,000 Americans in the Next Decade," *Stat News*, June 27, 2017.

FDA commissioner Dr. Scott Gottlieb's speech was made to the National Press Club in Washington, DC, November 3, 2017.

The dismissal of the director of the West Virginia pharmacy board was reported by Eric Eyre in "WV Board of Pharmacy Dismisses Director," *Charleston Gazette-Mail*, July 18, 2017.

Index